T0203255

Knowledge Needs and Information Extraction

To my son, Alexis.

Knowledge Needs
and
Information Extraction

Towards an Artificial Consciousness

Nicolas Turenne

Series Editor
Jean-Charles Pomerol

First published 2013 in Great Britain and the United States by ISTE Ltd and John Wiley & Sons, Inc.

ISTE Ltd
27-37 St George's Road
London SW19 4EU
UK

www.iste.co.uk

John Wiley & Sons, Inc.
111 River Street
Hoboken, NJ 07030
USA

www.wiley.com

Library of Congress Control Number: 2012950088

British Library Cataloguing-in-Publication Data
A CIP record for this book is available from the British Library
ISBN: 978-1-84821-515-3

Printed and bound in Great Britain by CPI Group (UK) Ltd., Croydon, Surrey CR0 4YY

Table of Contents

Introduction

The title of this book is both subversive and ambitious. It is subversive because few academic publications deal with this subject. There has, of course, been work done in robotics on artificially reproducing a "human" movement. One can also find more cognitive works about the way of reasoning – i.e. storing and structuring information to induce the validity of a relation between two pieces of information. However, the term "artificial consciousness" is not applicable to any of these works. There is probably a spiritual connotation which philosophers have dodged by calling the discipline "reason" or "rationality".

The book presents a theory of consciousness which is unique and sustainable in nature, based on physiological and cognitive-linguistic principles controlled by a number of socio-psycho-economic factors.

Chapter 1 recontextualizes this notion of consciousness with a certain current aspect.

In order to anchor this theory, which draws upon various disciplines, this book presents a number of different theories, all of which have been abundantly studied by scientists from both a theoretical and experimental standpoint. These issues are addressed by Chapters 4 (models of social organization), 5 (ego theories), 6 (theories of the motivational system in psychology), 7 (theories of the motivational system in neurosciences), 8 (language modeling) and 9 (computational modeling of motivation).

This book is a deliberate attempt to be eclectic – sometimes presenting fuzzy or nearly esoteric points of view. However, above all, it carefully highlights the context with validated and accepted theories drawn from academic disciplines which are recognized at the scientific and international levels: psychology, physiology, computing, linguistics and sociology. These are highly technical disciplines, with extensive analytical depth and a long history, from which it was necessary to isolate certain theories which are most relevant to the debate or controversial. The chapters which air the concepts of these academic disciplines are concise while attempting to give an exhaustive overview of the subject.

The theory presented in this book is based on the hypothesis that an individual's main activities are developed by self-motivation, managed as an informational need. This is described by Chapters 2 (self-motivation on a day-to-day basis), 3 (the notion of need), 10 (hypothesis and control of cognitive self-motivation) and 11 (a model of self-motivation which associates language and physiology).

According to approaches in philosophy and in the natural sciences (physics, chemistry, biology and geology), consciousness – be it real or artificial – must be observable in the long terms by the traces that it leaves by way of its situated actions. A potent argument, which is closely connected to the theory presented herein, holds that human activity is now highly dependent on new technologies (smartphones, open Web and Deep Web) whereas previously, only a minority of people produced written Web content. Given that the ratio of people to technologies is predominant, the idea is based on extraction of informations left, in an official capacity or otherwise, on networks and in digital archives. The subject of knowledge extraction from texts is, in itself, highly technical. Four chapters are needed to present the capacity of the approaches to reconstitute a pertinent piece of information based on different textual digital sources. These chapters are 12 (the impact of self-motivation on written information), 13 (non-transversal text-mining techniques), 14 (transversal text-mining techniques) and 15 (the domains of interest of text mining).

"A step toward artificial consciousness". The title edges towards production of artificial consciousness. The book does not present a computer program, a computation algorithm, the object of which would be to generate a form of consciousness. However, arguments are given in favor of extracting information from digital sources, which it would be possible to reproduce. When we speak of extraction, we wish to have parameters for a reading model, and therefore acquire the power of generativity in accordance with the same model. Thus, we would have the capacity to produce a digital data source, and therefore leave digital footprints which would suggest consciousness, but without an individual.

This may disappoint some readers, some of whom would like to see talking robots, and others dream of a unique consciousness which surpasses that of humans. The book describes a reality – individual and social, simple, universal and tangible based on the digital worlds of virtual reality.

Acknowledgements

For seventeen years, I have been musing about the cognitive and computational aspects of language processing. My work could never have been done in acceptable conditions without the support of a number of working groups who have put their faith in me, under the auspices of certain institutions: the University of Strasbourg (Dr. François Rousselot) and the *Institut National de Recherche en Agronomie* (INRA – National Institute of Agronomic Research) (Dr. Marc Barbier and Dr. Isabelle Hue). Several companies in Strasbourg were willing to take me on as a member of their team despite the risks of the innovative projects under consideration: the *Agence de Diffusion de l'Information Technologique* (Technological Information Dissemination Agency) (Jérôme Thil) and the company Neurosoft (Gérard Guillerm). My international collaborations have also been fruitful and constructive, and I should like to thank Dr. Vladimir Ivanisenko and Sergey Tiys (University of Novosibirsk, Russia) for their trust and their invaluable thinking on gene networks.

Chapter 1

Consciousness: an Ancient and Current Topic of Study

1.1. Multidisciplinarity of the subject

The subject relating to the study of consciousness covers a great many disciplines, which reflects the complexity of the concept, and makes it a multidisciplinary concept. From ancient times right up until the present day, thinkers, scientists and engineers wondered about the reality of thought, examining it through the lens of people's actions in their existence and the surrounding society. Philosophers have investigated the field of metaphysics; psychologists the role of the subconscious and the machinery of learning; computer scientists the possible modeling of an artificial plan of action; biologists the cerebral location for the process of decision-making; sociologists an organization of interpersonal interactions; managers a means of personal development; and engineers an optimization of the autonomy of automatons.

A number of factors contributed to a certain reticence to rationally study consciousness before the beginning of the 20th Century. One of the main factors relates to the dissociation of body and mind, which enabled the mind to be given a political and mystical interpretation in its religious form: the soul. The establishment of a stable secular republic in France on 31 August 1871 gave rise to a new era of thinking. Jean-Martin Charcot expounded his theory on hysteria in 1882. At the government's request, Alfred Binet created a metric intelligence scale in the context of the development of intelligence in children and anomaly detection. It was not until the Briand Law of 9 December 1905 that a strict separation between religious affairs and state affairs emerged – at least in France. Article 1: the Republic ensures freedom of conscience [consciousness] […]; Article 2: the Republic does not recognize, remunerate or subsidize any religion[1]. The uncircumventable dogma of daily life in France probably put paid to a great many intentions to carry out an analysis of consciousness. In the latter half of the 20th Century, work on consciousness related primarily to certain specific traits, such as the study of attention in developmental psychology, and the study of knowledge representation in artificial intelligence. We are still a long way from being able to explain why human beings think a certain way at a precise moment; however, thought is known by certain neurological mechanisms, which associate the faculties of reasoning, memory, motivation and language.

Consciousness is a cognitive mechanism which tends to produce actions in the context of situations. In everyday language, we can see concepts which are similar to consciousness, such as: intention, determination, appetence, motivation, faith, need and belief. These concepts are often held to be at the root of our decisions. They also have a great many points in common.

1.2. Terminological outlook

Intention comes from the Latin, *intentio*, which means "action of going towards". This is a deliberate action whereby we fix the goal of an activity or indeed the motivation which leads us to intervene. This concept can be broken down into three facets:

– the deliberate design of performing an action – a volition;

– the fact of setting oneself a certain goal – a firm and premeditated design – the same goal that we intend to attain;

– in the tangible concept, modulation of attention, to which consciousness gives a sense, a form.

Determination is a process which also underlies decision making. The word comes from the Latin *terminatio*, meaning "to set a boundary". The following are the three facets of this concept:

– action of determining, precisely delimiting, characterizing without ambiguity, clearly;

– resolution taken after having balanced several parts;

---

1 http://www.legifrance.gouv.fr/affichTexte.do?cidTexte=JORFTEXT000000508749.

– in philosophy, an action by which a thing, also subject to many different qualities, many different ways of being, is led to assume one state/quality rather than another.

In the same mold as determination, the concept of self-determination reaffirms the taking of a decision by its author. This is the fact of deciding for oneself, with no external influence.

The concept of belief, or credence, is more complex. It comes from the Latin *credere*, which means "to believe". It is a term which has been coveted throughout history by political figures to control the masses, and thus which has served as a shield and as a weapon. We can identify eight facets of belief:

– taking something to be true;

– having faith and offering submission of spirit relating to a religion;

– relying on someone and something;

– holding something to be likely or possible;

– adding faith to someone or something;

– having confidence in someone or something;

– having confidence in someone – in their talent or in their word;

– thinking, estimating, imagining.

The concept of faith is more far-reaching than simple subscription to religion, and relates also to the effects of belief on an individual scale. The word comes from the Latin *fido*, meaning confidence or faith. In symmetry to belief, we can distinguish seven facets:

– belief in the truths of a religion;

– dogma of a religion, intended to be believed as having been handed down by God;

– that religion itself;

– fidelity, meticulousness in keeping one's word, fulfilling one's promises, one's commitments;

– obligation which we contract, the assurance that we give of something by treatises, sermons, etc.;

– credence, confidence;

– testimony, assurance, proof.

A concept which leads us into the field of biology is that of need. The French word for this, *besoin*, comes from the Frankish *bisunni*, which means "great care". We can distinguish four facets of this concept:

– deprivation of something which is necessary;

– indigence, destitution;

– lack of food;

– instinctive motion, from a feeling which leads us to seek or do something.

Appetence is a concept which is very similar to need, but with the added detail that it also offers a dynamic. It comes from the Latin *appetere*, which means "seek to attain" (the same root as the word "appetite"). There are three distinguishable facets for this concept:

– a tendency and magnetism that all beings have toward that which can satisfy their instincts and needs – particularly physical needs;

– attraction for that which may satisfy a need or a whim;

– desire to use or buy a product or brand, experienced by an individual.

Finally, we come to the central concept in consciousness, which is motivation. The term comes from the Latin *motivus*, which means "move". There are only three facets for this concept:

– justification by giving a motive;

– reasons which make us act;

– will to achieve an objective.

1.3. Theological point of view

In Buddhist philosophy, appreciating the present moment is a state of behavior, a quest and in that sense, a motivation for optimism. To begin with, one is conditioned to believe that the "me", the ego, does not last, and that time does not pass, and is an illusion to the contrary, we follow the Buddhist commandment to become fully conscious of the present moment. Becoming aware of the fact that there is an "I" which forms an integral part of that moment – which is an instantaneous part of a temporally distributed ego – can condition subscribers to find themselves in the moment, which develops the motivation to detach oneself from time; even if it does not work, this stops time appearing to pass by – that is, Buddhists attempt to "live in the now". Thus, for example in a situation where an individual wants to enjoy the moment of a dinner, he can get away from the pain and anxiety of the disagreements over the dishes which will burn on the hobs and the uneaten food which will remain. If he tells himself "I may be able to gain a little respite from the pain and anxiety of this disastrous dinner, in which the fully-loaded hobs burn black as the uneaten dishes are taken away", each instant can be given over to savoring the dish of the moment.

Christian theology, exposed at its very beginnings to the agonizing dilemma of good and evil in human action, defined a concept peculiar to willpower, called "free arbitration of will", or simply "free arbitration". This is the faculty of a human being to determine himself freely and on his own, to act and think, in contrast to determinism or fatalism, which hold that will is determined in every act by "forces" which require it.

The French expression "*libre arbitre*" (of which "free arbitration" is the literal rendering), does not give a full enough account of the indissociable link which ties it to the notion of will. This link can be seen more easily in the more common English expression "Free will" and the German equivalent "*Willensfreiheit*". However, these expressions have the disadvantage of doing away with the notion of arbitration or choice, which is essential to the concept (Erasmus, Luther, Diderot, Saint Augustin, Fonsegrive, Schopenhauer, Muhm, Rouvière).

1.4. Notion of belief and autonomy

More recently, and still within the framework of lexicology, an international language called Kotava, created in 1975 by the linguist Staren Fetcey, expresses the verb "believe" in accordance with three different facets, one of which characterizes reflexivity of the belief relating to the individual himself – a form of self-belief, describing the individual who sees himself, represents or imagines himself. For instance, *I imagine myself eating* would be translated as *fogesestú*, with the prefix *fogé*, denoting self-representation; or *I imagine myself writing* would be translated as *fogesuté*.

Lexicology, which is an extension of linguistics, is in itself a good example of the enigma which enables an individual to concretize his autonomy and desires of action. In the natural order which anyone can observe, we find a hierarchy of natural objects, the majority of which are in a mineral state, and some in a living state. Of all living things, humans are the only ones to define plans in accordance with their surroundings, whilst retaining a high degree of flexibility about the range of their actions. In this sense, it is a peculiarity, and therefore an enigma. Religion has provided elements of a response to this puzzle. Biology and psychology have also made contributions. More globally, however, it is a particular cognitive state which appears peculiar to a state of consciousness which is not a very long way from the faculty of reasoning. We shall see the reason for this in Chapters 10 and 11. The uncertainty principle, chaos theory or Gödel's incompleteness theorems have, according to some people, brought new elements to this debate, but without being able to resolve the issue. The two academic disciplines which seem most likely to be able to give elements of a response to the question of free will are physics (which studies the laws of nature) and neurosciences (which study the function of the nervous system and therefore the brain, the decisional organ). Physics enables us to better understand the notion of determinism, while neurosciences touch directly on free will. Many writers state that we need motivation. In actual fact, this is not quite true: we *have* motivation.

1.5. Scientific schools of thought

The first cognitive science center was founded in 1960 at Harvard University by two psychologists: Jerome Bruner [BRU 56] and George Miller [MIL 56], who were interested in the mental mechanisms involved in language. Hoping to introduce greater formal rigor into social sciences than some of their predecessors such as Frederick C. Bartlett [BAR 25] and Jean Piaget [PIA 23], they worked with researchers in computer science, equating cognition to manipulation of signs, and viewed computers as a good model of the human mind. Stemming from the field of cybernetics (artificial intelligence or AI), this new way of looking at cognition would inspire the pioneers of artificial intelligence and give rise to an entirely new branch of cognitive sciences. In the mid-1980s, when the American psychologist Jerry Fodor [FOD 75] had just put forward his theory on the modular architecture of the mind and the computational theory of mind was beginning to gather momentum, in France, we witnessed the birth of a long-awaited institutionalization. The first association in cognitive sciences, the Arc (Association for Cognitive Research) appeared in 1981, founded mainly by researchers in computer sciences, psychologists and linguists. These researchers modeled their work on American cognitive sciences, which had emerged twenty years earlier. Thus, in the 1970s, before the creation of the Arc, computer scientists, psychologists and linguists came together on many occasions, to develop a theoretical computer science oriented at comprehension of language. These meetings were financed by INRIA (the French National Research Institute). The objective was that of artificial intelligence: to simulate cognitive functions. After having studied neurobiology, Patricia Churchland [CHU 86] put forward eliminative reductionism – i.e. the reduction of mental states to the underlying biological phenomena and the elimination of the psychological level. As a toehold, Churchland uses the trains of thought in the area of AI, which simulates functions of the brain as an automaton with input and output. The ideas of Gerald Edelman [EDE 87] have a considerable following amongst neurobiologists. Joint winner of the Nobel Prize in Physiology or Medicine in 1972, Gerald Edelman constructed a theory of memory and consciousness, based on the principle of progressive natural selection of the links which are established between neurones. His work constitutes an attempt to bring together neurobiology, evolutionism and genetics, where he defends his theory of neuronal groups. He believes that the mechanisms of perception and memory are based on the principle that, of an infinite number of connections which could be established during the brain's development, only certain pathways are stimulated by the subject's actions and the information given to him. Edelman [EDE 92] proposes a biology of consciousness, with emphasis placed on the processes of acquisition and modification by feedback of the acquisition on the innate potentialities. The model of consciousness has been influenced twofold by the revolution in cognitive sciences, inspired by computing (algorithms, memories, computation) and the neurobiological revolution (neuronal group selection, interconnection, neuromediators, psychoneurobiological representations). Neurosciences are the key to the processes of learning, social behaviors, neurological and mental dysfunction, foreshadowing a fundamental aspect of psychology.

1.6. The question of experience

For ethical reasons, few experiments have been performed on human beings to date. Dr. Rick Strassman, a neurologist specializing in *hallucinogenic substances*, was sanctioned by the US Department of Defense between 1990 and 1994 to inject a cohort of 60 healthy human patients and observe the effects of hallucinogenic substances [STR 96]. His research aimed to investigate the effects of the molecule *N,N*-dimethyltryptamine (DMT), a potent entheogen, or psychedelic drug, which he believes is produced in the pineal gland in the human brain. DMT is found in many and varied naturally-occurring sources, and is associated with human neurotransmitters such as serotonin and melatonin. There is a theory that DMT plays a role in the formation of dreams. Indeed Strassman also hypothesized that an individual who has a near-death experience causes the pineal gland to produce a relatively large amount of DMT, like in a dream-like state, which would explain the visions related by survivors who have come back from near-death experiences.

Oxytocin is a peptide hormone made by the paraventricular and supraoptic nuclei of the hypothalamus and secreted by the posterior pituitary gland (neurohypophysis). Its name means "quick birth". Indeed, it is involved in the process of giving birth, but in both men and women, it also seems to favor amorous social interactions, or which involve cooperation, altruism, empathy, attachment or the sense of sacrificing oneself for another – even for another who is not part of the group to which a person belongs [COO 02; BLA 56; BLA 60; BLA 64; UVN 03]. In certain situations, oxytocin can also induce radical or violent behavior for defense of the group – e.g. against another person who is refusing to cooperate. In these instances, it becomes a source of defensive (and not offensive) aggression.

Experiments relating to *isolation* have been conceived of. They are erstwhile, and only historical studies of archives relating to the subject reveal their authenticity. Of course, such experiments could never be countenanced in today's world, for reasons of human rights and ethics. In the Middle Ages, the Holy Roman Emperor Frederick II of the House of Hohenstaufen wished to know what sort of language and what way of speaking would be adopted by children brought up without ever speaking to anybody. Also, his chronicles tell us that the Franciscan monk Salimbene of Parma asked wet-nurses to raise children, to bathe and wash them, but never to prattle with them or speak to them, because he wished to know whether they would speak Hebrew, the most ancient language (or at least it was thought to be at the time) or Greek, or Latin, or Arabic, or possibly the language spoken by their biological parents. His efforts were in vain, because all the children died... indeed, "they could not survive without the smiling faces, caresses and loving words of their nurses". According to Aroles [ARO 07], the tale of children raised by wolves is a fallacy. Aroles is the only one to have conducted an inquiry into the question of the wolf-children by searching in the archives. Certainly, throughout human history, infants have been adopted by lone she-wolves, but apparently, never has a whole pack of wolves adopted a small child, be it Indian, Jewish or otherwise.

As we shall see in the coming chapters, we are not merely the product of our environment. We are the product of our biology. More globally, we are the product of mutual dynamics between the outside world, our internal world and our past and present behavior.

Chapter 2

Self-motivation on a Daily Basis

There is no shortage of examples of self-motivation to be found in our daily lives. We need only take the time to look.

2.1. In news blogs

In terms of the media and political information, certain current affairs arouse a polemic – particularly immigration. Sometimes, the impression given by the discourse on blogs gives immigration as being at the root of all problems, and everything comes back to that. It is impossible to ever break free of the issue completely. Any explanation for a fact, a phenomenon, a series of events, can be put down to mistrust or hatred of foreigners. From that point on, readers will believe anything, and particularly nonsense. As soon as a "newspaper" or a Website reports something: readers believe, they are certain, they are horrified/scandalized/revolted. This is *self-belief which is reinforced* because, since they already believe it, they make no attempt to verify the veracity of the information. The nationalism which underlies a fragmented, "isolating" and xenophobic political culture goes hand-in-hand with self-belief in a unique nation, alone and unequalled in the world (*anadelfo ethnos*: a nation without brothers or sisters).

2.2. Marketing

In the world of marketing, superstar salespeople are trained and motivated, animated, enthusiastic, persistent, have self-confidence, are sometimes arrogant, with no fear of outright rejection, driven by success, they have **firm self-belief**.

They know that they *will* sell; they see the positive side of everything. They see objections as "disguised buying signals". People who succeed in sales transfer their energy into argument (or, better put, into bartering), they create urgency, excitement about the product/service, and a desire to buy immediately – and of course, they close the deal. The world of art, just as eccentric as one might imagine it to be, is similar in many regards to that of marketing. Thus, Van Gogh's rejection of the established methods and pursuit of an alternative system, combined with self-confidence and determination were the fundamental ingredients of a creative entrepreneurial marketing practice. For many marketers of art, the main focal point seems to be to learn what others have done and to copy their procedures. For entrepreneurial marketers of art, these methods are adapted to satisfy the needs of the organization or, if these methods do not satisfy the requirements, alternative solutions are found. Salvador Dali is quoted as saying "At the age of six, I wanted to be a chef. At seven, I wanted to be Napoleon. And my ambition has never ceased growing since then". This illustrates assertive, proactive marketing where the choice is either to follow accepted marketing techniques according to traditional recipes, to become a super-chef adapting and improvising with the limited resources available in the organization, or conducting a higher level of creative entrepreneurial marketing, inventing new approaches. According to Mendel [MEN 98] the game with the transitory objective is in the prehistory of the act of "being able to". Through creation, I become master of the presence or absence of the mother. The game is often associated with any process of creation and self-confidence.

2.3. Appearance

Daily life offers situations of frustration or deviant behavior. An example is obesity. However, some people are unable to control their behavior. One of the explanations lies in lack of self-confidence. People suffering from low self-esteem also have the habit of putting themselves down. They constantly tell themselves that they are not good enough and that they are destined for failure. Over time, this negative self-talk becomes negative self-belief. In addition, they try and implant these seeds of negativity in the people around them. They also gravitate toward people who suffer from similar problems. The final result is that they feed off one another's negativity, and become much poorer individuals than they initially were. A high level of dissatisfaction is another indicator of low self-esteem. Some people spend all their time complaining. They see nothing positive in others, nor in themselves. Cynism eats away at their self-believe, and erodes their self-confidence. Conversely, people who value their own capabilities enjoy high self-esteem.

Visual appearance and the different means of correcting it require self-motivation, which can be altered by self-confidence. Simply put, attainment of a canon of beauty, losing weight, the dream of being as slender as a mannequin or simply being seductive – what some call "being popular" even at school age – can never be realized without self-motivation and solid self-confidence. The pressure is often greater for girls, making them attempt to attain an ideal stimulated by the world of "marketing", anxious to sell products, and knowing their compulsive consumer instinct.

2.4. Mystical experiences

We see cases of self-belief and powerful personal self-motivation in the context of esoteric cultures. The tales of out-of-body experiences evoke the endured and unwanted nature of the events, and incomprehension. This is interpreted as proof that we can have spiritual experiences without wishing to, which in fact expresses the opposite – i.e. self-conditioning or self-motivation. Another phenomenon which arouses therapeutic interest but which requires active participation of the audience is hypnosis. Some people claim that hypnosis can bridge the gap between dreams and objectives. In this theme, there is also a contribution of self-motivation in the guise of success. Mystic experiences are as old as time: they are attributable more or less to a conscious interpretation of one's intellect. According to practitioners, intellect astutely gathers together various elements from one's deep psyche and one's subconscious, to form a pseudo-logical system as intelligently as possible. The whole system feeds off strong feelings, emotions, which "energize" or "magnetize" the practitioner's vision or belief. In addition, the feelings of self-importance and value which every human being needs become "saturated", and one falls under the spell of this self-motivation to the point of sharing that feeling with those around them.

2.5. Infantheism

Infantheism is an example of a collective attitude which promotes the cult of the Infant God. This faith has become omnipresent in increasingly senile western countries. This cult of prostration before the neo-infant presents an image of itself as omnipotent under a new augur. Hence, it is a behavior stimulated by self-motivation because it comes from the individual and refers him back to himself – it is a self-cult, a cult of an idealized self. The ideal is reinforced by the difference in age [MUR 91].

2.6. Addiction

Clinical psychology and developmental psychology offer areas of study which examine pathological cases of motivation. In itself, this vindicates a possible alteration of a potential self-motivation system, and in itself, it is presented as an argument in favor of a systemic motivational system, because every natural system relies on equilibrium and state transitions which can be altered. In the real world, in the case of the process of drug addiction, psychosocial interventions need to be modified for patients suffering from schizophrenia with cognitive deficit symptoms and low self-confidence. Motivation improvement techniques are a central component of the treatment. Improvement of motivation reduces comsumption of the substance, and can be applied as a current intervention by a large-scale program. Prevention of relapses, based on a cognitive-behavioral approach, helps the patients to identify triggers, in the same way as for psychosis and substance abuse (e.g. stress response associated with social environmental factors). It also helps develop alternative strategies for when they find themselves facing high-risk situations. Relapses should be viewed as opportunities to develop strategies of adaptation with the patients, rather than as failures. At these times, the patients often feel demoralized, and it is important to remind them of their previous successes in terms of treatment.

Figure 2.1. *Statue of a "Border guard with his dog" in the Moscow metro (Revolution Square Station). The polishing evident on the dog's nose is attributable to the Russian supersition (still prevalent even today), which says that touching the dog's nose brings good luck to a hunt. This remained the case even after 70 years of materialistic communism, which destroyed the churches and purged popular belief. The statue itself was cast in the Communist era, by Communists*

In summary, no matter what life throws at us, no matter what our fears, no matter what the circumstances, we can get through it. Self-motivation and confidence are a large stride in the right direction. Take precautions to obtain this motivation and confidence, and everything becomes possible. To cite Lichtenberg [LIC 65], qualifying frenzy in self-motivation, "There are people that can believe everything they want. These are happy creatures."

Chapter 3

The Notion of Need

Our needs govern our consciousness by way of the mechanism of motivation. Our vital needs are a good illustration of this relation with motivation – although the primary vital need – the need to breathe – is usually felt subconsciously rather than consciously. Why? We must see individuals not only as being thinking entities, i.e. which are cognitive but also physical, but also as being mobile, unlike plants. However, respiration is a pressing need which does not support a tolerance to ubiquity as do other needs. It is a reflexive and instantaneous need – hence that unconscious feeling of a need.

3.1. Hierarchy of needs

Maslow's theory about human motivation establishes a hierarchy of needs to describe the motivation of a student [MAS 43; MAS 87]. Tennant [TEN 97] summarizes this hierarchy as follows:

– physiological needs – e.g. hunger, thirst and need for sleep;

– survival needs – the need for a secure space and a predictable world;

– needs for love and friendship – the need for meaningful relationships with other people;

– needs for self-esteem – these involve feelings of competence, confidence, credibility and respect of others;

– need for personal accomplishment – where full expression of the student's talents and potential can be demonstrated.

Practitioners of personal development are able to follow a social norm without being limited in their point of view and their beliefs, and can on occasion go beyond social means of behavior [TEN 97]. For some students today, even the first two levels of the hierarchy (physiological needs and security) are not guaranteed; they only have the motivation to keep themselves fed and keep a roof over their heads, and in some cases do the same for their families. If this requires them to spend long hours at some paid job, we can imagine that finding the time – and indeed the motivation – to integrate themselves socially and academically into an institution may be a challenge.

Needs beyond level 3 share the property of relying on a micro-certitude, which may extend to macro-certitudes, guaranteeing a stable progression of daily events – or by extension, more cosmological events (not to say poetic or esoteric).

3.1.1. *Level-1 needs*

Let us return to an explanation of level-1 needs. We have seen that *breathing* is nearly a reflex.

3.1.1.1. *Hunger*

Our bodies have to consume 400 kg of solid food a year; hunger is a sensation which occurs when the level of glycogen in the liver falls below a certain level, which usually precedes the desire to eat. This sensation, which is often unpleasant, comes from the hypothalamus, and then is triggered by receptors in the liver. Although human beings can survive several weeks without eating, the sensation of hunger usually begins to be felt a few hours after eating. Satiety is a sensation which is felt when we are no longer hungry, once we have eaten; this too is conditioned by the hypothalamus. This sensation is notably controlled by a number of hormones: leptin (discovered in 1994 – [ZHA 94]), ghrelin (discovered in 1999 – [KOJ 99]) and cholecystokinin (CCK) (discovered in 2002 – [WIE 02]). CCK was identified more recently by a British team working at Imperial College, London, and confirmed by researchers in Oregon and Australia. The hormone is secreted by the intestinal cells. The concentration of this hormone in the blood rises after having eaten, and remains high between meals, reducing the subject's desire to eat. When the concentration of CCK decreases, the brain interprets this as a signal of the beginning of hunger.

3.1.1.2. *Thirst*

Our bodies need to absorb 400 liters of water a year; thirst is a sensation of the need to drink, and is characteristic of a lack of water in the organism's cells. Under the control of the hypothalamus, thirst intervenes in the organism's behavior, alerting it so that it will respond to the need to drink. Thirst is related to the process of osmoregulation. Thirst is involved in maintaining the hydric balance. It regulates the intake of water by the organism, complementing the action of the antidiuretic hormone (ADH) which regulates the output of water. The mechanisms which regulate thirst are not perfectly known. Loss of water manifests itself by two phenomena, one at the intracellular level (2/3 of the hydric store), the other at the extracellular level (1/3 of the hydric store): osmotic pressure in the cells increases, while hypovolemia – a reduction in blood volume – causes a drop in blood pressure.

3.1.1.3. *Sleep*

Remember that our bodies drive us to sleep for the equivalent of 100 full days a year; sleep is a corporal state which results from active mechanisms called "sleep permissive" mechanisms. The alternation between sleep and wakefulness alternation is controlled by a two-pronged process: homeostasis and the circadian cycle. On the one hand, the circadian rhythm (a true internal biological clock), is aligned with the alternation of night and day (the nycthemeral cycle), by external synchronizing factors. In the whole organism, the circadian cycle results in a drop in body temperature, because of a cerebral hormone, melatonin [AXE 60], which is made at night by the pineal gland. The timetable of secretion of this hormone depends in part on genetic factors (whether the subjects are "morning people" or "evening people"), but is also modulated by external stimuli such as light levels, food supply, heat production and social environmental factors. On the other hand, the homeostatic process (the tendency to return to a state of equilibrium) is a sort of timer which alternates the periods of sleep and wakefulness. The propensity to sleep increases progressively throughout the day and then dissipates at night, during the sleep cycle. The molecular mechanisms at the root of this homeostatic process, however, are not yet known.

3.1.2. *Level-3 needs*

Level-3 needs cover the direct human relationships which socialize an individual. In this context, for young adults beginning to integrate themselves into society, and even for more mature adults, **sexuality** plays a major role in stabilizing their emotions and favoring certain friendships. The human sexual response comprises three stages: desire, arousal and orgasm. If desire is absent, the next phase will be compromised. Desire is sometimes referred to as libido – a term which denotes the level of desire and arousal for sexual activity. The libido is one aspect of a person's sexual activity, but varies enormously from one person to another, and also varies depending on the circumstances at a given moment. Libido is intrinsically linked to biological, psychological and social components. In biological terms, the levels of hormones such as testosterone are held to have a profound impact on libido; social factors such as work or family life also have an impact, as do psychological factors such as one's personality and level of stress. Libido can be affected by medication, lifestyle and relationship problems. Someone who has an intense libido or frequently indulges in sexual practices may be characterized by traits of hypersexuality, but there is no way of quantifying what a "healthy" level of libido is. Men's libido peaks in their adolescence; women's in their thirties. Certain theories, such as that advanced by James Giles, hold that libido is a social construct, intended to develop the feeling of incompleteness in one gender in relation to the other, and cause one gender to seek their own identity through relations with the other gender. Here, we can point out the denial of biology and of the organic elements of sexuality, which is also expressed (remember the third point of sexuality – orgasm) by elements of pleasure. In addition to its social character, sexuality is an operation performed by nature for the reproduction of the species, and mixing of the genes in order to best adapt to the environment. In that sense, it is a survival instinct, rather than a command to force people to live together. In view of this naturalistic observation, the stereotypical nuclear family structure – a man, a woman and a child – was developed to optimize the allocation of material resources and avoid interpersonal conflicts as far as possible. Sexuality is indeed a natural feeling and a need for every individual.

3.2. The satiation cycle

Certain theories have described the global process of the evolution of need in the form of a cycle. Thus, Vohs and Baumeister [VOH 05] described a cycle of "ethological" satiation. When the need is strong, a living organism tends to seek satisfaction, but when satisfaction is obtained the need expressed by the organism diminishes, only to re-emerge gradually over time when the satisfaction disappears. Going back to the example of hunger (a level-1 need), after a long time without eating, you feel hungry, which motivates you to seek and obtain food, but after eating you feel less of an urgent need to find food.

The other, higher-level needs (self-confidence, personal accomplishment) depend on multiple factors. They are conditioned by the satisfaction of lower-level needs. In this sense, they are more complex to apprehend and explain summarily for each individual. Conversely, there is no argument that necessarily suggests that higher-level needs are not structured according to the same arrangement as the needs in levels 1 and 3, for instance. Hence, these needs interfere with psychological and biological aspects.

Certain "innate" organized forms of behavior are present at birth; others appear after a period of maturation. We do not have to teach babies to breastfeed or to cry, toddlers to walk or adolescents to experiment with their sexuality. Neither do we have to create physiological motivators to deal with hunger, thirst, pain or somatic rewards. Similarly, small children are equipped with attentional selectivity and an interpretative tendency [VON 79]. The basic physiological functions are programmed at birth, as the result of accumulated ancestral experiences which are stored in the genetic code.

Even from the time when religion was still opposed to the investigation of the process of consciousness, and historically attempted to upset the course of the investigations and interpretations, we can see that this notion of need and systematic motivation could provide an interpretation of behavior. Notably Nietzsche [NIE 82], in passage 347, legibly interpreted the need for faith and for religious belief as being a search for a motivational state. "How much faith a person requires in order to flourish, how much 'fixed opinion' he requires which he does not wish to have shaken, because he holds himself thereby is a measure of his power (or more plainly speaking, of his weakness)". In the next chapter we shall see that a high-level process such as belief can be explained by a system which associates physiological mechanism and cognitive mechanism in a process of need.

Chapter 4

The Models of Social Organization

This chapter deals with the notion of social organization. This is the context external to the individual that enables him to formulate plans and perform actions in accordance with his motivational states and his needs [ROU 62; TÖN 87; SIM 08; MEA 34].

Many models of social organization have been advanced. Here we shall only cite those which are directly related to action and motivation.

4.1. The entrepreneurial model

The *entrepreneurial model* was described by Sarmiento *et al.* [SAR 07], who present the entrepreneurial attributes necessary to run a company. Of these, we can cite self-confidence and self-determination, alongside: realization of ambition, perseverance, a high degree of control, orientation of action, preference for learning by doing, a taste for the work, determination and creativity.

In the same vein as the entrepreneurial model but also centered around personal development, Covey [COV 99] describes a method of development and management which advocates proactiveness: the seven habits of highly effective people. Here, the human being is as much an actor as a receiver. The paradigm of the model is the way in which each person views the world – not necessarily how it really is. This is the map, not the ground. It is the optic specific to each person: the lens through which the individuals examine everything; it is forged by the education we have received and the accumulation of our experiences and our choices. The rules are as follows:

– be proactive, take initiatives; each person is the architect of his own life;

– know where you are going from the very beginning;

– prioritize the priorities;

– think win-win (there can be no friendship without trust, nor trust without integrity);

– seek first to understand others, and then to be understood;

– benefit from synergy;

– hone your abilities.

Proactiveness is a principle of one's personal vision, individual, institutional or community vision, depending on the case. To be proactive is to be dynamic, alert, vigilant, hardworking, perseverant, serious, diligent, enterprising, determined. This cannot be boiled down to taking the initiative. It involves assuming responsibility for one's own behavior (past, present and future). It is a question of basing one's choices on principles and values, rather than on moods and circumstances. It is a question of being an enactor of change; of choosing not to be a victim, not having a reactive attitude and not shirking one's responsibility for other people; of developing and applying the four gifts particular to humans: self-awareness, ethics, imagination and free will; of sparking change by opting to approach issues "from the inside out" and finally making the most fundamental resolution: to be the creative force in one's own life.

In order to stick with his choices, an entrepreneur must never give up at the first hurdle, but effectively get around the difficulties, and ensure that the final result is achieved, even if he has already done his bit of the work. He must always take initiatives, and follow the active projects through to the very end, constantly looking for solutions.

We can see that in both these entrepreneurial models, the motivational state plays a key role, and it is stimulated to produce actions which drive the person forward to decision and initiative.

Actions considered to be entrepreneurial may be based on any combination of behaviors and experience, involving a context (e.g. education, social class), cognitive skills (e.g. risk analysis, interpersonal skills), effects of attitude (self-perception, motivation), and the environment. Henderson and Robertson [HEN 99] remarked that the most frequently-mentioned adjectives were "motivated", "hardworking", "self-confident" and "determined", and the most commonly-cited keywords associated with the term "entrepreneur" were "risk-taking", "motivated", "ambitious" and "success". Similarly, a study conducted on students at a Scottish university found that the most common elements mentioned when asked to define entrepreneurism were "generation of ideas", "success", "creativity" and "opportunity". However, this opinion lacks realism as regards the influence of the innovation.

Kelman [KEL 1958] performed a great deal of research about behavior and organization applied to the process of social influence on commitment. Integration of the user's system of affective processes and personal norms into a model render a user's own beliefs crucial. Normative beliefs have an influence on behavior or differentiation of roles; in particular, this has been studied as regards gender roles by Wood *et al.* [WOO 97].

The opinion that emotion amplifies other capacities, or blocks them, is widely accepted [FRÉ 01]. Also, certain academics believe that emotion is the driving factor in motivation. The work of Forootan [FOR 07] showed that managers who have emotional relationships with their staff and who show their own emotions have a motivation which makes them compatible with the objectives and values of the organization.

4.2. Motivational and ethical states

Motivational and ethical states shape individuals, at the same time as those individuals, by their interactions, shape these states. An ethic based on autonomy – either of an individual or of a systemic whole – is an ethic based on universal moral principles, which do not depend on social or natural contingencies. They reflect the present context in which people interact: their circumstances, aspirations and motivations of individual life. This is an idealized vision of ethics, in which autonomous leaders exercise their freedom independently of the contingencies of nature or society. Management becomes the formulation of visions for an organization, independently of the nature and society in which that organization operates. In the Kantian sense of autonomy, acceptance of the visionary states of the top management by their underlings is tantamount to capitulation of their autonomy. Participation becomes a participant in the leadership of the leaders. If their actions are supposed to be ethical, from this point of view, then the individuals are assumed to be "connected to the world" and "committed to the whole".

Situativity theory offers an interesting framework for interpretation of consciousness by way of the notion of situation. Gibson [GIB 79] describes coupling between the environment and the individual, and sense and context, directly linked to perception but which are consistent with visions of the situated cognition [BRO 89; GRE 98; KIR 97; KIR 98; LAV 93; LAV 91; YOU 95]. Situativity theory states that thought involves interaction between the individuals and physical and social situations. Situativity theory constructs a theoretical framework whose central tenet is that cognition, thought and learning are situated (located) in experience. The importance of context in this theory is predominant, triggering the unique contribution of the environment to cognition, thought and learning. The argument is that cognition, thought and learning cannot be dissociated from (are dependent upon) the context. Situativity theory considers situated cognition, situated learning, ecosystemic psychology and distributed cognition. Two arguments play in favor of the application of situativity theory: one relating to the complexity of the environment, which may be nonlinear and multi-level; the other regarding individual responsibility and participation in a community (increasing "belonging"), which may be important for learning.

As we can imagine, social evolution is very rarely conditioned by fortune and chance; human beings can consciously design their own destinies. **Structuration theory** holds that the rules and resources which are mobilizable in the production and reproduction of social action are also the means of reproduction of the system. In this respect, human social activities are recursive because they are continually recreated by the actors, in which they express themselves as actors. In and through their activities, the agents reproduce the conditions which render these activities possible. The rules of social life may be considered to be generalizable techniques or procedures, applied for the adoption and reproduction of social practices. These rules which relate to the reproduction of institutionalized practices are the most important for sociology. Giddens [GID 84] defines the characteristics of these rules as intense vs. superficial, tacit vs. discursive, informal vs. formalized, weakly vs. strongly sanctioned. Signification, domination and legitimation are the three structural dimensions of social systems in structuration theory. Domination should depend on the mobilization of two types of resources: allocative resources refer to the capacities – or, more precisely, to forms of capacity for transformation – giving rise to control over objects, goods and material phenomena. Authority resources refer to types of transformative capacity, giving rise to control over the objects and the actors. [GID 84] pays a great deal of attention to the development of society in space and time – a reflection which seems crucial for human beings. As regards structure, Bhaskar [BHA 98] and Giddens [GID 84] define it as an entity which consists of stances and practices (Bhaskar) and of rules and resources (Giddens) which link them. Luhmann [LUH 88] argues that in Giddens' theory, society is mutually associated with the interactional domain in which the people interact. The society selects the interactions, and the interactions select the society; this is a form of an organizational closed cycle. We can imagine choosing to observe the society, and seeing communication networks activating other levels of communication, and forming closed subsystems which persist and are reproduced over time. We can also focus more closely on particular episodes of interactions between groups and individuals.

An alternative point of view to structuration based on *a priori* rules is self-regulation, leading to a theory of **social self-organization**. The details of changing circumstances choose the movements which are expressed, and the movements conforming to a wider global configuration of movements, a product of global emergence.

Turning back to the fundamental principles of self-organization which draws its principles from the observation of natural systemic behaviors in biology and physics. Juarrero's [JUA 99] theory about convection is based on physical metaphors for self-control and choice, determinate salient aspects of behavior. The metaphors are taken from simplistic physical systems in which a single process is at work, and laboratory models which have to operate up to a critical point. In living systems, criticality in itself emerges spontaneously: this is self-organized criticality [BAK 96]. Living systems self-organize to remain around critical states. The benefits may be elementary. Criticality allows for an attractive mixture of creativity and constraints. This creates new options for behavior and facilitates the choice of behavior to fit in with the circumstances of the behavior. Why is it that a creative nature gives rise to mystery in itself? In any case, the mystery is delimited on all sides by natural phenomena. The determined natural behavior comes from self-organized criticality – this is known as Juarrero's Conjecture [JUA 99], which suggested that intentional content keeps human beings in equilibrium around critical states. The intentional contents themselves emerge from dynamic structures. The intentional contents, as emergent structures, persist over the course of time by cyclic causality. They are a source of constraints which persist over time. The constraints limit the degrees of freedom of the interactions between the processes of the human body. The intentional contents remain stable over the course of time, whereas the movements of the body are changeable within rather brief periods of time. Constraints which change gradually or infrequently limit the possibilities of movement over more rapid timescales. However, [JUA 99] offered no proof in support of self-organized criticality: hence the application of the term "conjecture". She constructed a philosophical argument against conceiving intentional contents as representations and representations as efficient causes.

Now let us turn to a concrete case from daily life and which is also widely studied in developmental psychology; success in exams: a moment in life we all share, and which is unavoidable nowadays. The conditions for success in an exam are often tributary to capacities of self-organization. Motivation gives us inspiration to achieve our goals. It gives the student an incentive to grow, learn and develop capacities for self-organization. We build endurance based on motivation. In order to comprehend how motivation develops and how it is applicable to self-organization, we must learn to pay attention to certain stages in the phase of development. First, we have to make a promise to ourselves. This promise is to work via processes of self-development while we work on our subject, on our mental strength and this cultivates self-discipline. This in turn motivates us. Secondly, discomfort can affect us, and therefore we have to learn to understand and take control of discomfort. Discomforts are elements which worry us and often keep us apart by disturbing our attention. This is due to the fact that many people are unable to overcome discomforts. Often these people remain embarrassed, rather than attempting to put their finger on why and how they become uncomfortable. One of the greatest discomforts is the stress we feel before an exam. Even hearing the word "test" makes us uncomfortable. Discomfort leaves many people in this same state of mind until the test is over, when they realize that it was not so bad. If these people organized there study time, they would feel little or no stress during their exam. We must realize that assuming our responsibilities can keep failure at arm's length by way of a one-stage program. Time is important. By attaching value to time, we give ourselves space to organize our lives. Recognizing the value of time also helps to accept discomfort. Discomfort can either enable us to build ourselves up or break ourselves down. Thus, we have to learn to change our minds and our bodies to deal with our discomfort. It is possible to use subliminal learning through meditation to help control one's discomfort. Remember that discomfort causes anxiety and gives rise to embarrassment. This is due to the fact that some people will notice that you cannot deal with your discomfort and show signs of weakness and failure. When people lack motivation, they can find parts of the test where they lack confidence. Instead of letting these parts weaken their performance, it is possible to study harder in order to build confidence and gain better control over the weak parts. Studying harder helps to learn in many ways to solve problems. The exam may not be the source of the discomfort. Instead, the discomfort may relate to the position in which you are sitting. If you feel pain in this position, you must rearrange your body so that it is more relaxed. You can use internal dialog to debate what it is about the exam that discourages you. Using internal dialog, people often find that discomfort is a state of mind. The mind is powerful, and can keep us from succeeding. Using internal dialog, we can see that the problem of starting, of putting something on the blank page, was not a problem after all, and merely heightened our discomfort. This tends to have an effect on our capacity for organization. At certain times, we have to put ourselves under pressure in order to accomplish what we wish to achieve. For instance, if the exam taking place tomorrow is put back a week, this applies pressure to our work to finish the exam on time. Alternatively, it is possible to relieve the pressure on oneself long enough to finish the exam on time. When we feel ourselves disconcerted by the exam or the subject does not seem clear, there is also the possibility of asking for help or support. This is a human right. It is possible to invite a group of friends round to prepare and study for the exam together. Sometimes, it is sufficient just to write down one's plans for the day, in order to organize one's time and space so as to be able to meet one's obligations.

The problem of motivating crowds is a ubiquitous issue. It arises in any situation where a person wishes to affect or influence the behavior of others, including children's learning, training, politics, publicity, seduction, advice and psychotherapy and brainwashing. The concept of motivation seems to be a controversial key concept for self-organization and conduct of a dynamic of behavior since the beginning of the 1960s [PAT 64].

Certain values reinforce individuals' self-organization. Self-organization in itself can deliver different results when coupled with other factors such as focus, prioritization, collaboration, commitment, respect and courage. In a self-organized community, there is no real need for a hierarchy, in the strict sense of the term. Everyone is a leader, and everyone is a manager. An innocent communication, a sense of constructive criticism and constant iterations with prioritized goals and clear vision help to accomplish objectives. Self-organization applies to everything in life: the moment when we are forced to do something marks the beginning of a loss of conviction for that thing. This has to come from oneself; this must be motivated intrinsically. Self-organization harbors autonomy.

In today's world of highly complex organizations, we have to understand the nature of leadership as self-organized and as being close to ethics: an ethic of co-creation of identity and difference of thoughts in action.

Chapter 5

Self Theories

As mentioned in Chapter 1, religion played a leading role in the way in which consciousness was analyzed from a psychosomatic point of view for many years. Descartes [DES 73], who contributed a great deal to the foundation of analytical rationality, even in his time distinguished mind and body as being two separate entities.

Freud's [FRE 23] works in clinical psychology caused many ripples in terms of a consciousness dependent on the body and on its history. Yet Freudian studies still show a nearly non-existent relation with motivation. It was not until the post-war period that Hilgard [HIL 49], then President of the American Psychological Association, defended the idea that the self is a unifying concept in problems of motivation. Forty years later, and with the benefit of hindsight, this opinion has become unanimously recognized, and according to Graham and Weiner [GRA 96], it is clear that the self occupies center-stage in the field of motivation.

When an opportunity for decision-making arises, one of the primary activities is the collection of information on the subject and the possible alternative actions. The way in which the information is collected and the way in which it is processed are variables which have a significant bearing on the profitability of the decision. At this level, we find neither a single unique behavior nor an infinite range of behaviors. An individual's cognitive style represents the characteristic modes of function of that individual in their behavior of thinking and perception [KAK 04]. Jung [JUN 53] postulated that the human psyche is part of a "collective unconscious" which transcends space and time, linking one mind with another and a mind with nature. He associates the individual and the collective unconscious with original forms – *Jungian archetypes*. Although Jung [JUN 53] describes them differently, he holds that these archetypes are crucial for understanding of the links between conscious and unconscious aspects of the human psyche, and of the contour such that a person will "find themselves" in coincidence with the environment. On the basis of Jung's thinking [JUN 53], Myers [MYE 80] suggests that in the same way that different people are born right-handed or left-handed, they are just as predisposed toward extraversion (E) or introversion (I); perception (P) or judging (J); sensing (S) or intuition (N); thinking (T) or feeling (F). Extraverts are oriented toward the external world of people and things; introverts toward the internal world of ideas and feelings. Sensitive individuals are concerned with details and facts, whereas intuitive individuals prefer to focus on the possibilities, the future and the big picture. Thinking people make decisions based on logic and objective criteria, while feeling individuals base their decisions on the more subjective domains of sensation and emotions. Perceptive individuals tend to be flexible, open-minded and seek more information, while judging people want things to be stable and under their control. Judgmental individuals prefer to live in a planned, ordered way and decide on the path they wish to take; perceptive individuals prefer to live flexibly and spontaneously (see Table 5.1 below). Myers' theory [MYE 80] was developed into a model of sixteen basic personality types in accordance with four dimensions.

Dimension	Preference
Energizing (How a person is energized)	Extraversion (E) - personal energy gleaned by interacting with the world outside of human affairs.
	Introversion (I) - personal energy gleaned by thought and reflection.
Information acquisition (How a person pays attention to, the ways in which they look for information)	Sensation (S) - information collected through the five senses, with a focus on facts and concrete experiences occurring at present.
	Intuition (N) - information acquired as shapes and intuitions, with a focus on the inter-relational big picture, meanings and possibilities.
Decision-making (How a person makes decisions)	Thought (T) - conclusions based on analytical logic, with emphasis on impartiality and objectivity.
	Feeling (F) - conclusions based on personal values, with a focus on empathy and harmony.
Orientations (Lifestyles that a person prefers)	Judgment (J) - focus on closure, predictability, planning, organization and control.
	Perception (P) - focus on adaptibility, flexibility and openness to new information.

Table 5.1. *Summary of the dimensions of psychological preferences [MYE 80]*

At the same time as G. Jung, Goffman [GOF 59] advanced hypotheses about the self, also anchored in the social context and their interactions. He draws the distinction between a sacred, internal self and a self in itself consciously present among other people in daily interactions. [GOF 59] is an extension of the approaches of the famous founding father of sociology Émile Durkheim [DUR 93] with his argument according to which, interaction creates the self more than one's surroundings, but Goffman's perspective has more of an impact, in the sense that it focuses specifically on the self. Goffman set forth a point of view on the causal dynamics of how interaction contributes to the formation of popular preconceptions, believing that the self is a dominant causal force at the micro-level. People come up with strategies, create and cooperate in teams in order to present a positive self. The person, who will either succeed or fail in his/her effort to generate a positive self-image, is simply a cornerstone, around which a collaborative structure is constructed over a certain period of time. Thus, the means to produce and maintain selves are not to be found within that cornerstone. The self is a sacred symbol of interaction, according to Goffman [GOF 59], following in the footsteps of Durkheim [DUR 12]. The force which generates the sacred symbol of the self is attributed to symbols (drawn from social interactions) which represent it once the symbols are formed. Organization is attributed to the sacred self, because it is the sacred symbol affirmed in multiple interaction rituals which shape our daily lives.

However, Goffman's argumentation is unclear, because the use of the terminology is complex and not always consistent. In his book [GOF 59], the self is used to denote the positive value that an individual receives in an interaction, which Goffman refers to as being a facet in a quest toward an ulterior motive. Goffman presented the individual as a strategy working in the present with a view to a positive self, but he does not explain the mechanisms or the capacity to make strategies.

More recently, a model advanced by Greenwald and Breckler [GRE 85] divides the self into the multiple audiences to whom it is presented (other people, oneself or other people with whom one is a co-participant). We can associate each of these audiences for the presentation of the self with a different motivational facet of the self: the public self, the private self and the collective self. [GRE 85] interpret the self (or the ego) as an organization of cognition, characterized by three information-control strategies. These three strategies, or cognitive biases, are: (1) *la beneffectance* (beneficence and effectence [competence]), the tendency for self to be perceived as effective in achieving desired ends whilst avoiding undesired ones, (2) *cognitive conservatism*, the tendency to resist cognitive change, and (3) *egocentricity*, the tendency for judgment and memory to be focused on self.

Some hypotheses of the theories of the motivational system, associating cognitive functions and neurology, as we shall see in detail in Chapter 7, highlight five primary motivations for the self (Lichtenberg *et al.*, [LIC 92]). They established their hypotheses and categories of motivational systems based on empirical data drawn from the study of children's development. The paradigm helps to understand the mutual relationship between motivation and ego. Each system is an entity with probable neurological correlations:

- the need for physiological regulation (physical health);

- the need for attachment and ulterior affiliation;

- the need for assertion and exploration;

- the need to react by aversion by way of antagonism or withdrawal;

- the need for sensual delights.

Motivational systems offer a gateway between theoretical models and clinical phenomena. These systems are often operational throughout our lives, and can be seen in the discourse of each individual. Lichtenberg *et al.*, [LIC 92] suggest that these five motivational systems work to develop, maintain and repair the cohesion of the self and self-organization. The switch from confrontation to exploration is an example of the potency of the natural motivational systems.

On an anecdotal note, it is interesting to note that one of the sons of Ferdinand de Saussure, the founder of structural linguistics, was a psychoanalyst. We shall see the importance of language in cognition later on, in Chapter 8.

Chapter 6

Theories of Motivation in Psychology

6.1. Behavior and cognition

An individual has a certain number of dimensions which modulate his/her personality (LEW 35; VYG 35; MCF 03]. The theories of the ego reveal glimpses of some of these dimensions. In addition, psychology, as a major science, has been able to touch on dimensions of the personality focusing on capacities for learning and therefore attention and motivation as an open-ended question. Individual differences are marked, for instance, by dimensions such as hostility/empathy, the property of which may help to better understand aggressive or insensitive forms of psychology. Numerous hypotheses have been put forward, which it is our intention to explore in this chapter.

After 20 years of studies in the 1960s and 1970s in the wake of the behavioralist movement, developed in the 1930s and 1940s by – in particular – Ivan Pavlov (1849-1936), John Watson (1878-1958), Burrhus F. Skinner (1904-1990), Clark Hull (1884-1952) and Edward Tolman (1886-1959), the existentialist humanist movement, aimed at psychological development to improve a learner's mental state, died down in the 1980s, ceding the stage to cognitive processes and the "information processing" view of human functioning. This cognitive revolution, as implied, was influenced by the technological advances and the advances of computational sciences, which have become a metaphorical signature of the movement. More than their humanist predecessors, the new wave of theorists focused on mental and internal events, but this investigation was at the root of cognitive functions such as the encoding and decoding of human thought, and problem-solving more than reflecting on the nature of the self. Over the past two decades, the prominent figures in psychology and education have indicated a major re-orientation of the critical issues of human functioning, and the self has, once again, become the major focal point of interest for research in psychology and educational practices as regards scholarly motivation.

In developmental psychology, it has long been recognized that there are many different forms of intelligence coexisting. According to Gardner [GAR 82], everyone is possessed of a mosaic of intelligences. Uniform teaching at school takes no account of these differences: each pupil has a spark in him/her. It is up to the educators and the institutions around the pupils to detect what might encourage these sparks. Particularly by encouraging children to have the confidence to work independently but also to develop social skills so as to be able to work as part of a team, it is possible to "kindle that spark".

6.2. Theory of self-efficacy

Turning away from the indifference of behavioralists to cognitive-reflexive processes, Bandura [BAN 89] postulated that individuals have a self-system which enables them to exercise a measure of control over their thoughts, feelings and actions. Moving in this direction, Bandura reawakened the nearly-abandoned field of investigation into the self in the study of human processes which William James [JAM 90] had initiated a century before. In Bandura's theory, individuals are perceived as proactive and self-regulated (or self-organized) rather than reactive and controlled by biological or environmental forces.

Bandura introduced the notion of *self-efficacy* as a key concept in his theory, defining it as the belief in one's own capabilities to organize and execute the courses of action required to manage prospective situations. This judgment has a profound effect on the choices that people make, the effort they invest and the way in which they persevere to deal with challenges. Pintrich and De Groot [PIN 90] showed that self-regulation, self-efficacy and exam stress emerge as being good factors on which to base a prediction of school performance. Schunk [SCH 00] even suggests that belief in self-efficacy could predict up to 25% of school performances (greater than the pedagogical processing of the effects).

The major breakthrough in relation to the work of behavioralist theorists was Bandura's triadic reciprocality model. In this model, Bandura postulates that the individual, the behavior and the environment are inextricably interlinked to create a tendency in an individual. Bandura [BAN 86] believed that the reflexive self is the only human capacity, and through this self-referent form of thought, individuals evaluate and alter their behavior and means of thought.

Investigations into English-language learning in Brazilian students reveal that motivation is not a linear phenomenon, and that small changes caused by the students' experiences can lead to a radical change in motivation (Menezes de Oliveira e Paiva [MEN 11]). On the other hand, motivation can evaporate when faced with monotonous activities in the classroom, but recrystallizes if the learner comes into contact with a different teacher, a new establishment, or interesting experiences outside of school. For instance, one student says that the only thing she learnt in school was to hate learning the English language. She lost her motivation in school, but it came back when she began to take private classes. She says that her teacher not only taught her not to be afraid, but also to love the language. Therefore she began learning English as a primary subject, her motivation crumbled, she began to hate the course and eventually abandoned it. Later, she traveled to Canada and lived there for six months, and when she came back to Brazil she joined another university and became an English teacher. Motivation is a changeable phenomenon, which can be strengthened or weakened and which can vary depending on the educational establishment and social experiences. One Brazilian student mentioned that she hated repeating dialogs but loved listening to music. It is interesting to see that a student's degree of motivation varies from one student to another, in similar situations.

Beliefs in self-efficacy have been characterized as mediators of our behavior. All of them are very important, and have an impact on our change in behavior. Our beliefs in our self-efficacy also have a high degree of significance in determining our motivation. Bandura observed that people regulate their level and the distribution of their effort in accordance with the effects that they expect to attain by their actions. As a result, their behavior is easier to predict based on their beliefs than on their current actions.

Self-efficacy is a key concept for the theoretical framework of Bandura's socio-cognitive theory [BAN 86], and concrete illustrations can be found in daily life, particularly in educational psychology. For instance, some students may be very confident in their own ability in mathematics, but if the results that they expect are not very optimistic (a poor jobs market, a high degree of competition for a limited number of available jobs), it is unlikely that they will keep their beliefs in their own efficacy. Conversely, a weak belief in one's self-efficacy may be revived by interesting results and potential rewards. If the individuals lack the necessary skills, no amount of self-efficacy will deliver the desired performance, but increased effort, persistence and perseverance can improve their skills and therefore lead to better performances.

Adolescents' development, view as an agent (agentic state) offers an analytical perspective to show that self-regulation is not a willful act. Self-regulation requires the development of self-regulatory skills. In order for a feeling of efficacy to be created in individuals, they must learn to monitor their healthy behavior and the cognitive and social conditions for which they commit, develop sub-objectives to motivate and guide their efforts, employ a range of strategies instead of sticking with a single technique, develop incitements for self-motivation and social supports to sustain the effort necessary for success, and apply multiple self-influences systematically and persistently [BAN 05].

Bandura [BAN 86] suggested that self-efficacy relies on two dimensions which he terms "outcome expectancy" and "self-efficacy expectancy". The first dimension means the estimation that a person makes of the probable consequences (impact) of carrying out a task, as their expected level of skill. A certain behavior or action will yield certain results, which corresponds to general teaching efficacy. The second dimension is the conviction that one has the capacity, the skill and the means with success to adopt the behavior or perform the actions required to produce the desired outcomes. This is consistent with the concept of personal teaching efficacy.

Learning and problem-solving, alongside self-regulation and metacognition, can only be understood by considering both the emotional and cognitive processes, instead of the social environment. Life is breathed into this personal dynamic by the students' aspirations of self-development, and it refers in a learning model to their process of self-management, involving self-evaluations or self-judgments, self-interpretations, self-regulation and states of self-awareness. Malmivuori [MAL 01] illustrates and underlines these processes of a higher-level self-system, whose central role becomes particularly apparent, regarding the difficulty in learning mathematics. In [MAL 01], the investigation is restricted to the case of mathematics, but the results are also applicable to any individual learning process in scholastic educational contexts. The study combines socio-culturally determined contexts for the learning of mathematics and affective responses specific to the situations, and personal to the students, and the activity of self-regulation in the learning of mathematics at school. One of the most important environmental factors behind pupils' self-regulation, the behavioralist-motivational dynamic and self-motivation relies on pedagogical conditions and the beliefs, practices and objectives of the teacher. Often, the aspects which favor self-regulation and adaptive orientation styles in school learning are linked to cooperative learning contexts, and to the difference in competitive class structures.

In addition, a high degree of self-efficacy creates feelings of calm to help deal with difficult tasks, increases optimism, decreases anxiety, raises self-esteem and favors resilience.

According to Bandura [BAN 89], cognitive function involves knowledge – mainly specialized knowledge – and cognitive skills. This is partially true if Hart and Risley [HAR 80] are to be believed, and it involves skills but also a natural system. Hart and Risley illustrate the effectiveness of a motivational system by pointing to the fact that language is developed through natural interactions initiated by children, whose activities arouse their interest and greatly incite them to improve their communication skills. If necessary, they receive standard guidance to generate optimal learning conditions.

Knowing the factors – be they planned or fortuitous – which can alter the course of a life enables us to provide guides to help favor future values. At the personal level, this requires cultivating the capacities to practice self-direction. This includes the development of skills, confidence in one's own ability to exercise control, capacities of self-regulation to influence one's own motivation and actions [BAN 89].

Our beliefs in our own skills are also influenced by verbal persuasions that we receive (Pajares and Lapin-Zeldin [PAJ 00]).

Individuals' beliefs in their self-efficacy determine their level of motivation, as reflected by the effort that they put into a task and how much time they are prepared to persevere in order to overcome obstacles. In the reciprocal causation model, the individuals partly determine the nature of their environment, and are influenced by it. Self-regulatory functions are constructed on a personal basis, founded on various experiences rather than simply being the product of an implanted environment [BAN 89].

Middleton *et al.*, [MID 05] put forward the definition of elite athletes; they confirmed the co-presence of twelve factors: self-efficacy (the athlete's judgment or belief in his/her own capacity to succeed, to attain a specific objective), the mental-oriented concept of themselves (a vision of themselves as being mentally strong when faced with adversity), potential (believing that they have an inherent capacity or the capacity to develop, improve or to have an innate ability), attention to a specific task (an unwavering concentration of the mental processes on a task, so as to minimize any disturbance of concentration), perseverance (persisting to remain constant for an idea, a task or a question in relation to obstacles, discouragement or adversity), familiarity with a task (having a good understanding and being used to the task and the adversity), personal records (internal motivation or a guide to continue with personal performances), the value of a task (the level of importance or significance that success in a task holds for an individual), commitment for a goal (the act of connecting, intellectually or emotionally, with a goal or during an action), positivity (the process of being positive and remaining positive in the face of adversity and challenges), minimization of stress (process acting toward a reduction of one's emotional reactions when faced with adversity), positive comparisons (the sentiment of feeling better in the face of adversity and obtaining a psychological and competitive advantage over one's opponent).

6.3. Theory of self-determination

A number of fairly similar theories have come to light, with explicit highlighting of the importance of motivation as an intrinsic psychological dimension. A long line of theorists, including Rank [RAN 30]; Piaget [PIA 52]; White [WHI 59]; Rogers [ROG 61]; and Ryan and Deci [RYA 00] argued that individuals are intrinsically motivated to develop their understanding and their capabilities. These theories have common ground which is well expressed in the *theory of self-determination* advanced by [RYA 00]. These theories of intrinsic motivation are based on the distinction between intrinsic motivation (whereby people will perform an activity "off their own bat") and extrinsic motivation (people have an ulterior interest in doing an activity, to receive a reward). As Eccles *et al.* [ECC 98] showed, the distinction between intrinsic and extrinsic motivation is reflected as being fundamental in the literature on motivation.

Flux, which is a subjective pleasure, felt when one is completely and optimally engaged in a difficult activity, can be viewed as a blueprint of intrinsically motivated activity (Czikszentmihalyi [CZI 75]). Frederickson [FRE 01] suggests that positive emotions, such as individuals' interest in expanding their momentary action/thought repertoire, are what build their psychological, intellectual, physical and social resources.

The orientation of motivation relates to the underlying attitudes and the goals giving rise to an action – in a manner of speaking, it is the "why" of actions. As an example, we can cite a student who may be very motivated to do his/her homework by curiosity and interest or, alternatively, because he/she wants to obtain the approval of a teacher or a parent. A student may be motivated to learn a new set of skills because he/she understands the usefulness or the potential value, or because learning these skills will enable him/her to get a better grade and the privileges that the new grade brings with it. In these examples, the degree of motivation does not necessarily vary, but the nature and focus of the motivation which attests to that degree very probably will change. In the self-determination theory advanced by [RYA 00], a distinction is drawn between different types of motivation based on the different reasons or goals which are behind the action. The most elementary distinction is that between intrinsic and extrinsic motivation. Three decades of research have shown that the quality of the experience and of the performance can vary fairly greatly depending on whether an individual is acting on an intrinsic or extrinsic motivation. Behaviors which are intrinsically motivated, which are established in the interest of satisfying innate psychological needs for competence and autonomy are the prototype of a self-determined behavior. Behaviors that are extrinsically motivated are those which are established because they are instrumentalized for a separable consequence, and can vary in the extent to which they represent self-determination. Internalization and integration are processes by which extrinsically motivated behaviors become more self-determined.

6.4. Theory of control

The notion of control has been integrated into certain theories to parameterize the regulation of actions. Control theories (Connell and Wellborn [CON 91]; Skinner [SKI 95]) focus on the belief that people have in relation to the way in which they (or their environment) control their achievements. In all these theories, a number of factors are touched upon which affect motivation.

In this vein, we find *self-regulation theories* which study how individuals regulate their behaviors in order to succeed in a task or an activity. Zimmerman [ZIM 89] enumerated three processes in which self-regulated learners are engaged: self-observation (monitoring their own activities), self-judgment (making an evaluation of their own performances) and self-reaction (modulating their reactions based on the results and performances). Self-determination theories, discussed above, also relate to self-regulation.

Along the same line, we also find theories relating to volition. According to Corno [COR 93] and Eccles *et al.* [ECC 02], the term "volition" refers both to the strength needed to accomplish a task and an assiduousness of pursuit. Kulh [KUL 87] lists a number of strategies for volition (cognitive, emotional and strategies for motivational control) to explain the persistence to face distressing elements. Searching for educational support aimed at identifying appropriate moments to give help is very similar to self-regulation and to the concepts of volition. Giving help when a student is not making any effort may result in the student's work decreasing. However, according to Newman [NEW 94] and Eccles *et al.* [ECC 98], searching for an instrumental aid may favor motivation whilst keeping the children engaged in an activity when they are having difficulties.

6.5. Attribution theory

Attribution theory accounts for the interpretations that individuals attribute to the results of their actions and how this determines the expectations of future achievements. Weiner [WEI 85] classified attributions using three dimensions: the locus of control, the stability and the controlability. The locus of control, also known as the locus of causality – a term of attribution for autonomy in the sense of [RYA 00], is a dimension which may be internal or external depending on whether or not the success is attributed to internal causes (which depends on the learner). The stability dimension determines whether the causes change over the course of time or not. The controlability dimension draws a distinction between the controllable causes of attribution such as competence/efficacy and uncontrollable attributions such as aptitude or mood.

Blanchard and Frasson [BLA 04] present factors for motivation of performance. The elements which affect motivation of performance are many. In the literature on the topic, those which occur most frequently are individual goals, the social environment, emotions, intrinsic interest in an activity and self-confidence. There are relations between these factors, so that they cannot be viewed as being mutually independent.

As explained by Eccles *et al.* [ECC 98], research shows that a learner can develop goals relating to their ego (if they wish to maximize the probability of a good evaluation of their skills and create a positive image of themselves), goals involving the task (if they wish to master the task and improve their skills) or indeed goals based on decreasing workload (if they wish to minimize the effort). In fact, the goals are usually said to be performance-oriented (involving the ego) or mastery-oriented (determined by the task).

As it affects their self-confidence, the social environment is an important factor in individual motivation. Parents, peers, the school, personal specificities (such as gender or ethnic group) and pedagogical contexts have a high impact on a learner's motivations to succeed ([ECC 98; ECC 02]. Ego-based goals are particularly strongly liked to the social environment. If a learner has such goals, the importance of the evaluation that this environment has of him/her will be higher. The objective of this type of learner is to maintain a positive image of him/herself and surpass other learners. For instance, in some cases where they are likely to fail, a learner may decide not to attempt a task for fear of being judged by their peers. These learners believe it preferable that their peers should attribute the failure to a lack of effort than to a lack of capacity. This is commonly called the "face-saving tactic".

The integration of emotions into distance learning is an increasingly popular technique which needs to be improved. O'Regan [ORE 03] emphasized the fact that current practices in distance learning produce negative emotions in the learners more often than positive emotions. This means that emotional control must be developed in distance learning. A great many publications explain that emotions can act as motivation activators (Petri [PET 96]. Reciprocally, motivation can also influence one's emotions. Thus, [ECC 02] and [ECC 98] say that, in Weiner's attribution theory [WEI 85]:

– the dimension of locus of causality is more closely connected with affective reactions and the success of attribution is close to internal causes, and these dimensions should develop pride and self-esteem;

– attribution linked to external causes should develop gratitude; failure of attribution linked to internal causes should produce shame;

– failure of attribution linked to external causes should produce anger.

In his volition theory, Kuhl [KUH 87] proposed strategies to explain persistence when a learner is faced with distraction or other possibilities. One of these strategies refers to emotional control, the goal of which is to keep inhibitive emotional states such as anxiety or depression under control ([ECC 02]). What it is interesting to note, in view of the experiments conducted by [ORE 03], is that learners reported emotions discussed by Weiner [WEI 85] and Kuhl [KUH 87] as being linked to a lack of motivation.

An individual is intrinsically motivated by a learning activity when he/she decides to carry out that activity with no external need, and without being rewarded. According to a number of works, we witness differences and individual orientations as regards an intrinsic interest. Certain learners will be attracted by difficult tasks and the opportunity to overcome challenges. For others, curiosity will be a major element in the intrinsic interest. A third category of learners seek activities which will develop their skills and their mastery. In addition, [ECC 98] cited Matsumoto and Sanders [MAT 88] for proof to suggest that high levels of characteristics related to intrinsic motivation facilitate positive emotional experiences. As we saw briefly above, distance learners often suffer from a lack of positive emotions. It is assumed that this is partly due to a lack of motivation.

Different sorts of self-confidence can affect a learner's attributional motivation. A learner may have expectations of a result before engaging in an activity. If the expected results are poor, the learner may decide not to try. A learner may also have expectations of efficacy, which means he/she believes he/she can adopt the behaviors necessary in order to succeed in the activity. Self-confidence is also proposed in control [CON 91; SKI 95] and intrinsic motivation theory [RYA 00] in relation to the control that a learner believes he/she has over a task and its realization. According to [ECC 98], a number of works have confirmed the positive association between an internal locus of control and scholastic achievements. [CON 91] suggested that children who believe they are in control of the results of their actions should feel more competent. They also made the connection between beliefs of control and needs for competence, and hypothesized that the satisfaction of needs was influenced by features of the social environment (such as the autonomy achieved by the learner). In his model of attributional motivation, Skinner [SKI 95] describes a belief in control as an expectation that a person has of being capable of causing the desired events. Distance learning has the advantage of giving learners the belief or illusion that they have control (i.e. autonomy) over their activities and achievements.

6.6. Standards and self-regulation

Self-regulation in terms of motivation and behavior can be expressed as a guidance of internal standards, which are distinguishable into *aspirational standards and social/moral standards*. Let us first look, though, at how such guidance emerges.

Motivational factors, which influence the use of an established model of knowledge, undergo significant evolutionary changes. During childhood, imitation functions are there to ensure an interpersonal response. By way of mutual modeling with adults, babies enjoy ludic intimacy and acquire experience in terms of social reciprocality. Later on, the parents cease to imitate the actions of the baby, but remain attentive to the babies' demands which adopt modeled forms, extending their skills. That which continues to serve as a social function for very young children is conveyed in a new instructional vehicle for the parents. This transition requires babies to enter into a cognitive process, based on observed regularities involving the social effects that their various imitations are able to produce. In order to help their children learn functional values of modeling, parents imagine results that are salient, recurrent, consistent and closely linked with the actions of the baby [PAP 77]. With increasing cognitive developments, babies become more able to judge the probable results of their actions. Such expectations of results serve as incentives for observational learning. What has an incentive value for babies also changes with experience. At the very earliest stage, babies and young children are primarily motivated by immediate sensory aspects and social effects of their actions. During the course of their development, symbolic incitements mean results, and the exercise of mastery and self-evaluation reactions require an increase in motivational functions. Children learn very early on that models are not merely sources of social reward but also sources of skills to better apprehend their environment. The benefits of an effective action and the personal satisfaction this brings with it become powerful incentives to modeling. Hence, development increases the extent and complexity of the incentives which motivate children to gain knowledge through modeling and to use what they have learnt. Having looked at cognitive social theory from the perspective of development, we must mention observational learning as part of a more general process of social and cognitive development. Observational learning is also one of the fundamental means by which cognitive skills are developed and extended. Consequently, a complete theory would have to examine not only the cognitive mechanisms of observational learning, but also the determining factors in social learning describing cognition.

In the French adage "*en forgeant on devient forgeron*" (literally "it is by smithing that one becomes a smith", or more roughly rendered, "Practice makes perfect" or "Live and learn"), the results serve as a destructured way to inform learners of the characteristics of appropriate behavior. By observing whether certain actions work or not, individuals eventually construct conceptions of new forms of behaviors and adopt them at the correct time.

In cognitive social theory, learning from the effects of action is a particular case of observational learning. In learning based on direct experience, individuals imagine conceptions of behavior based on observation of the effects of their actions; in model-based learning, they derive the conceptions based on observation of the behavioral structure, which is modeled.

Parental advice and sanctions have an enormous influence on the process of socialization. However, neither parents nor other adults with a significant role can always be there to guide children's behavior. Hence, successful socialization requires a gradual substitution of internal controls and direction of external sanctions and mandates. Once the capacity of self-control is accomplished, self-expectancy and self-sanctions serve as a primary guide, a motivating or deterrent factor. Without internal standards and self-sanctions, people would behave like weather vanes, constantly changing direction to conform to any and every ill-timed influence which comes to court them. Theories which seek to explain human behavior by only the product of external rewards and punishments represent an incomplete image of human nature, given that individuals have the capacity for self-direction to enable them to exercise control over their thoughts, their sensations and their actions by way of the consequences that they impose on themselves. Psychosocial function is regulated by reciprocality between self production and external sources of influence.

As mentioned above, self-direction can result in guidance of internal standards which are divided into aspirational and social/moral standards. The capacity to exercise self-influence by personal challenges and reactions of evaluation of one's own achievements provide a fundamental cognitive mechanism for self-motivation and self-direction. The motivation is based on aspirational standards involving a process of cognitive comparison between internal standards and personal achievements. Motivational effects do not stop at the standards themselves, but rather at self-reactive influences. This includes affective evaluations of oneself and of one's achievements in order to adjust to the standards, and an adjustment of one's personal standards to keep them in check [BAN 88a; BAN 83].

Standards motivate people by encouraging self-evaluation in an activity. Individuals seek self-satisfaction by fulfilling evaluated objectives, and can intensify their efforts because of discontentment, due to the action of sub-standards. Perceived self-efficacy is another cognitive factor which plays an important role in the exercise of personal control over motivation. Whether negative differences between the internal standards and the achievements are motivating or discouraging is partly determined by the beliefs of the individuals, according to which they can achieve the goals which they have set themselves. People who endure self-doubt as regards their capabilities are easily dissuaded by failure.

People who are more certain of their own capabilities intensify their efforts when they fail, in order to achieve what they want, and they persist until they succeed. The standards that the individuals set for themselves at the beginning of their attempt are apt to change, depending on the progress that they make. People may keep their original standard, lower their ambition or adopt a standard which responds to more of a challenge.

Finally, the third component, self-influence, in continuous regulation of motivation, relates to readjustment of personal standards in the light of one's attainments. Csikszentmihalyi [CSI 79] examined what, in activities, favor the pursuit of stimulation in life's projects. The common factors deemed likely to render self-motivation long-lasting include the taking up of personal challenges in accordance of one's own perceived capabilities and imagining oneself making progress as regards a desired goal.

Viewing an organization as controllable increases the perceived self-efficacy to manage it, whereas viewing it as relatively immovable decreases self-confidence in managerial efficacy (BAN 89).

The efficacy of aspirational standards to regulate motivation and action depends partially on the way in which we project them into the near future. A short-term standard is useful to mobilize self-influence and direct what we do here and now. Long-term standards are too far removed in time to offer incentives and guide our current actions. We often find too many competing influences in close proximity for distant cognitive events to exercise enough control over our current behavior. Sub-objectives do not just federate self-reactive motivation factors; they also help to develop self-efficacy and an intrinsic interest [BAN 81]. Without standards against which to measure their performances, individuals have very little on which to base themselves to gage their own capabilities. The results of a sub-objective provide an increase in mastery indicators which improves people's perception of their own efficacy. Individuals appear to maintain interest in activities in which they feel themselves effective and from which they derive self-satisfaction. Standards associated with challenges give rise to long-term involvement in tasks necessary to acquire skills which favor the interest. When individuals focus on and master high levels of performance, they receive a feeling of satisfaction. Satisfactions derived from the realization of an objective create an intrinsic interest.

A number of theories of self-regulation are based on a system of monitoring negative feedback. The system works as a regulating factor or a motivating factor for action by way of a mechanism of reduction of divergence. A perceived divergence between the performance and a referential standard triggers an action to reduce the incongruousness. Decreasing the divergence plays an important role in any self-regulation system. However, in a system of negative feedback monitoring, if the performance exactly matches the standard, then the individual does nothing. A regulatory process whereby matching with a standard causes inertia does not correspond to human self-motivation. Such a negative feedback monitoring system should give rise to cyclical action which leads nowhere. However, people also cannot be incited by an action if they do not receive feedback telling them that their performance is not in correspondence with the standard. Human self-motivation relies on the production of divergence as well as reduction of it. This requires regulation with predictive action and a feedback loop. Individuals motivate themselves by way of regulation with predictive action, adopting performance standards which create a state of imbalance and thus drive them forward, based on an anticipated estimation of the amount of effort that will be required to achieve the goal. Upon receipt of feedback, they make adjustments depending on the effort expenditure required to achieve the desired results. Once individuals have attained a standard that they were pursuing, they generally set themselves a higher standard. Adopting ulterior challenges creates new motivating divergences which must be overcome. In addition, however, overcoming a hurdle is more likely to further develop the individual's aspirations than to decrease performance in order to conform to an outdated standard. Self-motivation involves a dual cyclical process of imbalancing production of divergence, followed by a reduction in the divergence to redress the balance and restore equilibrium. Motivation has been explained by certain theorists in terms of innate motivating factors. According to Piaget [PIA 52], the divergences between the cognitive patterns that children already possess and the perceived events pose an internal conflict which motivates them to explore the source of divergence, so that the internal patterns are altered to adjust to contradictory experiences. Empirical tests of this type of self-motivating factor show that the mere divergence of the experience does not necessarily ensure cognitive learning. However, if the disparity between the perceived events and the mental structure were, in fact, automatically motivating, everyone would be highly knowledgeable about the world around them, and would constantly progress toward ever-higher levels of reasoning. Observation shows that this is not the case. In a social and cognitive vision, individuals function as active agents of their own motivation. Self-motivation by cognitive comparison requires that we draw a distinction between the standards of what we know and the standards of what we would like to know. This latter set of standards, coupled with perceived self-efficacy, exert a selective influence on the basis of which, numerous activities will be actively pursued. Aspirational standards determine which divergences are motivating and which activities people will push themselves to master. The intensity of self-motivation varies in a nonlinear fashion, depending on the level of divergence between the standards and the achievements. Relatively easy standards do not pose enough of a challenge to arouse a great deal of interest or effort. Other, slightly more difficult standards maintain high levels of effort and produce satisfactions by way of the realization of sub-objectives. A set of established standards which are far beyond an individual's potential may be demotivating, favoring discouragement and a feeling of inefficacy.

In operational domains which involve the accomplishment of efforts and cultivation of skills, the internal standards which are selected as a mark of adequacy are progressively altered as knowledge and skills are acquired and challenges are met. In many subjects of social and moral behavior, the internal standards which serve as bases to regulate one's behavior are more stable. This means that the individuals' views or what is wrong or right and what is good or bad do not change from week to week. Over the course of socialization, the individuals develop moral standards based on a variety of influences [BAN 86]. This includes direct instructions of precepts of moral conduct, reactions of approval or disapproval of one's conduct by significant people in one's life, and moral standards modeled by others. Individuals do not passively absorb moral standards based on each and every random influence which occurs and affects them. Rather, they construct generic standards based on evaluative rules which are prescribed, modeled and taught. This process is complex because the individuals who serve as examples and influencing factors in socialization, be it intentionally or unintentionally, often exhibit inconsistencies between what they practice and what they preach.

In addition, individuals usually differ in terms of the standards which they model, and even the same individual can model different standards in different social contexts and fields of conduct. Reflexive evaluation reactions provide a mechanism by which standards regulate behavior. Anticipated pride and self-appraisal of one's actions which match or diverge from personal standards serve as regulatory influential factors. Individuals do things which give them self-satisfaction, meaning and personal value. They refuse to behave in a way in which violates their moral standards when to do so would make them ashamed of themselves. Thus, self-sanctions ensure conduct which is in conformity with internal standards. The influences on self-management are not governed solely by moral standards. The actions cause reflexive reactions by way of a process of moral reasoning in which the conduct is evaluated in relation to the environmental circumstances as well as personal standards. Situations with moral implications involve a great many decisional ingredients which not only vary in terms of importance but to which we can attach a more-or-less preponderant weight, conditioned by a series of particular events during the course of a given moral situation. Thus for instance, judgments about the reprehensibility of a particular form of behavior should vary depending on the nature of the transgression, the degree of violation of a standard, the contexts in which it takes place, personal and situational motivating factors perceived for it, the immediate and long-term consequences of an action, whether it causes personal injury or damage to property, and the characteristics of the people to whom the action is done and their feeling of guilt. Thus, in view of moral dilemmas, individuals must extract, weight and integrate morally relevant information in the situations in which they find themselves. Factors which are given a large weight in certain sets of circumstances may be ignored or considered less important depending on a number of conditions. This process of moral reasoning is guided by multifaceted rules about how to combine different kinds of information to judge the morality of a particular behavior (Lane and Anderson [LAN 76]; Surber [SUR 85]; [BAN 89]).

6.7. Deviance and pathology

Most people think that joy is a form of happiness. However, joy means more than happiness: i.e. joy is a satisfaction which leads us to lose ourselves in delight, inspiring us to attain our objectives. Joy is an exaltation which causes heart palpitations and drives motivation to go forward. Here we can clearly see a link between physiology, emotion and motivation [GOL 39]. Problems may arise and derail this physiological cycle of emotion/motivation. Some scientists have observed that an obsession with self sentiment is responsible for an alarming aggravation of depression and other mental problems. Several different levels of health problems can be seen:

– mood problems:

- depressive disorders,

- dysthymia,

- suicidal and para-suicidal behaviors,

- bipolar disorders;

– anxiety problems:

- panic attacks,

- agoraphobia,

- social phobia,

- specific phobias,

- general anxiety disorder,

- obsessive compulsive disorder (OCD);

– traumatic chaos:

- post-traumatic stress disorder (PTSD) and acute stress,

- dissociative disorders,

- reduced distress tolerance;

– sexual disorders;

– eating disorders;

– cognitive-behavioral pain management;

– addictions.

6.8. Temporal Motivation Theory

Steel and König [STE 00] developed temporal motivation theory (TMT). They suggested an explanation for motivation support: the time delay. The idea is as follows: objectives which are substantially separated and distant in time from one another reduce the efficacy of the expectation and of the value. The only bad thing about proximity is that by breaking a major objective up into regularly-spaced sub-objectives, each sub-objective may become easier to achieve and therefore less satisfying. Consequently, there is a critical point beyond which any further subdivision of an objective will decrease the motivation for realization below the level that can be compensated by the decrease in time delays between objectives.

All in all, private life and perceived security are related to the confidence that a user has in a system to finalize a transaction securely and maintain privacy of a personal piece of information (Lallmahamood [LAL 07]).

Historical research on self-coherence has provided conclusive proof that individuals declare a tendency to behave in accordance with the belief they have in themselves (Festinger [FES 57]; Heider [HEI 58]; Cialdini [CIA 93]). More recently, Bosson and Swann [BOS 01], and Swann [SWA 02a] noted that individuals seek evaluations from significant other people, i.e. feedback to validate their behavior. Also, Swann and Pelham [SWA 02b] found that individuals strategically select, from their social environment, that which may give them positive reinforcement. Based on these works, we may imagine that consumers must be motivated to select exploration spaces which are compatible with their subjective knowledge [MOO 04].

6.9. Effect of objectives

Pajares *et al.* [PAJ 00] found significant correlations between task-oriented objectives and performance-oriented objectives. Both these types of objectives are founded upon self-regulatory practices which yield positive results such as acquisition of skills or mastery of a task both on the scientific and academic levels.

6.10. Context of distance learning

In the domain of distance learning, we find three main avenues of research on the subject of motivation: 1) research focused on planning of motivation (del Soldato and du Boulay [DEL 95]; 2) focused on the "attention, relevance, confidence, satisfaction" (ARCS) model (Keller [KEL 87] and 3) focused on social cognitive theory (Bandura, 1986). Motivational planning includes tactics and practical strategies which are used depending on the learner's motivational state. Three parameters are used to create motivation: effort, confidence and autonomy. Motivational planning is correlated with domain-based planning. Keller's model has been used as a principle for design in order to develop the process of motivation-based learning. Certain recent publications use this model to induce a motivational state in a learner interacting with a system. For instance, de Vicente and Pain [DEV 02] found 85 motivational rules for a human/computer interface to deduce a student's motivational state.

6.11. Maintenance model

Heine [HEI 06] proposes to explain individuals' self-motivation with a meaning maintenance model. Individuals have a need for meaning – a need to perceive events through the prism of mental representations to expect relations between them which organize their perceptions of the world around them. When individuals meaning logic is mistreated, they produce alternative representations as a way to regain meaning – a process termed fluid compensation. Compensation that frames the meaning is well adapted to the deterioration of self-esteem, the sensation of uncertainty, personal rejection and mortality salience.

6.12. Effect of narrative

As Rowe *et al.* [ROW 07] point out, challenges, curiosity, monitoring and fantasy are key factors when dealing with intrinsic motivation. They also show that a narrative-centered (or discourse-based) approach can develop motivation for learning.

6.13. Effect of eviction

An individual also shows their complexity in their economic interactions with the world. Bruno Frey's seminal work [FRE 97] on the "crowding out" effect theoretically supports the role of intrinsic and extrinsic motivation. The first form of motivation appears through the satisfaction of one's immediate needs. Given that there is no external and indirect recompense, such a satisfaction can only be the result of two psychological mechanisms: one related to obligation and another based on pleasure. Pleasure-based mechanisms refer to fluxes of satisfaction ensured by an activity such as playing a game or accomplishing a challenge may be associated with a reward. Obligation-based mechanisms refer to the pursuit of objectives defined by oneself or obligations defined by social and personal standards – e.g. an environmental ethic or fiscale morals [FRE 97]. In the case of extrinsic motivation, an activity implies indirectly satisfying one's own needs, involving financial consequences, but can also involve other forms such as effects on one's reputation or confidence, which may serve as a springboard in the recruitment market or promotion of external control over one's own activities (monitoring). Extrinsic motivations may form the basis of economic practices of price-changing, by deliberate manipulation of the financial sanctions and rewards, in order to serve individual interests that coincide with those of the collective.

6.14. Effect of the teacher–student relationship

An educator must believe in the process, and in the students' capacity to accomplish the objective of a college degree. The process whereby the belief becomes reality is a slow one, but when enough students have completed the process to degree level, positive feedback reinforces the belief (Armington [ARM 03]).

6.15. Model of persistence and change

Some psychologists view motivation as a process which involves perservering or, conversely, sparking a change. The change gives rise to a new resolution; it also causes a break in persistence through lack of motivation. Thus, motivation can be interpreted as a probability of change which characterizes resistance or denial depending on the states that the context allows for in terms of transition to the change. The probability is not an ineffable given, but rather can evolve over time depending on the events or on the individuals and their capacity to resist. Thus, it is not a constant piece of information. Contexts also and indubitably exert a not-insignificant influence. In other words, the situations introduce a degree of agreement and disagreement, becoming parameters for estimating this probability of transition which, in any case, is expressed in terms of ambivalence, the present state or a new state.

6.16. Effect of the man–machine relationship

A person's psychology and relationship with the world extends into the relationship of humans with technology, which has been studied by Norman [NOR 04]. According to him, individuals treat objects and technology in three different ways. Firstly, a visceral treatment involves emotional, preset and automatic responses: swift judgments of good and bad. Secondly, a behavioral treatment involves cerebral treatments which control daily life, and can cause responses which are more sophisticated than visceral treatments. Thirdly, a reflexive treatment involves recall and reasoning, reflexive about the experiences and actions of the past, and an evaluation of them with a view to planning future actions. What is important here is formulated as four components for the design of a user-friendly human/computer system: function, comprehensibility, usability and physical sensation. These physical components must be gathered together in an accessible model of the system, offered to a user.

Chapter 7

Theories of Motivation in Neurosciences

7.1. Academic literature on the subject

A request for keywords such as "motivational system" or "motivational systems" turns up 265 documents from between 1965 and 2011 on PubMed, which is the largest database of biomedical literature in the world, hosting 22 million articles. This means two things. The first is that the subject is a complex one to deal with, particularly in terms of experimentation and ethics surrounding human beings; the economic consequences may not be as evident as for cancer. Then, the rate of publications on this subject has increased greatly over the past few years (179, which equates to 68%, between 2000 and 2011). The subject is beginning to occupy a slightly more important place in current affairs. In this chapter, we discuss a number of these works which have made their mark on physiology relating to the brain's motivational system.

7.2. Psychology and Neurosciences

The question which psychologists ask themselves is whether they can identify the cause or causes of a disorganization responsible for observable symptoms of an individual's high-level cognitive functions, simply by explaining a malfunction at the level of the cognitive system. Neurosciences, for their part, have until recently assumed that the physiological systems responsible for functions such as sleep or neuro-endocrine regulation must, by definition, be able to be reduced to elementary biological mechanisms. More modern neurosciences attempt to break with this methodological trend, assuming the existence of more complex mechanisms that are capable of interfering, e.g. with a person's emotional state.

7.3. Neurophysiological theory

The cognitive aspects of motivation began being taken into account with the works of neurophysiologists such as Pribram and Morton [PRI 76], Luria [LUR 80], Posner [POS 92], Damasio [DAM 94] and LeDoux [LED 96]. The subject is still greatly associated with neurosciences.

Fowles [FOW 94] puts forward a psychobiological model which involves a theory of motivation derived from the literature about animal learning, offering an attractive theoretical bridge between neurochemical influences and phenotypical characteristics as regards psychiatric disorders. This model associates aversive motivational systems and a separate interactive appetite which control activation of the behavior (appetite) and inhibition (aversion).

Derryberry and Tucker [DER 06] analyzed the links between the neurophysiological mechanisms and their internal states associated with motivation, personality and psychopathology. They postulated an interdependent and separable system, divided into two systems: an appetitive subsystem and a defensive subsystem (Figure 7.1). These subsystems are balanced and associated with the cortical functions. Deregulation of these subsystems can cause pathological conditions. A certain region of the brain plays a defensive role in case of aggression; in the case of a possible flight, a region is activated, and in another case a defensive reaction is invoked. The appetitive subsystem's reaction is the opposite to that of the defensive subsystem; hence, the maximum activity of the appetitive subsystem occurs when the defensive subsystem is inactive. If the defensive subsystem is operating to maximum capacity, people experience anxiety, analgesia or depression; and for the appetitive subsystem, hyperactivity or anxiety. These subsystems ensure that children build representations of the world which serve their motivational needs.

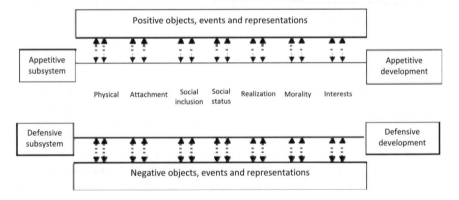

Figure 7.1. *Illustration of the interaction between motivational development subsystems and the environment [DER 06]*

The cingulate region in the cortex is described as providing a directive motivational thread which is articulated in terms of distal, proximal and axial components in the dorsal premotor regions (Goldberg [GOL 85]) (Figure 7.2). Thus, the cingulate region can give us an active and conscious sense of the organization involved in voluntary action. The construction of an appetitive neural system has been the topic of many scientific works. The underlying circuit has been discussed in terms of the "food seeking system" (Panksepp, [PAN 98]), and of the "behavior facilitation system" (Depue and Collins, [DEP 99]). The most primitive appetitive system described by [PAN 98] calls on the regulations of active process by states of need (such as hunger) and by the functions to activate exploratory behavior combined with an emotional state of desire. In the face of this, the circuit proposed by Gray and Collins [DEP 99; PIC 01] is more recent and is designed to detect conditional signals of recompense and sanctions. Given such signals, the circuits facilitate an approach behavior oriented by positive incitements by emotional states of expectancy (given an expected reward) and relief (given a punishment). The current neural circuit underlying appetitive motivation has not been well described. It seems to be distributed vertically through the brain, using the same structures as are involved in the defensive functions. Dopamine is the neuromodulator used for both subsystems (Pickering and Gray [PIC 01]).

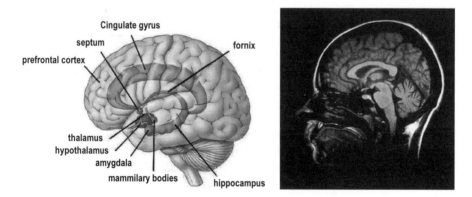

Figure 7.2. *Limbic system of the human brain. Left: diagram of the modules (http://www.unites.uqam.ca/cnc/psy4042/emotion.pdf); right: image of the brain from a scanner*

Panksepp [PAN 98] described an instinctive motor system that would be the neural source of joy and sadness (fundamental emotions). The reason for this might be a stage of the development of the human brain, imbuing it with curiosity for art and technique.

Derryberry and Tucker [DER 06] do not rule out the possibility that a child, who is equipped with a highly developed defensive subsystem, could learn in a higher-stress environment. The defensive and appetitive systems regulate three types of peripheral systems (the motor system and the autonomy and endocrine systems), giving rise to a complex behavior. In case of defective regulation, appetitive motivation often leads to frustration rather than gratification. Tests in the field of neurology show that people suffering from significant lesions to the cingulate cortex and the mediodorsal nucleus manifest akinetic mutism or pseudodepression. We see a paradox in [DER 06], where the authors claim that the motivational system is guided by emotions such as fear, although it is supposed to be this system which causes these emotions. The motivational system is described as an autonomous structure which stimulates attention and memory; above all it is characterized by its immediate effects and its pathological derivatives in extreme configurations. The motivational results for the appetitive subsystem are pleasure and frustration; those for the sub-defensive subsystem are pain and relief. Ascending efferent projections of the neurons, releasing dopamine, serotonin, norepinephrine and acetylcholine are engaged in different combinations during motivational states. These neuromodulators act to regulate common cortical processes and facilitate the storage of the information in memory. These motivational circuits are part of the limbic system. The system described here is not specific like deliberate acts of searching for information in the long-term memory, where internal dialogs take place. This corresponds to cognitive operations which, as yet, are not well known. The process of self-organization, whereby the motivational systems are sensitive in terms of choice of representations, is highly sensitive to the environment, to the point where different profiles of individuals self-organize in different ways. The view of development explains personality traits such as extraversion and neurosis, but proves less robust when it comes to explaining more specific behaviors.

The idea seen in the previous chapter of a balancing act between reduction of divergence and expansion of divergence holds water, and is a useful principle when studying behavior. It is interesting to note, however, that these ideas are echoed in the family of theories on neurobiological motor systems, which has received a great deal of attention from numerous personality psychologists and social psychologists (e.g. [DEP 93; FOW 93; GRA 94; LAN 95; CLO 98; DAV 98; DEP 99; DAV 00]). Most of these theories postulate the existence of a set of mechanisms which take care of appetitive motivation and approach behavior, and a rather separate set of mechanisms which take care of aversive motivation and avoidance behavior.

7.4. Relationship between the motivational system and the emotions

Lang and Davis [LAN 06] argued that there was a motivational circuit in the brain, centered on the amygdala, which manages human emotions. This neural circuit of approach/appetitive and avoidance/defensive developed fairly early on in the evolutionary history of human beings, in the primitive cortex, the subcortex and the midbrain (or mesencephalon), for behaviors fundamental to the survival of the individuals and propagation of genes for generations to come. Thus, events associated with appetitive rewards, or which relate to pain and danger, engage attention and rapid information-gathering more than do other input sensors. Motor indicators also facilitate metabolic regulation and anticipative responses and mobilize the organism to prepare for action. These discoveries were made during work on animals to better understand psychophysiological (cardiovascular and neurohumoral) aspects of emotion and behavioral aspects (control of worry, "immobilism") and define how these aspects are mediated in the circuits of the brain. Similar results are described for experiments performed on humans, showing similar forms of activation in the brain and the human body in response to emotional indicators, which co-vary with the affective valence and increasing emotional excitation of the individuals.

In terms of biophysiological factors of intrinsic motivation, we find evidence that gonadic steroids (testosterone and estradiol) play a role both in activation of the stress channel to trigger effective motivation and in frustration/satisfaction (HAL 10). It seems that progesterone plays a part in affiliation motivation, and arginine vasopressin (AVP) in achievement motivation. Brain imaging shows that the need for competence, affiliation and achievement modulate the activity in a central motivational circuit formed by the striatum, the amygdala, the orbito-frontal cortex and the insular cortex when non-verbal social intentions are being processed.

Recent works (see [CHE 08] have shown a fundamental cellular mechanism which can have quite a significant impact on pathological drug-seeking behavior. Rats were deliberately sensitized to cocaine and show persistent cellular memory in the brain's reward center even after several months without the drug, whereas their non-sensitized peers do not have such memory. In rats that were given a mechanism to self-administer cocaine, the long-term increase in neural communication, called synaptic plasticity, is similar to that relating to self-administered food or sucrose, but with a crucial difference. The plasticity due to cocaine taking remains even after three months of abstinence, but the increase in response to natural rewards disappears after only three weeks. A surprising finding is that rats which have been given passive inoculation with infusions of cocaine do not exhibit plasticity in the dopamine neurons in the ventral area. This shows that dependency is caused by factors other than the pharmacological effect of a drug, and illustrates the significance of active choice.

Lang and Bradley [LAN 10] showed that studies in neuroscience and the psychophysiology of the treatment of emotion can be performed experimentally as regards reflex reactions, neural structures and functional circuits to explain human evolution over the course of the millennia. Their point of view offers a vision of the expression of emotional states governed by motivational circuits of the brain which developed early on in the history of the evolution to ensure the individuals' survival and of their progeny. These circuits react to memorial and environmental indicators, of either appetitive or aversive nature, which mediate appetitive and aversive reflexes. They adjust the sensory systems and mobilize the organism for action, and are thus at the root of positive and negative emotions. These works evaluate the reflexive physiology of emotion, both autonomous and somatic, by looking at the feelings aroused by the perception of an image, with imagery of memory. These experiments are performed in the context of reward or punishment, using electroencephalograms (EEG) and nuclear magnetic resonance (NMR).

7.5. Relationship between the motivational system and language

Some major works in cognitive neurosciences (Gazzaniga [GAZ 92]) give language a central role in elaborating a higher-level consciousness model. Gazzaniga worked with "split brain" patients. He uses the notion of an "interpreter", which is a sophisticated communication module to describe the specific capacity which resides in the left hemisphere of the brain, which he holds is the locus of the formation of human belief. The term "interpretation" defines a contour of functional capacity for integration and narration, recognizing the meaningful importance of language and memory. This interpreter sheds light on the tendencies that individuals have to give explanations for themselves and for others. These effects of separation of the two halves of the brain were modified when Gazzaniga partially severed the corpus callosum of a patient to minimize the extremity of epileptic seizures. The corpus callosum is a sort of immense cable of 200 million nerve fibers which fully activate the linguistic left brain (in right-handed people) based on how the relatively nonlinguistic right brain reacts. The very silent right brain communicates with the left by electrochemical means. In principle, the hemispheres of the brain inform one another and coordinate through the corpus callosum. There are other areas in which such coordination operates, but these areas are minor. Because the linguistic left brain in right-handers activates consciousness, the left hemisphere is considered to be dominant, and plays a directing role in coordination of the multiple silent modular parts of the right brain. The modules of the right brain perform very specific tasks. The capacity to identify faces and facial expression, to locate oneself in space, to order things chronologically, to move and to identify colors is the result of the function of these modules. Thus, they all have their own memory, volition and interests. When the parts of the right brain which activate perceptions are damaged, these capabilities are lost. However, Gazzaniga recognizes that 95% of cerebral activity is unconscious, and that a large proportion of conscious activity is produced by images and non-verbal actions.

7.6. Relationship between the motivational system and need

We shall close this chapter, which borders on neurology, by mentioning the work of Konrad Lorenz [LOR 70], one of the rare winners of a Nobel Prize (1973) for physiology on animal behavior. His work, in ethology, began with the observation that the explanation of hunger given by psychoanalysis does not fully account for animals' food-seeking behavior. Seeing his pet starling chasing imaginary flies, he came up with the idea that the seeking was triggered not by hunger, because the starling was well-fed, nor by the presence of flies: it is executed automatically under the influence of autonomous endogenous motivation. Ethologists prefer the term "motivation" to the concept of impulsion, which is deemed too vague. In ethology, motivation is held to be genetically passed on to create emotion and appetence. Appetence characterizes a domain of behavior: prophylactic, submission, domination, reproductive, verifying, social contact, accumulation, trophylactic, achievement, altruism and exploration. Motivation is also to be distinguished from instinct, which associates hereditary coordination with an external stimulus. Ethologists believe humans have lost instinctive behaviors, which have been replaced by motivated behaviors. Deregulation of certain appetences leads to physiological problems. The explanation is to be found in biology. Neurosis is a consequence of the distortion of a reproductive appetence (libido); obsessive compulsive disorder is a distortion of the appetence for verification of the survival conditions, due to deregulation of the glutamate in the cortico-basal ganglia circuit made up of the orbitofrontal cortex, the anterior cingulate cortex, the thalamus and the striatum (Wenner Moyer [WEN 12]). Certain cultural and social appetences stem from biological appetences. For instance, the exploratory appetence would be at the root of a passion for travel, but also passion for knowledge by moving from the concrete to the abstract realm of knowledge; this appetence would be the driving force behind scientific research. Random exploratory appetence would be behind bargain-hunting, one of the motors of our economic system founded on consumerism. Genetics and endocrinology account for certain appetences – e.g. oxytocin for altruism and testosterone for domination. Lorenz holds that the study of behavior belongs more at the level of appetence, owing to the observation that motivation can be seen in vacuous conditions which are difficult to implement.

Chapter 8

Language Modeling

8.1. Issues surrounding language

The *question of language* is a three-pronged one. We find a philosophical question which tends to try to explain why human beings are the only species to express themselves using high-level language, and when this ability originated. Another more political issue is that of mastering the function of a language, to use it as an instrument of harmonization of exchanges within a nation and of regulation toward an international stage. The third issue relates to the explanation of cognitive phenomena and the impact of language in everyday life. This third issue is related to the two previous ones, but is more pragmatic, involving concepts of psychology, brain function, social interactions and modern technologies which can be used to create models.

8.2. Interaction and language

The role of language is certainly far more important than simple regulation, because it is necessary for sophisticated *interaction* between individuals. Interaction "between individuals" may, first and foremost, involve oneself, particularly given that – as we saw in Chapter 5 – a component of the personality is introversion; i.e. the absence of introversion is symptomatic. Introversion is accompanied by monologues, which begin to occur very early on in the development of an individual's cognition after simple phonetic mimicry. Monologue uses language as a tool for internal communication to establish one's ideas, express associations between concepts and decide on actions, either through interaction with other people or in an internal mode involving self-analysis. The absence of monologue, but in introverted mode, relates to behavior which only requires sensing and direct analysis of external informations, e.g. getting out of bed, going to the toilet. In the case of preparing breakfast, which appears to be a primitive need, we already see internal communication come into play, e.g. knowing where the bowl is; whether there is enough coffee; how much time is left to eat in order to avoid being late for work, etc.

8.3. Development and language

Studies in developmental psychology showed that the majority of our vocabulary is acquired by reading between the ages of 7 and 20; beyond this age, the amount of words stabilizes at 73,000 clearly-understood lemmas (see Table 8.1). These studies, aimed at measuring the efficacy of a language-teaching technique, show that the complexity of a language is not yet known [EHR 78]. They do not show the whole **complexity of a language** and the underlying associations – i.e. the key to the complexity: the generalized lexical combination, which goes beyond analysis of the immediate constituents.

age	0-5 mths	6 mths	11 mths	12 mths	2 yrs	6 yrs	7 yrs	8 yrs	9 yrs	10 yrs	20 yrs
number of words	0	2	30	100	200	400	1100	2200	3700	5100	73000

Table 8.1. *Distribution of the number of words learnt by an individual (source: [POT 03; NEW 01] and http://www.ac-bordeaux.fr/ia24-2/Docdepartemental.pdf (2003)*

8.4. Schools of thought in linguistic sciences

Language has been studied as a cognitive object for a very long time. 4,000 years ago, the Chinese created dictionaries which served to code the design of a pictogram. More recently, modern grammars of European languages were created between the 16th and 18th Centuries. More recently still, in the late 19th and early 20th Centuries, academics began to wonder about meaning beyond philosophy and beyond metaphysics, in systemic terms.

The **history of linguistics** is divided into four largely dominant phases: structuralism (1900-1935), distributionalism (1935-1960), universalism (1960-1985), lexicometry and ontology engineering (1985-2012). This last phase draws very heavily upon computational methods resulting from the reign of computer technology in most academic fields. Grammars can be divided into three major classes: generative grammars, dependency grammars and syntagmatic grammars, whose formalisms are highly varied and relate to Boolean logic or predicates, probabilities or vectorial computation. We shall describe these phases in this chapter in order to gain a fuller understanding of the link between linguistics and cognition – a link the evolution of which appears to coincide with that of psychology, going from analytical trains of thought to behavioralist ones, to the cognitivist trains of thought today.

The most pronounced element from the prehistory of linguistic theories goes back to the works of Ferdinand de Saussure [SAU 16], who defined a theory of paradigmatic and syntagmatic axes with a matrix of semantic traits to describe expressions in a language. We find the Russian philological school, which studied the structure of stories and the poetic functions, but also the emergence of a field of linguistic statistics with the mathematician Markov [MAR 16], who methodologically and rigourously revisited a 19th Century school of thought: stylometry (Dittenberger [DIT 81]; Lutoslawski and Leroux [LUT 90]) about the attribution and dating of texts (Shakespeare or Plato for instance) by studying the frequency with which certain words appear [THI 87; LOW 95; HOL 95; HOL 98; RUD 98; LIS 08]. Later on, the English school, in the 1930s and 1940s, became greatly interested in these aspects of distribution of words generally in a text, with thinkers including Trier [TRI 31], Zipf [ZIP 33] and Harris [HAR 54].

European structural linguistics was developed thanks to the course which Swiss linguist Ferdinand de Saussure taught at the University of Geneva between 1906 and 1911, published posthumously in 1916. At the start of the 20th Century, the European powers were few, colonial and extremely rich. There was an explosion in the arts, giving rise to an abundant and lyrical body of literature, but also to literary criticism. In the wake of Saussure's work, the Moscow Linguistic Circle was formed in 1915, supported by the avant-garde poet V. Maïakovski, in response to neogrammarians who were making literary interpretations based on the influence of words evolving over the course of time and society. Later, for political reasons, this circle of thinkers moved to Prague, creating the Prague Linguistic Circle under the aegis of N. Trubetzkoy and R. Jakobson [JAK 56]. The objective of the Circle was to approach literary criticism by rigorous study of the literature and particularly of rhetoric, and it gave rise to a linguistic theory based on metaphor and metonymy. The Linguistic Circle of Copenhagen with V. Brondal and L. Hjelmslev [HJE 35] joined this movement. The movement remained active until the 1930s. Under the influence of Chomsky, it re-emerged in the guise of functionalism, particularly with A.K. Halliday [HAL 85]. Even in Antiquity, language was the subject of controversy, and the Middle Ages also provided their share of definitions about grammar. The structuralism begun by Saussure and further developed by the Prague Linguistic Circle was the first discipline to consider language as an entirely separate system. Human language groups sets of random objects together; these sets are organized into systems which are defined simply by the relationships that exist between these objects; this model is constructed based on a set of real-world data, collected and brought together, and covered by the term *corpus*.

DEFINITION 8.1.– The corpus used must satisfy several conditions: it must be in computer format; include a minimum number of texts; present a minimum level of comprehension and coherence; ideally describe only one theme in each text; not rely on implication, undertone, irony or antiphrasis.

It was Bloomfield [BLO 33] who would redefine a new way of thinking, which we can call distributionalism. The distributional method consists of segmenting a lexical string into distinct units, defined by their own environment, and the IC (immediate constituents) method defines a combinatorial analysis of these units, from the minimum unit to the highest-level units (from the morpheme to the statement). This theory is marked by the fact that the divided elements have meaning in the physical world. Thus, there is a close correlation between the structure of the language and the real world. While distributionalism dominated linguistics between 1930 and 1960, toward the end of this period it underwent slight methodological changes, based on the fact that the immediate constituents can go beyond the context of the sentence, and therefore the notion is disambiguation appeared by paraphrase-analysis.

Chomsky's "utopian and universalist" project (1965) changed the stakes at the end of the 1950s. It placed the emphasis on the logical formulation of statements, in the tradition of the logicians from the early 20th Century such as G. Frege and B. Russell, keeping the attention of the research community focused on linguistic computing for nearly 25 years until the late 1980s. The influence of this project related to the development of a model able to generate and validate any sentence using transformation rules. Such models are known as *generative grammars*, or universal grammars, the prerequisites of which postulate the existence of rules which describe the validity of a sentence no matter what the language and who the speaker, but dependent upon the speaker. In this respect, they differ from grammars such as that of Montague [MON 70], whose approach is similar (categorial grammar, or probabilistic *tree-adjoining grammar* (TAG) in its most recent forn). Chomsky organizes the complexity of languages into several orders of logic of construction of associations between simple character strings (e.g. tokens or single words). We must define the framework of this grammar in order to better comprehend its limitations. The grammar of a language is defined by four elements; the grammar has an equivalent representation in graphic form, whereby the nodes may be terminal or non-terminal, and are linked one after another to form paths. A path is a rule. Nodes can be linked to themselves – hence the notion of recursiveness which is a principle of reasoning peculiar to human beings:

– T (sets of words): is the set of terminal nodes;

– N: is the set of non-terminal nodes;

– R: is the set of rules;

– S (S ∈ N): is a starting symbol (e.g. a letter of the alphabet).

The rules define the laws of construction of the language: its grammar. In English, for instance, the structure: *subject + verb + complements* is an element of grammar. Human languages (vernacular languages such as French or Chinese) and computer programming languages are some examples of languages. According to Chomsky, there are four families of grammar, with increasing complexity. The regular grammar is the weakest; then come context-free grammars, context-dependent grammars and finally unrestricted grammars. Unrestricted grammars have no rules. The time needed to determine whether a phrase is correctly defined is not decidable. Context-dependent grammar can be represented as follows:

$$(N \cup T)^* \rightarrow (N \cup T)^*$$

The right-hand argument is smaller than the left-hand one. The grammar is context-dependent because the replacement of a non-terminal element with a terminal element may depend on the elements around it, and therefore on its context. Context-free grammar can be represented thus:

$$N \rightarrow (N \cup T)^*$$

In the left-hand argument, there is no longer any context, which means that the non-terminal elements are treated individually. Finally, the regular grammar, the least expressive, is represented as follows:

$$N \rightarrow T$$

$$N \rightarrow NT$$

To give an example of a regular grammar, let us consider a string which begins with an **a** and ends in a **z**. It can contain between 0 and n signs '=', separated by 1 to n signs '-' between them. Thus, some valid words are {az, a=z, a=-=z, a-=-=-z, a----- z}. The regular grammar associated with this situation would be:

$T = \{a,z,=,-\}$

$N = \{S,A,B\}$

$S = \{S\}$

$R = \{ S \rightarrow Az, A \rightarrow A-, A \rightarrow B=, B \rightarrow A-, A \rightarrow a, B \rightarrow a \}$

Skinner [SKI 57] called into question the approach of behavioral psychology to the study of the mind and language. He extended the application of the same principles of operant conditioning to communication. This approach begins with the observation that if a person asks another person for an object, the fact of receiving that object in return reinforces the asking behavior, thereby increasing the probability that the subject will later repeat this behavior in similar conditions to obtain the same kind of result. Skinner formulated a theory whereby communication is viewed as a particular behavior intended to obtain very precise consequences by way of other individuals. He distinguishes several levels of abstraction depending on whether the stimulus is explicit or not. Thus, describing what we see (Tact) is not the same as describing what is going on elsewhere, or what has happened or will happen at a different time (Intraverbal). Chomsky criticizes Skinner's position and the broader one of Piaget: relating to the capacity of individuals to produce new statements.

According to Chomsky, the regular grammar may perfectly well describe the morphology of a natural language such as English, but he recognizes that context-free grammars are necessary to deal with complex associations. The schools of thought in linguistic computational sciences "outside of the United States" have moved on from Chomskian ideas to concentrate on Wittgensteinian grammars (higher-level grammars, which sometimes have no rules), whereby the constitution of corpora of texts serves as a fertilizer to nourish the identification and validation of expressions. Chomsky's sphere of influence has endured in the form of different variants of syntactical analysis (GB/PP/MP, LFG, G/HPSG, Minimalist program) which have even introduced the usage of syntactic dependency (syntactic functions, headed constituents, framework of subcategorization, c-command).

A corpus is a meaningful set of documents on a subject or a context of usage of the language (definition 8.1). For instance, interviews with young people in the suburbs of large cities can be significant of the language of young people in peri-urban zones. These grammars are called Wittgensteinian, because in the 1930s, Wittgenstein [WIT 53], a philosopher and logician, was the first to recognize the limitations of mathematical logic using premises and conclusions to single-handedly account for all the processes of construction and description of a general language. That said, it is possible to refute this argument when we are no longer operating in the axiomatic context of description of the general language. In highly specialized texts, regular structures appear often for obvious social and cognitive reasons: a jargon is used between specialists. These structures are often the subject of controversy, and hence the element of strong consensus of non-comprehension, and on the topic of these controversies – for reasons of comprehension – concepts are employed which are the object of consensus about the state of comprehension. These concepts therefore form stable expressions (sequences of words) which are reused between different writers. In general, these stable elements of language are few (a few hundred or a few thousand expressions) for reasons of economy and strategies to avoid multiple interpretations. Thus, a whole school of information extraction from concepts has developed around these morphological analyses. In particular, it is possible to base extractions on markers found in a dictionary, and possibly declinations. For instance, the verbs in a language are fairly easily distinguishable. However, in a more practical, applicative context, proper nouns and common nouns which are the object of controversy are also elements of languages which are fairly easily "extractable". Classic examples are the names of proteins in documents and the names of authors in scientific publications. There are extensive databases in existence on the names of genes. Given the context of their use, the names of genes are not hugely ambiguous, even if they correspond to a common noun. For example, in flies, there is a gene called *ebony*. However, in use cases which describe the genetics of flies, the mention of *ebony* never means the wood: always the gene. To analyze names of authors, we can use a field of bibliographical notices and cutting rules to pick out, at the right point, the series of surnames with the initial of their first names. Alternatively, in mid-text, we would use trigger-words which are morphological sequences which precede the expression to be picked up on. For instance, in the expression "President Chirac", the expression "President" would be considered a trigger. When it comes to answering a question: "Where does Chirac live?" put into a search field for documents, the analysis cannot content itself with the surface text, using a few trigger words such as "address" in the vicinity of the name, or dictionaries comprising the addresses of every city in France, which would be identified in the vicinity.

At this point, we leave behind the morphological and syntactical level, and enter into the universe of semantics [GRO 94; KLE 90; RAS 87; RAS 95; RAS 01]. The extraction of named entities is, in itself, a semantic analysis in the weak sense, because knowing that a text is talking about Chirac is in itself a semantic analysis. We qualify the meaning of a text using a signifier of palpable reality – interpretable and comprehensible for everybody. However, this is minimalist semantics. General semantics acts not on unitary forms but in a holistic manner, which makes a language a language, by its combinations which are finite in quantity but are extremely numerous.

We can appreciate the enormous influence of Chomsky's theory and of a universal grammar by looking at the interests of American military defense in terms of espionnage and the Cold War in the post-war period. The idea of having translation performed by a machine was advanced by Weaver and Booth [WEA 49] at the University of Washington, when the earliest computers appeared on the market. The machines were then considered as huge dictionaries (not even portable), and "translation" was reduced to a word-for-word operation. In 1964, the American government commissioned a report on automated translation. This report, known as **ALPAC** (*Automatic Language Processing Advisory Committee*), established that automatic translation had no future either in the short or long term. This stopped research dead in most countries, through lack of funding.

8.5. Semantics and combination

The gradual construction of a text is done by a *combination of different levels of scale*. The alphabet is a set of letters, forming words by combination, which in turn can form more complex words, which in turn combine to form sentences which are combinations of specialized words (action words such as verbs, descriptive words such as nouns, qualifying words such as adjectives, and so on). Sentences can reveal combinations of expressions, desolidarized from their syntactic constraints (article-noun, noun-verb). These combinations ensure flexibility in the variability of associations, enabling us to pronounce different judgments for the same situation, expressed differently by a group of speakers, or to describe different situations expressed in the same way for a group of speakers.

At the same time as Chomsky, justifying the gap in combinatorial semantics, Zellig Harris [HAR 54; HAR 68] created the first Department of Linguistics at an American university in 1945, and developed structuralist linguistics inspired by linguistic practices. This theory, although not widely implemented at the time, inspired the linguistic school of corpus processing in the 1980s. Harris rationalized the ideas of the philosopher Leonard Bloomfield [BLO 35], who had created the American school on *distributional linguistics*, in parallel to that of textual statistics founded by George Zipf [ZIP 35]. Although Chomsky was one of Harris' students, Chomsky's work proved more immense and more Platonic, with the ambition of converging into an innatist and universal grammar. Harris converges toward analysis of sub-languages, which can also be called speciality languages, showing how a sub-language in a restricted domain may have a pre-existing external metalanguage, expressed by phrases in the language but not in the sub-language – something which is not accessible to the whole language. Harris was largely influenced by the anthropo-linguistic hypothesis advanced by Sapir-Whorf [SAP 21], claiming that the structural differences between language systems can be placed in parallel with non-linguistic cognitive differences, in an indeterminate manner, in native speakers of a language. Harris proposed finite graphs and primitive informational entities to represent the information. However, he limited the power of representation of the information to the sub-languages of sciences, and, furthermore, for a well-organized science at a particular moment. Furthermore, beyond scientific sub-languages, Harris also developed the idea that objective information is channeled by elementary expressions such as paraphrases.

8.6. Functional grammar

The ALPAC report altered the expectations that we could have of structuralist works, giving the green light to develop alternative schools of thought, even though these new schools of thought did not immediately appear. Thus, the distributionalist school continued in spite of the omnipresence of the transformational universalist theory. M. Halliday [HAL 84] is behind the **systemic and functional grammar**, which continues in the structuralist tradition but is greatly inspired by empiricism. This is a descriptive grammar employed in corpus linguistics by contextual exploration. Functional linguistics can be qualified as "radical", in the sense that they consider that the only organizing force in language is the pressure of evolution, over the course of time and in usages, and selective toward greater efficacy in communication by selecting the syntactical, lexical and grammatical elements which are necessary. From this perspective, some have compared this approach to a Darwinist grammatical method. Linguistic functionalism rejects formal logic and the lexis/grammar dichotomy. Halliday's conception of grammar, or lexico-grammar, is based on a global theory whereby the language is a social semiotic resource, in the wake of Sapir [SAP 21] and Firth [FIR 52]. He specified that theoretical categories, and their interrelations, construct a model of language; they are intertwined and mutually defined. Theoretical categories are, for instance, a metafunction, a system, a level, a class, a realization. Conversely, descriptive categories might include, e.g. a clause, a preposition, a subject, a concrete process, a theme.

The functional property of lexical or speech items was revisited by diachronic approaches seeking to understand the emergence and transformation of the language [LAB 68; GOF 81]. In particular, the theory of the "invisible hand" by Keller [KEL 94] attempted to explain the change process self-organized on a global scale, that is to say, not intentional on the part of the speaker participating in change. It is based on the concept of lexical redundancy from economic events and its use by a social group.

8.7. Meaning-Text Theory

The first linguistic theory based on syntactic dependency stems from Tesnière's model [TES 34]. One of the most successful was *Meaning-Text Theory* championed by I. Mel'čuk [MEL 84], whose interpretation-based model of the complexity of a natural language on the inventory of possible combinations, which Mel'čuk estimates to extend to several million for a single language. This is one of the theories which draw a clearer distinction between semantic, syntactic and morphological notions. In particular, the authors set apart semantic and syntactic dependencies, deep and surface lexises and deep and surface elements of grammar. They clearly separate the rules of sub-categorization, word order, agreement and rection. In this field, we can take Piaget to be correct over Chomsky, who presents the learner as a passive sponge which accumulates elementary knowledge in specific interactional situations. We can also take as correct autonomic systems which aim to treat natural language as "collection/restoration" of associations in particular contexts of information seeking, like a prompter in a theater. Obviously, the prompter is neither the scriptwriter nor the director, but he/she is part of the regulation. The meaning-text theory (MTT) clearly separates the different levels of representation of a sentence: semantic representations are graphs of predicate/argument relations, syntactic representations are non-ordered dependency trees and morphological representations are progressions.

8.8. Generative lexicon

Generative lexicon (GL) is a theory of linguistic semantics which focuses on the distributed nature of compositionality in natural language (Pustejovsky [PUS 91]). GL was initially developed as a theoretical framework for encoding selectional knowledge in natural language. This required making some changes in the formal rules of representation and composition. Perhaps the most controversial aspect of GL has been the manner in which lexically encoded knowledge is exploited in the construction of interpretations for linguistic utterances. The computational resources available to a lexical item within this theory consist of the following four levels:

– Lexical Typing Structure: giving an explicit type for a word positioned within a type system for the language;

– Argument Structure: specifying the number and nature of the arguments to a predicate;

– Event Structure: defining the event type of the expression and any subeventual structure it may have, with subevents;

– Qualia structure: a structural differentiation of the predicative force for a lexical item.

8.9. Theory of synergetic linguistics

One theory which models lexical semantics by way of its distributions is the theory of *synergetic linguistics* (Köhler [KÖH 86; KÖH 05]). This theory aims to integrate the separate hypotheses and laws into a complex model which not only describes the linguistic phenomena but also provides a means to explain them – e.g. with biological constraints. The explanation is based on the central axiom that language is a self-regulating and self-organizing system. According to this theory, it is impossible to account for the existence, properties and change of linguistic – and more generally, semiotic – systems without the aspect of the (dynamic) interdependence of structure and function. Genesis and evolution of these systems must be attributed to repercussions of communication on structure. This view of language as a system that develops in reaction to the properties and requirements of its environment by adaptation mechanisms in analogy to biological evolution makes it possible to set up a model on the basis of synergetics. The synergetic approach is a specific branch of systems theory and can be characterized as an interdisciplinary approach to the modeling of certain dynamic aspects of systems. Synergetic modeling in linguistics starts (first step) from axiomatically assumed requirements which a semiotic system must meet, such as the coding requirement (a semiotic system has to provide means to create meaningful expressions), effective methods of encoding and decoding, of memory saving and minimization of effort. These requirements can be subdivided into three kinds:

(1) language-constitutive requirements,

(2) language-forming requirements, and

(3) control-level requrements (the adaptation requirement, i.e. the need for a language to adapt itself to varying circumstances, and the opposite stability requirement).

The second step is the determination of system levels, units and variables which are of interest to the current investigation. In step three, relevant consequences, effects and interrelations are determined. Here, the researcher sets up of systematizes hypotheses about dependences of variables on others, e.g. with increasing polytextuality of a lexical item, its polysemy increases monotonically, or, the higher the position of a syntactic construction, the less its information. The fourth step consists of the search for functional equivalents and multi-functionalities. Step five is the mathematical formulation of the hypotheses set up so far – a precondition for any rigorous test – and step six is the empirical testing of these mathematically-formulated hypotheses. In this way, for each subsystem of language (i.e. the lexical, morphological, syntactical etc. sub-systems), models of arbitrary complexity are created. The elements, the system variables, represent linguistic units or their properties, while the specific links between these elements are universal hypotheses, which obtain the status of laws if they have been intensively tested and corroborated.

8.10. Integrative approach to language processing

Some approaches, which are less linguistic-computational and are more anchored in *integrative approaches to language-processing*, have emerged in different communities whose needs are expressed by means of processing of electronic documents. These approaches are based on light processing using external resources (dictionaries) [TUR 98c], light surface treatments (suffix analysis) and extraction of weak dependencies (co-occurrences) [NEE 61; REI 86; PHI 89; HIN 90; SMA 90; MAR 91; MIK 92; NIW 94; TAN 96; EDM 97; LEN 97; TIS 99; TUR 00; MIM 01; MEI 05]. The domains are google-style smart information searching (electronic document management) ([SAL 83; VAN 79), storage of company memory (management of company knowledge), semantic analysis of social networks [MIC 88; COU 90] and extraction of named entities. These applicational frameworks use various approaches. Some excellent examples are:

(1) supervised machine learning from examples working on linear separators such as Support Vector Machines (SVM);

(2) semi-supervised machine learning techniques using nonlinear classification distances such as neural networks or graph analysis techniques;

(3) approaches combining extraction of associations and graphical user interfaces (GUIs);

(4) but also context analysis methods such as semantic memory with probabilistic formalisms of analysis of links or Markov chains.

Currently, applications draw a great deal on light approaches for purposes of extraction of useful information: one might cite socio-semantic networks to study the interface between scientific domains and debates in society; information-seeking approaches in large heterogeneous databases where the texts are mixed in with sound, video and semi-structured documents such as forms; approaches to identification of specific objects in large collections of technical documents (such as names of genes and their associations forming complex networks); semantic Web interfaces which make it easier for a user to navigate around a complex site which includes navigation and interaction, such as e-business sites for reserving hotel rooms, for which the terminological and domain ontologies (organization of knowledge) may prove effective in terms of speed to conclude a transaction. Less mainstream purposes such as spying on information flow and analysis of political debates around election time prefigure similarly illustrative uses. These applications involve several actors with different ambitions, a user wishing to identify a piece of information for his/her own purposes, a tool to process digital information using algorithms, and a use context which includes a vast quantity of data – possibly heterogeneous. Issues relating to interfacing and storage (sometimes in delocalized mode) mean these applications become very complex in order to manage the comprehension of the common language by a machine. This is also true for languages which are specialized sub-languages and are therefore contextualized and less ambiguous. This complexity can be seen in the burgeoning number of actions to perform. For designers who require coordination and fairly long periods of time to manage a project, the next step is difficult to imagine. It is also difficult to get to grips with the tools, for users who have to change their habitual practices, and therefore require training.

8.11. New spaces for date production

Indeed, the logics of data production and use on the *Internet* are greatly changing the relationship individuals have with society; the Internet has become a hidden face of our existences as much as a tool and an instrument of communication or purchase. As of 2012, two billion individuals are connected to the Internet the world over, creating a network comprising 200 million servers. When we list the languages spread throughout the world (*lingua francas*) and the languages used to publish on the Internet, we find that there are few differences [ATW 07]. The Internet does not address the crushing weight of languages in the interface which people are faced with in terms of these new technological and societal universes. On the contrary, 80% of the electronic information available online has been produced in the space of the past five years. This information is unstructured and is therefore similar to natural language. New challenges mean that we risk information overload to identify the emerging needs (e.g. the exchange of emotions over social networks) and master new potential capabilities (e.g. distance learning). These requirements give rise to motivation, and particularly because of the use of natural language.

Rank	Language	Primary country	Native speakers (millions) (2009)
1	Mandarin	China	1213
2	Spanish	Spain	329
3	English	United Kingdom	328
4	Arabic	Saudi Arabia	221
5	Hindi	India	182
6	Bengali	Bangladesh	181
7	Portuguese	Portugal	178
8	Russian	Russia	144
9	Japanese	Japan	122
10	German	Germany	90.3
11	Javanese	Indonesia	84.6
12	Lahnda	Pakistan	78.3
13	French	France	70.8
14	Telugu	India	69.8
15	Vietnamese	Vietnam	68.6
16	Marathi	India	68.1
17	Korean	Korea	66.3
18	Tamil	Sri Lanka	65.7
19	Italian	Italy	61.7
20	Urdu	Pakistan	50.8

Table 8.2. *Distribution of the number of speakers of the most widely-spoken languages (source: http://www.ethnologue.com/ethno_docs/distribution.asp?by=size)*

Languages	Percentage of Web pages (2000)	Languages	Percentage of Web pages (2012)
	Total		
English	68.39	English	56.0
Japanese	5.85	German	6.6
German	5.77	Japanese	4.9
Chinese	3.87	Russian	4.8
French	2.96	Spanish	4.6
Spanish	2.42	Chinese	4.4
Russian	1.88	French	4.2
Italian	1.56	Italian	2.2
Portuguese	1.37	Portuguese	2.1
Korean	1.29	Polish	1.5
Flemish	1.01	Arabic	1.2
Swedish	0.93	Flemish	1.1
Danish	0.44	Turkish	1.1
Norwegian	0.40	Swedish	0.7
Finnish	0.38	Persian	0.6
Czech	0.32	Czech	0.6
Polish	0.27	Korean	0.4
Hungarian	0.16	Romanian	0.4
Catalan	0.14	Greek	0.4
Turkish	0.14	Hungarian	0.3
Greek	0.09	Thai	0.3
Hebrew	0.06	Danish	0.3
Estonian	0.06	Vietnamese	0.3
Romanian	0.05	Javanese	0.3
Icelandic	0.04	Finnish	0.2
Slovenian	0.04	Norwegian	0.2
Arabic	0.04	Bulgarian	0.2
		Slovak	0.2
		Hebrew	0.1

Table 8.3. *Distribution of the number of Web pages in the most widely-used languages (source: http://www.ethnologue.com/ethno_docs/distribution.asp?by=size)*

To treat the lingua franca as a contiguous, abstract and unchanging unit would be utopian. Currently, mastery involves dealing with *speciality languages*, just as Sapir anticipated in the 1920s in an isolated manner when analyzing Native American dialects, and Harris later on in a more rationalized context. Sager [SAG 75], continuing in the vein of Harris' work, illustrated the efficacy of treating corpora in the field of medicine, which produces a phenomenal amount of literature. The database PubMed serves as a demonstration of this, and supplements the exploitation of such a database by using modern data mining techniques, particularly by integrating other kinds of databases – more specific but still useful (notably the gene base or free-access biological database).

We can cite the more philological but insightful work on social networks in the texts of Francis Andersen (Andersen and Forbes [AND 78]), who studies the distribution of Biblical characters and their associations. Andersen integrated a base of texts from the original Hebrew Bible, called the Leningrad Codex, between 1971 and 1979 in electronic form. Today, thanks to the Internet, we can create a corpus of 100,000 summaries of articles on any subject in biology in the space of a few minutes – i.e. generate the list of documents and download them to one's personal computer. Thus, we must doff our hats to the laborious and painstaking work of the pioneers in corpus linguistics and linguistic computing. Andersen divided the orthographic words of the Bible into grammatical segments. A linguistic dictionary was generated by a computer, including the grammatical information on every segment in order to study the concordances between the sought words (e.g. characters in the Bible). This work on corpora did much to contribute to the advances made in lexical semantics.

8.12. Notion of ontology

In spite of their elegance, these systemic and lexical approaches do not always lend themselves to spontaneity and reactivity of interaction with a user of an information system in the broad sense or the Internet, via online services and supports as smartphones and laptop computers may require. The notion of *ontology* is an old one, like numerous philosophical concepts. We can cite Porphyrian trees which date from the time of Plato, and the terminological nomenclature of Roget's categories [ROG 52] around 1830, which he took 20 years to establish. In the modern sense, the ontology is reduced to a hierarchy of concepts, the structure of which benefits from relations between types, categories and terms which are gradually associated. Obviously, the networks can vary from one domain to another. Hence, we again see the advantage of corpora to be able to extract useful terminological expressions and practiced by experts in a domain and integrate them into an ontology: this is acquisition of knowledge. The nature of the links between concepts and the levels of hierarchy are established by abstraction of a domain which either it is possible to study using a corpus, or which must be established beforehand [SKU 91; RES 92; SUS 95; RIL 97; RIL 98; HEA 98; PLO 98; TUR 99;

REI 03; SHA 03; HAR 04; SPY 05; YAO 09]. For instance, it is known in bioinformatics that the names of genes vary over the course of time and between species, owing to the fact that a gene is assigned a provisional name when it is discovered. We are dealing with an abstract relation of synonymy, which is highly complex to manage automatically. In biological hypotheses which involve a limited number of genes – around a hundred – it is prudent to deal with this issue manually in a dedicated table which will be taken into account by an information processing system. When we wish to reason about a hierarchy of concepts or validate the structure of a concept as a function of the attributes which it receives in a form, acquisition is no longer enough, and we enter the domain of representation of knowledge with associated metalanguages [TUR 08]. These metalanguages can justify the coherence of the hierarchy if a new concept is introduced (i.e. consistency), or of the nature of the links that exist between two concepts (i.e. subsumption); Bertrand Russell's [RUS 03] old logic and F. Gottlob Frege [FRE 92] and its sympathic properties of validity of propositions surfaces once again, and will be judiciously used to infer (i.e. deduce) new relations and therefore new knowledge.

8.13. Knowledge representation

Although they were developed independently in the early 1970s, **frames** (Schank and Abelson [SCH 77]) and **scripts** (Minsky [MIN 75]) have many points in common. The key idea involved in both frames and scripts, borrowed from work in cognitive psychology – particularly in the field of knowledge acquisition – is that our knowledge and our perception of concepts, events and situations which we create are organized around prototypical contents and particular characteristics which we expect in relation to these concepts, events and situations. Hence, a script is a structure made up of frames, possibly with overlaps. It represents a set of events, with certain temporal, spatial and causal relations. The descriptions of the events may be only partial. Given that the combination of frames is usually fairly open-ended, it is easy to describe unusual events or infer behaviors or events not explicitly described, based on prototypical structures. The SAM program, developed by Schank and Abelson, was able to recognize and represent simple sequences such as the following well-known example:

> *Joe went to a restaurant. Joe ordered a hamburger. When the hamburger came, it was burnt to a crisp. Joe stormed out without paying.*

The system, in view of this description, was able to infer that Joe had not eaten the hamburger, even though no explicit mention was made of what he did and did not eat in the restaurant. The system, which was highly advanced for its time, was able to explain its reasoning by referring to the contrast between the standard restauarant script and information not found in this text. For instance, the lack of information about the eating of the hamburger, among other factors, leads to this deduction. The restaurant script is given below: it involves eight elementary frames. This script is represented informally for ease of reading:

– Script (restaurant (Customer, Restaurant, Food)):

- Enter (Customer, restaurant),

- Call (Customer, Waiter),

- Order (Customer, Food),

- Bring (Waiter, Food),

- Eat (Customer, Food),

- Pay (Customer, Manager, Food),

- Exit (Customer, restaurant), If: human (Customer), human (Waiter), human (Manager), food (Food).

Thus, frames and scripts offer a rich and flexible method of representing fragments of specialized knowledge in an organized manner. They replicate an essential characteristic of our understanding of processes encountered by assimilation to prototypical situations which we have learnt. Furthermore, in an extended context, Piaget suggests adaptive processes which enable us to change the prototype over time. This is a highly economic approach, without systematic development of very complex inferential forms for every new situation. The frames are adaptable and revisable.

In another scenario, similar to a Roget-style semantic network, the Polish linguist A. Wierzbicka [WIE 72] advanced the hypothesis of the existence of a nucleus of semantic universals (also called *primitives*), which cannot be broken down, which would form a "universal mental alphabet", or "atoms of thought". This work fits in with the theory known as Natural Semantic Metalanguage (NSM). Although this form of structure of knowledge corresponds to the image of a stable transmission of structured knowledge, we can see that it works for colors – for which the range of concepts is well established – but for smells it works less well. Locally, though, the representation may represent an advantage to identify the resilience of a structure of knowledge.

A *conceptual graph* is a formalism of representation of knowledge and reasoning. This formalism was introduced by John Sowa [SOW 84], who proposed conceptual graphs as a formalism of knowledge representation pivoting between logic and natural language. He showed how the join of the graphs associated with the words of a sentence could serve to construct a graph which should represent the entire sentence. Three ingredients in this type of formalism should also serve as an aid to reasoning: the graphical interface from first-order logic, the diagrammatic system for first-order logic, and the formalism of knowledge and reasoning representation based on the graphs.

Description logics, also known as *descriptive logics*, are a family of knowledge representation languages which can be used to represent the terminological knowledge in a domain of application in a formal and structured manner [BAA 03]. The name, description logic, relates on the one hand to the description of concepts used to describe a domain and, on the other, to the logic-based semantics which can be given by a transcription of the first-order predicates into logic format. Description logic was developed as an extension of frames and semantic networks, which did not have a formal logic-based semantics. Most description logics divide knowledge into two parts:

– terminological information: definition of the basic notions or derivatives and how they are interconnected. These data are "generic" or "global", true in all models and for all individuals.

– information about the individuals: these data are "specific" or "local", and only true for certain particular individuals.

All the known pieces of information are then modeled as a <T, A> couple, where T is a set of formulae relating to terminological information (the T-Box) and A is a set of formulae relating to information about the assertions (the A-Box). Another way of seeing the separation between these types of information is to associate the T-Box with the rules which govern our world (e.g. physics, chemistry, biology, etc.), and associate the individuals of our world with the A-Box (e.g. John, Mary, a cat, etc.). The basic tasks of deduction can be used to define relatively complex tasks such as:

– Searching: given a concept, finding the individuals mentioned in the knowledge base who are instances of that concept.

– Realization: given an individual mentioned in the knowledge base, finding the more specific concept, in accordance with the subsumption relations, of which that individual is an instance.

For instance:

Let S be a knowledge base <T, A> where:

– T={STALLION = HORSE $\cap$ $\forall$Sex.Male}

– A= {shadowfax: STALLION}

The formula of T says that male horses are stallions, and the formula of A says that the horse *Shadowfax* is a stallion. The formal semantics which we impose upon ourselves in the definition enables us to verify that S has at least one model (i.e. it is coherent).

The WWW Consortium (http://www.w3.org/) recommends norms and directions of reflections about new faces of the Web. Notably, it adopted the language OWL (Web Ontology Language) based on description logics to describe relations of concepts on Internet pages and facilitate information extraction.

Chapter 9

Computational Modeling of Motivation

9.1. Notion of a computational model

Computational models have attained maturity in terms of perfection, variety and adaptability to numerous parametric situations. We find such models in various domains of computer science: artificial intelligence (AI – multi-agent approaches, artificial neural networks, probabilistic networks), theoretical computing (formal languages) and complex systems (self-organized models). Physicists have abstractly demonstrated a theorem of free will, and it is interesting to look at this theorem in order to understand the rational side of motivation. It is the only rational framework which deals with the issue. Computational approaches simulate a degree of reflexiveness, which is limited and is independent of natural language. All told, the formalisms proposed do not model self-motivation, but begin to approximate this concept by way of slight autonomy (internal motivation) or cost/benefit parameters (external motivation).

9.2. Multi-agent systems

One of the flagship formalisms to conceive of an artificial autonomy – which is, in itself, a model of a dynamic social network – is the *multi-agent system*. Ermolayev *et al.* [ERM 05], for instance, define actors and associated concepts in a multi-agent framework, which they call Dynamic Engineering Design Process (DEDP). Figure 9.1 presents the ontology of an actor in this model. An actor is the abstract representation of a person who performs tasks and executes atomic activities resulting from the transformation of design artifacts (Hewitt *et al.* [HEW 73]).

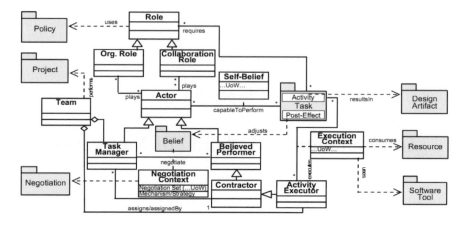

Figure 9.1. *Schema of the ontology of an actor in the DEDP model [ERM 05]*

The main property of an actor is his capacity to perform a task. An actor is capable of performing tasks in the context of an "organizational role" that he plays, in the sense that he possesses subjective knowledge such as: (1) the compound or singular nature of a task; (2) if he can perform that task himself or whether he could allocate it to another actor. This knowledge constitutes the actor's self-belief.

The architecture of an agent is a multi-layer architecture, hybrid and multiple in association with other agents. These agents are intentioned to take care of political, cultural and business aspects, and of rules of business. These agents adapt their behavior on the basis of the likely success of a plan, and on the estimation of cost, time and the value in the choice of a plan. An intelligent multi-agent system is an ecosystem of autonomous cooperative components, each of which maintains constant interaction with its environment. An intelligent agent has to be autonomous, cooperative and adaptive. The basis of self-belief involves the agent's reflexive knowledge about himself and his public, private and semi-private knowledge (Pěchouček *et al.* [PĚC 02]). Wagner and Diaconescu [WAG 09] also described an agent by virtue of his self-belief (the agent's knowledge about himself).

Pezzulo and Calvi [PEZ 04] described the means of implementation – i.e. the dynamic of belief and objective in a multi-agent system. They also showed the interwoven web between epistemic structures, motivations and activity of autonomous agents, adopting a situated and constructivist view [PIA 75]. An objective may be triggered by desires, as well as by increasing/decreasing pressures, by plans and even by the actors' beliefs. Desires are internal, pilots for higher layers to lower layers and the trigger for objectives: a unique characteristic for self-motivated systems. Desires are maintenance conditions (i.e. fluid variables to be conserved for a given period of time); the further the desires are from the reality of the conditions, the stronger they are and the more motivation they provide. In certain circumstances, they can also give rise to new objectives. Sometimes the contribution of desires can be viewed as normative ("adverbial"), in the sense that they pose constraints on the progression of the objectives (e.g. behaving politely). Thus, they are useful for the development of a lower version of standards.

The organization of the interaction between the individuals and the components of the system affect the aggregate behavior, and how the organization itself appears (Kirman [KIR 99]). In today's world, a considerable proportion of the resources in an economy is devoted to the acquisition and distribution of information [BAY 87]. However, in standard economy models, the information necessary to ensure efficient allocation of resources is minimal. This contradiction between the abstract models and the real world is easy to account for. In the models, communication only relates to prices, but in the real economy, the agents communicate with one another, observe one another and are influenced by the behavior of other individuals. Thus, it is helpful to take account of direct interactions between individuals, the consequences of those interactions and the modification of the role of the price which results from this. In the financial markets, for instance, it is worth mentioning a number of points. A common argument regarding the evolution of prices of a financial asset is that, if it were predictable, the agents could earn money. Thus, the only evolution possible is a series of random spikes and dives – hence the idea that the price of assets must follow a random pattern, a notion which dates from Bachelier [BAC 00]. Of course, this argument is set against that which holds that if there is a predictable structure in the series of prices, it can only be exploited if the agents are capable of perceiving it and if they learn to do so. Thus, as Brock and LeBaron [BRO 96] showed, technical rules for exchanges have a precision value in the financial markets. Of course, once this is understood, their predictive power should disappear.

Most researchers working on social systems consider that a micro-level theory of individual decision-making must take account of a considerable degree of unpredictability and random chance. Everyone is exposed to a wide variety of different influences, which are superimposed upon one another. Consequently, we cannot hope to describe human behavior using a deterministic model. Helbing *et al.* [HEL 11] developed computational models based on agents. They used the theoretical framework of game theory, coupled with a success-oriented model, imbuing the agents with two (simplistic) rational micro-motivations: (1) imitation of winning strategies and (2) migration toward places with higher yields. They studied the importance of the range of interactions between agents to maintain cooperation and thus demonstrated that migration motivations cause structural effects and the emergence of forms such as groups with similar strategies and segregation of differing strategies. The social environment influences individuals' behavior, which at the same time shapes that social environment. Individuals tend to group together in order to increase the number of neighbors with whom they can interact.

Why individuals come together in cities, groups or networks, and why they exhibit extravert and "social" behavior, are among the most fundamental questions in sociology and other behavioral sciences ([HOB 84; PAR 25; PAR 37; SCH 71; SCH 78; GRA 73; AXE 84; COL 90]. These two questions are mutually correlated, as social interactions requiring a certain degree of adaptability and coordination to favor cooperation. Otherwise, most interactions would fail or would end in conflict [AXE 97; HEN 04; WIN 09; RAU 09].

A category like an emotion, or a mood, constantly being updated by an emotion system, is declared as a belief in an agent's cognitive layer. This means that an agent becomes cognitively "conscious" of each of his own emotional states, which is fairly decisive to be classed in terms of emotional categories [BEC 06].

Agent coordination systems are sensitive to the phenomenon of data accumulation, as they are used in pervasive systems and cloud computing. There are a number of works on coordination systems which include self-organization of the data (i.e. a swarm system); however, they organize their data using naive approaches whereby the elements are either totally similar or dissimilar (a 1|0 approach for data matching). Although this approach is useful for general systems where the diversity of data is great, the data are rarely considered to be entirely similar, which leads to situations where the data do not organize themselves well. An organization method may appear through ontology management – notably through the very well-known Wordnet, which is a lexical ontology defining relations between concepts. The data are seen as concepts which are related to other concepts: tuples (associations of data) are guided toward another tuple at a rate which is proportional to the strength of the relation of the tuple. Pianini *et al.* [PIA 10] demonstrate that this approach leads to a good mechanism which self-organizes the data in a mass-data environment.

Saglimbeni and Parisi [SAG 11] implemented simulations in which living organisms have two motivations: eating food and avoiding being captured by a predator. In order to stay alive, the organism must be capable of finding food (energy) and water in the environment. The organism looks for food and water when the level is low. We refer to these two components as adaptive components of the organisms: the cognitive (or tactical) component and the motivational (or strategic) component. The simulations suggest that there are two types of individuals who do not tend to reproduce: individuals who are not good at finding food (tactical or cognitive problem) and individuals who are too afraid of predators to look for food (strategic or motivational problem). The information gleaned from the body (input) is used to decide which action to undertake. The study shows the ambivalent side of the motivational system, associated with a cognitive signaling system. A parallel may be drawn with a motivational system based on a close relation between a cognitive sub-system of language on oneself and a motivation/action subsystem.

Nichols [NIC 93] explains that a point of view is a set of beliefs held by an agent. A belief is a state of disposition – a belief, and therefore a point of view, belonging to an agent. A state of disposition is supposed to indicate the possession of a belief by an agent toward a certain form of behavior but does not guarantee it. One consequence of approaching problems from different points of view is that the beliefs attached to a point of view may be inconsistent with those of another point of view. Fagin and Halpern [FAG 88] formalized this in a local reasoning logic which allows agents to hold beliefs that are inconsistent with incoherent situations. One reason for which individuals hold inconsistent beliefs is that the beliefs tend to come in "groups" without interaction. Each part of an agent's mind may contain different beliefs about the same objects, which means accepting different points of view about a certain set of objects. Three other ideas are based on logic: implicit and explicit belief, consciousness and limited resources. An agent's implicit beliefs include all the consequences of his explicit beliefs. Consciousness enables agents to reason with just the beliefs of which they are "consciously" aware – i.e. those which they consider to be pertinent. The limited resources available to an agent may also restrict his reasoning – e.g. to satisfy real-time constraints with a certain response time.

9.3. Artificial self-organization

During the period from the 15th to the 19th Century, many developments were made in science, which came to imply a vertical operational principle: a set of laws must be able to explain all natural phenomena; the rest is absorbed by stochastic theories. However, in 1889, H. Poincaré [POI 90] attempted to solve the three-body problem and showed that, in such a case of interaction between the bodies, the system is not integrable. This means that it is not enough to know all the physical laws governing the behavior of each particle in order to know and predict the behavior of these particles. The term "**self-organized system**" appears to have been used first by W.R. Ashby in 1947 [ASH 62] in the field of cybernetics. As for the notion of self-organization, it was applied only for technical systems and was primarily associated with control. We can identify five key characteristics of natural self-organization:

– The elements of self-organized systems are autonomous in the sense of a cycle of autonomy. These systems may be functional with an external control (control parameter).

– A phenomenon of natural self-organization appears in macroscopic forms. Even with the naked eye, we can see forms of self-organization achieved by living organisms (colonies of ants, swarms of bees, human crowds, herds of animals, schools of fish, flocks of birds) as seen in Figure 9.2.

– The interactions between the elements in natural self-organized systems are fixed (e.g. the interactions between liquid molecules in hydrodynamic systems, the atoms in a laser, the bacteria or the cells in biological systems).

– In most self-organized systems, the control parameters are represented by a flux of energy (matter), and the change of parameters of control is given by a change in these quantities.

– Most self-organized systems are invariant in size; self-organization phenomena take place when the number of participating elements is independent (number of molecules in a hydrodynamic phenomenon, number of species/cells in biology).

Figure 9.2. *A tornado-shaped cloud of birds formed near Lake Mogan in Turkey (photo courtesy of Gonulalan, Caters News Agency/SIPA)*

As regards artificial self-organization, there are four main points to be highlighted: "technical" emergence, the construction of forms of behavior, self-organized generation of forms of behavior and scaling of the forms of behavior. We find various types of emergence: combinatorial, creative or thermodynamic. Self-organization in computational approaches is largely associated with combinatorial algorithms which we can see in multi-agent systems. Thus, the emergence in such a system is a "combinatorial" emergence. Self-organization is a process in which a form emerges at a global level of a system only, based on innumerable interactions between the system's low-level components. In addition, the rules governing the interactions among the components of the system are executed using only local information, without reference to a local form. In summary, a form is an emerging property of the system, rather than a property imposed on the system by an external structuring influence. If there is a structure formed by positive or negative feedback then collective self-organization becomes possible (Camazine *et al.* [CAM 01]; Weisbuch [WEI 90]).

Self-organization is interesting as a social process, as a communication practice and as an event. Self-organization, as a concept of a process (ontic, description of the being), has more to offer than as an ontology (properties of the fact of being). In the living world of self-organization, we see relations and activities, communication and production, an identity and conflicts. Self-organization is any process taking place on open-ended systems, feedback loops and co-evolution leading to a competitive advantage. Ilya Prigogine put forward the hypothesis of spontaneous self-organization appearing far from states of equilibrium and in which individual behavior or specific circumstances can play an important role [PRI 84]. Complexity theory states that a radical change is possible in self-organization, but this change, or emergence, is particular and dependent upon specific circumstances. The change is not predictable: it genuinely is emergent. These states must lead to a form of social complexity theory and keep more deterministic systemic theories at arm's length.

Sansores and Pavon [SAN 08] proposed a mechanism of self-organization to model adaptive multi-agent systems inspired by an approach from psychological motivation. The motivation behind this approach is an internal state or condition which serves to activate or energize a behavior and give it a direction. In order to increase the robustness of this particular behavior, they suggested the existence of a reinforcement mechanism based on the agents' past experience as controlling feedback. The aim of this mechanism is to mimic the adaptation exhibited by entities of complex systems comprising numerous autonomous entities which take local decisions, leading to an organized overall behavior in the system. Such organization is achieved autonomously in different ways, which thus adapt to a task and to the environment.

9.4. Artificial neural networks

In a slightly different theoretical register – that of *artificial neural networks* – Marshall *et al.* [MAR 04] hold that self-motivation is an emergent property caused by competing pressures which come about as a result of the attempt to balance predictability and novelty. They proposed a relatively simple architecture of recurrent networks and an algorithm by way of which, systems are strongly coupled for learning of prediction and control. In this model, the better the predictive system becomes at anticipating the consequences of the actions of the control system, the more the novelty diminishes and the behavior of the predictive system becomes more closely linked with that of the control system. When the novelty decreases, the rate of error generated by the predictive system becomes smaller and more fragmented, which can cause the error to fluctuate around its average value or even disappear completely. Thus, the control system has a greater degree of difficulty in attaining new parts of inputs for a sensor in time. As the performances of the system decrease, a robot appears to "lose interest" in aspects of the inputs to a sensor which would previously have captured its attention. The coupling between the predictive and control systems begins to weaken, because the control system is no longer paying as much attention as effectively to what is happening as before. As the predictive system loses its ability to effectively predict the control system's responses, the novelty once more begins to dwindle. At this level, the novelty of another stimulus may attract the system's attention, although in this experimental framework, the development of a robot has never found another focal point. This scenario may potentially serve as a habit-forming model. More generally, the interwoven web of predictability and novelty offers a fairly rich framework to explore open-ended learning and skill acquisition in developmental robotics.

9.5. Free will theorem

In 2006, physicists John Conway and Simon Kochen demonstrated a theorem called the "*free will theorem*". The free will of an entity A is defined as the capacity that A has to take decisions which are not defined by a function (in the mathematical sense of the term) of the information to which A has access – i.e. the information available in A's "cone of past light". Thus, the theorem states that if an experimenter has free will, then elementary particles have free will as well. Philosophers generally consider that experimenters have enough "free will" to choose the way in which they organize their experiments in a way which is not determined by past history. From this, the theorem deduces the surprising fact that if this is true then the particles' response is no longer determined by their past history. The proof of the theorem relies on three axioms, which Conway and Kochen call "fin", "spin" and "twin". The spin and twin axioms can be verified experimentally:

– "Fin" axiom: there is a maximum speed for propagation of information (not necessarily the speed of light). This assumption rests upon causality.

– "Spin" axiom: the squared spin component of certain elementary particles of spin one, taken in three orthogonal directions, will be a permutation of $(1, 1, 0)$.

–"Twin" axiom: It is possible to "entangle" two elementary particles, and separate them by a significant distance, so that they have the same squared spin results if measured in parallel directions. This is a consequence of (but more limited than) quantum entanglement.

Conway and Kochen begin by demonstrating if we accept the "spin" axiom, which all quantum physicists consider to be true because it conforms to the results of their experiments, then a certain quantity measured by these physicists cannot pre-exist before the experiment. This quantity cannot be inherent in the structure of the particle being studied. This is a sardonic nod to the "materialistic" conception of the universe. However, we may imagine that this quantity is instantaneously "calculated" based on the information available in the universe accessible to these particles just before the measurement is taken. Yet this "free will theorem" demonstrates that this is not so, on condition that the experimenters have free will and that we accept two other axioms called "fin" and "twin" which are also held to be true by physicists. The theorem also delivers a fatal blow to so-called "hidden variable" theories, which hold that there exists a wave of reality, and that the particles have more properties than quantum mechanics assigns to them, but that these properties are "hidden" and only manifest themselves during the "reduction of the wavepacket" following a measurement. In fact, the free will theorem proves that hidden variable theories are all false (or inconsistent with restrained relativity), without using quantum mechanics, because it is simple mathematical reasoning which does not exploit any physical property of the particles. According to Descartes, determinists have always believed that one day it would be possible to describe the universe as the evolution of a system from an initial state according to deterministic laws, i.e. which do not vary over space and time. The reasoning employed in this demonstration is in the same vein as chaos theory and the theory of self-organization, and shows – without using free will, and using only the three "fin", "twin" and "spin" axioms – that no theory using laws independent of spacetime can predict anything other than the result of certain measurements of the spin on particles. Conway and Kochen do not prove that free will exists, and the theorem does not mean that determinism is necessarily wrong. If the universe is entirely deterministic, then human beings have no free will and the theorem is inapplicable. However, if there is indeterminism, i.e. free will in humans, the same is also true for the elementary particles. The definition of "free will" used in the proof of the theorem results simply from a terminological and interpretative equivalence with "is not determined" by the initial conditions, which may prove debatable from a philosophical point of view by the fact that this only applies to deterministic models. The cognitive, attentional and regulatory aspects of the self are intimately interconnected by pervasive links with emotion and motivation, which do not give an account of a purely deterministic nature.

9.6. The probabilistic utility model

Young [YOU 07] elaborated a model of the self described by action and knowledge by way of an economic *probabilistic utility model*. An individual is concerned with the self-image if its utility function does not only depend on that individual's actions, but also on their beliefs about what kind of individual they are. This two-pronged motivation problem makes it difficult, and in certain cases impossible, for an individual to learn who they are by basing this judgment only on the observation of their own behavior. However, it is possible to find very simple situations, involving only two actions and two possible identities. For instance, we may consider an individual to be made up of an observant Self who has beliefs but not preferences, with an initial uncertainty as regards that individual's true identity, and another self who has preferences and takes actions. The Self is a familiar entity to a purely economic individual who simply maximizes a utility expectancy function, whereas the self is a separate aspect of the individual, a sort of impartial spectator who attempts to deduce who the Self really is by way of proof. The difficulty lies in the fact that the utility function of the Self contains the opinion of the self as one of its arguments. More precisely, let "I" represent a finite set of n possible Selves, which is also qualified as identities or types. A Self is defined by its utility function, which includes two arguments: the actions, and the beliefs of the self about who the Self is or could be. "A" denotes a finite set of actions available for the Self. Let "p_{ia}" be the probability that the Self i will perform an action $a \in A$, and let "p_i" be the probability distribution on A. The beliefs of the self are composed of probability distributions $\theta = (\theta_1, \ldots, \theta_n)$ on I, where θ_i is the probability that the self will actually choose the correct value for the Self (i). Let us suppose, for argument's sake, that "i" assumes the belief vector which is given, and that the utility function of "i" assumes the following separable additive form:

$$u_i \left(p_i, \theta \right) = \sum_{a \in A} u_{ia} \theta_j + \sum_{j \in I} v_{ia} \theta_j$$

where u_{ia} is the "intrinsic" utility of i performing the action a, and v_{ia} is the utility of the self-image, which is the utility that i draws from the self's belief that i is actually "j".

We suppose that the self's *a priori* belief is given by the vector θ. Let θ_{ja} denote the self's *a posteriori* belief that the Self is j in the knowledge that the action a has occurred. One imagines that you are, in fact, the Self i. Because you are rational, you choose the actions which maximize your expected utility. This would suggest maximizing p_i.

$$u_i \left(p_i, \theta \right) = \sum_{a \in A} p_{ia} [u_{ia} + \sum_{j \in I} v_{ij} \theta_{ja}]$$

However, this is deceptive, because the posterior values θ_{ja} depend not only on p_i, but also on what each possible Self would do if it were the true Self. Thus, instead of this second expression, we need to write:

$$U_i \left(\mathbf{p}, \theta \right) = \sum_{a \in A} p_{ia} [u_{ia} + \sum_{j \in I} v_{ij} \theta_{ja} \left(\mathbf{p}, \theta \right)]$$

where $p = (p_1, p_2,\ldots, p_n)$, and every p_i maximizes $U_i(p, \theta)$ in view of the strategies of the other possible Selves. The quantities $\theta_{ja}(p, \theta)$ are calculated as follows. Given that a occurs, the self's *a posteriori* beliefs are:

$$\theta_{ja} = f_j \ (a, \mathbf{p}, \mathbf{\theta}) = \frac{\theta_j \ p_{ja}}{\Sigma_k \ \theta_k \ p_{ka}}, \text{if} \sum_k \theta_k \ p_{ka} > 0$$

denoting the *a posteriori* probability distribution as $\theta_a = f(a, p, \theta)$. The profit functions $U_i(p, \theta)$ defined by the previous two expressions constitute a set of n individuals out of the various possible Selves, which we can call the "set about the knowledge of the Self".

9.7. The autoepistemic model

The *autoepistemic logic* is a logic of self-belief, because the meaning of the modality K in the autoepistemic logic is the same as that of MK (which may be known) in the modal logic S4F [KON 89] (Schwartz and Truszczyński [SCH 92]). Consider a formal language which is sufficiently rich to enable the user to declare arithmetic propositions – e.g. the following proposition: for any n, there is an m such that $m > n$, or indeed the same proposition more symbolically expressed: $\forall n, x, y, z$ $[(n \geq 3 \text{ and } x \neq 0 \text{ and } y \neq 0 \text{ and } z \neq 0) \rightarrow (x^n + y^n \neq z^n)]$. This also enables a user to make declarations such as "I think φ", or its abridged form "Bφ", where φ is another declaration in the language. The language is also closed in finite applications of Boolean operations: $\neg$, $\vee$ and $\wedge$. We use the symbol L to denote the collection of all declarations in that language. The totality of the beliefs of a decision-maker who takes a decision, or his belief system, is a subset $B \subseteq L$. We impose the following postulates on B:

(1) B is consistent. This means that we cannot deduce a contradiction based on the declarations in B. In particular, B cannot include a declaration φ and its negation $\neg\varphi$ at the same time.

(2 -) B is deductively closed. This means that if φ_1, ..., φ_n is a finite collection of declarations in B and φ can be inferred from φ_1, ..., φ_n by the rules of calculation of the predicates, then $\varphi \in B$.

(2 +) The set $\{\varphi \in L \mid B \varphi \in B\}$ is deductively closed. Postulate 2 (2- or 2+) holds that the decision-maker is fully aware of all the logical consequences of his beliefs. This state is sometimes called "logical omniscience". This practical point of view is a strong hypothesis. That said, no realistic decision-maker has that capacity at any point in time. In addition, it is not clear what a weaker and adapted postulate might be, so that each rational individual would have a clear possibility to produce a logical inference. It should be evident that, even with such an idealization, the

decision-maker's self-belief cannot be complete. To prove such a result we need only to require that the decision-maker be able to perform a handful of deductions; the logical omniscience postulate is declared here merely because it seems more natural than a finite and specific collection of rules and axioms in the demonstration. Postulate (2+) holds that the decision-maker is not only capable of making logical inferences, but also that he is conscious of making them.

(3a) B contains arithmetic axioms (e.g. the Peano axioms with the mathematical induction scheme).

(3b) B contains the following axioms concerning the self-belief operator: for each φ, $\varphi \in L$, $B(\varphi \wedge \varphi) \longleftrightarrow B\varphi \wedge B\varphi$;

$B\varphi \vee B\varphi \rightarrow B(\varphi \vee \varphi)$;

$B(\neg \varphi) \rightarrow \neg B\varphi$.

In this formal language the operators $\rightarrow$ and $\longleftrightarrow$ are defined in terms of $\vee$, $\wedge$ and $\neg$ in accordance with their traditional usage [CHA 94].

A logic which combines reasoning about belief with the autoepistemic logic facilitates a description of the processes of revision of the beliefs of an agent who is able to absorb the facts observed about behaviors. The review of attitudes takes place in response to discourse acts [APP 88].

Chapter 10

Hypothesis and Control of Cognitive Self-Motivation

10.1. Social groups

Social groups have a real existence nowadays, with geographic but also digital links, of urban or professional origins. These groups are all the more significant, given that more than three in four people on the planet live in a town or city. Promiscuity and interdependency make the idea of absolute autonomy in towns an illusion. Even going to the market is tantamount to involving oneself in an organized social life and obeying a dependency upon food – a fundamental dependency. Groups are fairly furtive depending on their own motivations, obviously.

In a population capital, we can find groups who follow certain fashions, such as "goths" or bourgeois-bohemians ("bobos"). A bobo is an inhabitant of a large city, who lives in a Haussmann-type building with reduced floors, appreciating "vintage", the difference between the rustic and the refined, the sporty and the distinguished. The name is strange: one imagines extravagance of style and spiritual disorientation. Bobo is a qualifier of one's social language – a label one receives like a medal to validate their peaceful but non-ritualistic existence. It is presence and visibility that count, acting like a modern ritual for the benefit of a select majority, and no longer a select minority. This is a new model of the microcosm, served with democratic sauce. "I decide to adhere to it if I like it and I have the time to follow it", with a little money of course, but within reason; in any case, this is not seen too often. The group affords the individual a state, rather than a status which would include demand and legitimacy, expressing a common denominator corresponding to a given time and place with a situation of existence, and by which an individual feels close to happiness, or at the very least experiences a feeling of wellbeing because of this state. Possibly also a feeling of success in life. We have gone from a trait of social description to a trait of psychic description. From fashionable group to emotion. We can fairly simply sum up an easily-interpretable variety of types of emotions without going into the almost binary caricature of love (positive emotion), fear (negative emotion) and contemplation (neutral emotion). If we let ourselves go with the diversity, we can list seven types of emotions: joy, sorrow, fear, anger, surprise and disgust, and contemplation could also be added to this list. Now let us consider the question of how much time to attach to these emotional states. We know that, on a daily basis, an individual spends on average eight hours sleeping, and an hour eating and drinking. We are left with fifteen hours, which is 900 minutes. Nobody can be satisfied 100% of the time, unless we model the world in his image and in accordance with his view of things. Thus, we allow ourselves states of psychotic frustration which range from 20 to 50% of the time, leading an individual to be dissatisfied. Hence, it is possible to calculate the number of combinations, and divide the 900 minutes up into one or two periods of satisfaction which are equal to the half the total time.

(a)	1	2	3	4	5	6	7	8	9	10
(b)	1	2	3	4	5	6	7	8	9	10
(c)	1	2	3	4	5	6	7	8	9	10
(d)	1	2	3	4	5	6	7	8	9	10

Figure 10.1. *Division of 10-minute slot into two periods and positioning of four boundaries. (a) the full 10 minutes; (b) positioning of the first boundary; (c) positioning of the second boundary; (d) both periods*

Figure 10.1 shows an example of the division with 10 minutes. For our 900 minutes the number of possibilities to position four boundaries is at most $450 \times 450 \times 450 \times 450$, equating to over 41 billion combinations, which must be viewed in the light of all the possible combinations of the seven emotions in each minute: 7^{900}; this number is greater than the number of atoms in the universe, and no computer could count this on silicon bits (or fingers of a hand) in less than a century, and yet a human being will certainly experience moments of satisfaction, even without being aware of it. Hence there are factors which lead us to believe in instants of satisfaction, without which non-selective combinatorial would not allow these factors which lead us to believe in the feeling of satisfaction. That which leads us to believe in the feeling of satisfaction is comparable to a belief. In our interpretation and according to the model outlined in this chapter and the next, self-motivation is a driving force. According to such a model, self-motivation is not a form of belief, but rather *leads to* belief. Self-motivation is natural but controlled, and also steams from a requirement. It means a cognitive stimulus of belief, and thus an immaterial need which is less visible than thirst (dry mouth) or the need for sleep (muscular fatigue). It is similar to an unlearned stimulus, upon which the outside social world has a controlling influence rather than an influence of acquisition. Thus, it is a self-organized form which, it must be emphasized, is not visible. It is not enough to say that we are motivated in order for things to work. This is not the Coué method of reinforcement of one's self-confidence or voluntary optimism (autosuggestion), although sometimes self-control can also act on one's self-organization because the self is also an element of the social world; in the sense of psychoanalysis, the self is divided into several selves, including a social self. The cognitive aspect is embedded in cerebral mechanisms which touch on various subsystems, the main ones of which are the language system which manages communication and the motivational system which manages the reaction to immediate survival needs. These two arguments – cognitive need and deep brain action – mean that cause and effect are intermingled and confused. Hence, the consideration of an action has hitherto been interpreted by the influence of blind belief or of a spontaneous and arbitrary desire for action. If we perform this action, it is not because we need to do so, but because chance has decided that this action should be performed and/or because of external conditions, intrinsically linked to the action (e.g. I decide to go for a bike ride because it is sunny, or because I associate cycling with sport and sport with losing weight, and therefore I want to lose weight). In fact, our hypothesis which governs action is made up of an innate physiological need whose coordination is piloted by language in a self-organized form.

10.2. Innate self-motivation

We introduce the concept of *innate self-motivation*: controls stemming from the outside world, because of a belief or a spontaneous intention. Since only the effect is visible, cause and effect are confused. The history of religions and archaeology give us some clues, dating from the time of the first *homo sapiens* around 100,000 years ago. The first people were nomads, they lived in small tribes of around twenty people, and began to develop a primitive language in order to survive during a period of mass migration. This sparked cultural development, forged around belief systems, which were particularly useful to help manage community life. This story continues even today. Although in France, 29% of people identify themselves as atheist   (China: 47%,   UK: 35%,   Russia: 32%,   Japan: 31%,   Brazil: 15%, Germany: 15%, USA: 8%, Spain: 6%, Poland: 6%), and are bathed in an omni-technological and technocratic civilization, 70% are not. Religion is a set of principles and life rules, brought together in the form of a doctrine. The faithful, who respect a religious creed, are accepted into a community of varying size. They may be expelled if they do not respect the doctrine – and in certain historical periods, this expulsion was at the risk of their own lives. Religion shows major weaknesses when it comes to providing creditable explanations for natural phenomena. Yet this does not shake the mechanism of belief. It is not the mechanism of belief which is robust in the face of criticism and capable of standing the test of time, but rather that which is above the mechanism: the innate self-motivation which is invisible and is confused with belief. This is even more so because language plays a part in the elaboration of self-motivation, whereas the same is not true of other mechanisms of desire such as sexuality, thirst or the need for sleep: in this case, language is solely descriptive and not performative in any way – hence the utilitarian and neutral nature. We can teach in a language; we cannot imagine a hammer hitting itself or another hammer. The reflexive nature of the tool is somewhat frustrating from a dialectic point of view; a tool is indeed a tool to be used on objects other than itself. Hence that elusive, ephemeral aspect of innate self-motivation. This psychological mechanism to last as long as possible and touch as many people as possible is fundamental: it has been perfected in the biological sense in our brains in parallel with the current use of language. Belief is a judgment – not a proof; nor is it a mechanism. Religion offers a framework, which claims to be generalist and closed to other beliefs. Yet we can conceive of as many beliefs as there are objects and activities on the earth; while this number is not infinite, it is a very large number. The political management of a complex situation leads a group of people to think alike. Political guidance in order to create mass belief gives rise to a uniform dominant train of thought – manipulation of which is one of the means. We can list a number of types of retrospective control over self-motivation: communication, cost–benefit ratio, social representation, relational environment, perception, the need for identity, seduction, historic precedence, economic moral influence and ergonomic complexity. This is to say nothing of optimism (a posture of perceiving good results) and pessimism (a posture of perceiving obstacles) which are very unclear concepts, created to explain motivation whose essence is neither social nor genetic. We can compare these two postures to the cost–benefit factor.

10.3. Mass communication

Mass communication is a controlling element. It operates not as an internal transmission vector on an individual level, but rather as a way of absorbing outside messages which give him convincing arguments filled with conviction. This procedure of communication is neither centered on oneself nor interpersonal, but rather is addressed to a mass of people. Turning back to the example of bobos (or by extension, metrosexuals, fans, socialites) imitation of those around us is not enough, on its own, to account for the sentiment of satisfaction. "Boboization" or "gentrification" has its origins in the United States with the movement of "Yuppies" (YUP: Young Urban People) in the 1980s. The phenomenon reached France in the early 2000s. It propagates like a nomadic model, which is not geographically localized, in concurrence with other urban cultural models such as a ghetto model or a model of a familial or doctrinal microcosm.

Hence, there are other factors of control. The level of life causes a kind of aptness, with purchasing power in a model of civilization governed by an excessively "credit card economy", independent of a more long-term political ideology but dependent upon the economic system which tends to satisfy or create the desires of one consumer but rather of a group of consumers. We have gone from the model of a fridge for "housewives under 50" (a commonly-used group in segmentation for marketing) – in the knowledge that all housewives are targeted, and therefore that only one social group is considered – to the model of a fridge for cozy apartments or numerous families – which corresponds to a social tightening of the targeting. For this purpose, mass media basing their actions on studies of trend operators use crowd analysis techniques based on the image and attitude which they wish to reach or to construct. In all its forms – audio or video on the Internet, adverts displayed on the subway, or in a public situation in a large room – publicity seeks to capture the audience's attention and attempts to make it impossible to avoid having your attention caught. In that sense, given that on average the eye or the ear is drawn to around ten messages a day – equating to around 4000 messages per year – this can influence models of activity, which may be called into question and possibly abandoned.

Marketing bases its procedure of sensitization on these two participative notions of an urban individual: membership of a small group and sensitivity to the capture of signals and changes (sights, sounds and smells) which have benefited the survival of the human race. Indeed, an individual's social cognitive space is evaluated by managing at most 200 relations in terms of interpersonal exchange (Gonçalves et al. [GON 11]). A concrete illustration of this is the social networking site Facebook, which in May 2012 had 901 million members with 130 friends on average per account. The auditory, olfactory and visual sensors have been developed over the course of evolution by vertebrates in order to guard against predators and find food; they are highly effective survival tools. When the signals change rapidly, this causes concern; if a habit is formed, we may become accustomed: the signal becomes a habitual element of the day-to-day environment. The frequency of the signals reinforces their importance and their impact. The crucial factor here is the frequency of exposure rather than the duration of that exposure.

10.4. The Cost–Benefit ratio

Publicity is not, in itself, a change. However, it proves effective to rally an audience. It does not involve a contribution or an estimation of that contribution. What is mentioned in works on motivation – particularly external motivation – is the capacity to evaluate the situation using the *cost–benefit ratio*. For each intention an action, or a series of actions, for each action requires an effort or an expenditure. It is conceivable that – as in the case of a patron in the Middle Ages – the expenditure may be an act of kindness. However, this reasoning is that of rich people. The statistical distribution of revenue *per capita* (this example is taken from France, but can be extended to numerous other countries without too great an error margin) shows that less than 1% of the population earn less than €6,000 a month, which leads us to think that very few people live in material comfort. For the other 99% of individuals, it proves crucial to obtain the benefit – particularly in case of need. I work to earn money: money which will serve to keep a roof over my head and food on my table. The same could be said of self-motivation. The benefit is a satisfaction; the cost may be the physical effort or the money spent in order to obtain that satisfaction. Collecting coins or stamps may prove to be a consuming passion in terms of time spent, probably enjoyable in terms of amassing a collection of rare coins or stamps, but one still needs to have means to spend time searching for these rare stamps, or be able to afford to buy them. Here we can see that the mention of a cost–benefit ratio does not necessarily mean earning money, although – it cannot be denied – that possibility may fuel self-motivation in some people. Money is usually involved on the side of costs if we have to talk about saving. This apparently highly materialistic factor sometimes takes emotional forms and often social forms. Consider the example of an artist who supports a humanitarian action, and thereby consolidates a positive aura in the eyes of a large audience. Life experience teaches any individual – who, in addition, is an urban dweller in most cases (77% urbanization rate in France and 51% in China in 2012) – that it is easier to spend than to earn, or to re-sell than not to buy. Poor and middle-class individuals find themselves immersed in a mediatized and ultra-liberalized society which drives spending with the constraint of limited resources. This causes a reflex of restraint and therefore reasoning of ironing out the cost–benefit ratio. We could speak of this factor – the cost–benefit ratio – as being active, in contrast to the previous factor which is rather passive in view of the individual's reaction.

10.5. Social representation

Social representation leads us to the third factor. This factor results in complex relations between an individual's environment in his daily life and his cultural space. This space is constructed from notions reminiscent of fairytale images, models stemming from the collective unconscious such as prototypes and stereotypes, education on the basis of a communal doctrinal model, or indeed an idea of protocol. This factor is passive. An individual absorbs representations from an extremely early age. Tales and myths are typical examples of this. In "Snow White and the Seven Dwarves", the story shows that narcissism is not a virtue. The myth of the dragon – a creature with no archaeological reality – symbolizes male strength. Stereotypes are rarer and more universal than prototypes. They are almost intercultural – e.g. the image of the rich represented by a sports car with a five-zero price tag. Prototypes correspond to more local representations. They synthesize a complex reality whose salient elements, the most indicative for a class model, are easy to memorize (the "communication" factor) and to interpret to support decision-making (the "cost–benefit" factor). We can see here that the factors are interdependent. Social representation is an elastic form: highly cultural, and therefore dependent upon the type of organization and life history as a function to political isolation or economic evolution (European versus Japanese industrial bourgeoisie; or Peruvian village versus Russian village). The culture of Adidas, McDonald's and Disneyland has been very widely disseminated across the globe. It is an intercontinental culture which is comprehensible, accessible and cheap; the welfare check of culture. It is not a non-representation but a "new wave" representation, amalgamated and culturally indifferent and universalist, which juxtaposes prototypes and stereotypes of various domains, with powerful and proselyte marketing, well-known logos accompanied by innumerable accessories. Once adopted, social representations are difficult to shake, and validate a compatibility of ritual and ceremonial ways of life: such is the object of their utility. In this sense, social representation is a powerful controlling factor over motivation.

10.6. The relational environment

The near **relational environment** – a super-school in the broad sense, encapsulating the institutional schools – plays the role of a catalyst. This is the fourth factor. An individual, in his/her daily reality, is familiarized by regular visual contacts and/or verbal exchanges with around 200 people per week. This occurs with very close individuals (siblings, cousins, friends), those of medium closeness (neighbors, players at a sports club, office colleagues or classmates), or distant individuals (street vendors, the neighborhood inhabitants). Virtual networks facilitate exchanges with both known and unknown people, with no limitations. In practice, the coherence of the exchanges is limited to around 200 people. Essentially, between a depressive person battling isolation and a party animal, the social context varies from 1 to 300 people. It is difficult to conceive of an individual's cultural neutrality by his/her relational context, if only to preserve the moral tranquility of his/her cultural space, saturated with representations or political or doctrinal traditions. As we can see, this tranquility, which is a dependency from one's childhood but which is highly influential, has a relation with the "representation" factor. The effigy of the individual who is cut off from his/her social and relational environment is similar to that of a vagabond with no roots and no ties, in constant erratic movement, living like an autistic person, minimizing interpersonal exchanges. Similar but less nomadic are hermits, who retreat from public life to devote themselves to activities of mystical reflection. In both these cases, we can hardly say that the social environment does not play a part – it does, but rather it is an antinomic role, a sort of repulsion, so the influence exists. Both the vagabond and the hermit are familiar with city life. In reality, we find precious few examples of individuals who live alone and have not experienced some form of group life. The influence of interactions with the social environment is complex and has given rise numerous domains of research in sociology. Notably, the impact of relationships over computer-based social networks is not yet well known in detail (impact on recruitments, emergences of polemics, construction and deconstruction of amorous relationships, etc.).

10.7. Perception

The biological functions of *perception* in interface with the outside world plays a motivating role. These are what one might call low-level functions, which relate to sensory perception and sensory memorization. This leads to *in fine* considerations about the ergonomics relating to situations strongly linked to physical comfort in terms of series of gestures, the feeling of stress and memorization of these phenomena. Stress can be caused in very varying ways. For an online computer system, the response time does not necessarily play a part overall, but the constancy of the response time can result in a user's feeling uncomfortable or frustrated. In this case, sensory perception is not involved directly, but its interrelation with emotion is; for instance, the vision of the result which takes a long time to arrive. One of the important aspects relates to vision and notably the mirror neurons which were suggested in the early 1990s in animals and studied in 2010 in humans. These mirror neurons are activated when an individual observes an action in another individual and reacts to replicate that action. Thus, they play an important role in learning and mimicry. In that sense, observing actions in other people which we cannot ourselves reproduce may give rise to a feeling of difficulty, frustration and therefore ergonomic discomfort. This perception factor is very similar to the "environment" factor, except that it accentuates the reality on the environment–perception exchange more than on the actual nature of the environment. On the other hand, the environment need not necessarily be hugely social: in the case of choosing a sport, one can choose a collective, team-based ball-game with a heavy influence on the social context, or an individual swimming sport which is not greatly influenced by the context.

10.8. Identity

An individual builds an *identity* for him/herself which serves as a reference point. This identity, in the form of a reference, creates feedback control to regulate conformity. Conformity validates actions and situations which disturb the identity framework as little as possible. The identity is not only administrative and geographically localized: it defines boundaries which may be linguistic, professional and technical skills, cultural, political and spiritual. Visual and cognitive habits construct an identity which can change between 0 and 30 years of age, after which point it becomes stabilized and difficult to transform. The identity exists by a set of knowledge states but without necessity. The identity is a product of the familiar and societal education to counter the process of exclusion from a group, not on the scale of a tribe but of a large company, a city, a region or a state. The desire for identity is also a composite of the "perception" and "social environment" factors. Identity enables us to legitimize and include an individual's production in a collective in order to justify his/her contribution and possibly make progress. The archetype of the absence of identity is the figure of a stateless person who disembarks in a country in exile. The feeling is largely tainted emotionally by a sentiment of wrenching and injustice. On the other hand, multiple identities are characteristic of the symptoms of schizophrenia. Ultimately, identity exists: it is unique and exerts an influence on one's actions.

10.9. Social environment

The "social environment" factor evoked the social context in terms of composition – i.e. structure. The nature of the interactions already takes account of an actor and goes beyond the environment. Roughly speaking, the quality of an interaction is twofold: cooperative or competitive. The competitive framework will be viewed more as a motivation inhibitor; the cooperative framework, on the other hand, will be a driving force and act as a control to improve motivation. In that sense, we can speak of a *seduction* factor. This perspective of seduction is an extension of a more fundamental need associated with reproduction and sexuality. Human beings, although they have constructed increasingly sedentary social groups and sophisticated civilizations from that point, cannot avoid the fact that they belong to the animal kingdom. In Europe, only 5,000 years ago, they were cannibals. Biological needs are always very present, as mentioned in Chapter 3 (eating, drinking, sleeping and procreating). Primarily, this last need means identifying a partner and mating. The search for a partner has long been a source of social cohesion to keep peace within families, villages or states. Beyond the need for alliances to create a family, alliances may be conceived of in different circumstances: alliances for games on the beach, professional alliances at the office, courtesy alliances for good neighbors, and so on. We are not overly far from the adage "birds of a feather flock together" because the strategies and contexts are multiple but they do exist. Both in order to seek a sensual pleasure and to obtain promotional gratification, seduction plays an effective controlling role. A world without seduction is a world of convention, which can indeed be appropriate for effective rules for life (e.g. regulation of a school) but which can also be a source of boredom when one is limited to such a world. Perception impacts on shared emotion, where for instance parents use fear to produce a stress, so that their children will pay attention to what they are saying. A great many adolescent practices which adults deplore are intended to attract attention in an attention-based economy. Adolescents use fear to attract their peers' attention. Adults are by no means innocent of this either! Both adolescents and parents develop an acute sense of what will attract the attention of their interlocutor. Attention is the lemma of contemporary society.

10.10. Historical antecedence

An individual, just like the society in which he/she lives, *is* by virtue of what he/she *has been*. He/she benefits from a cultural heritage and a history from the very earliest of ages. He/she also is by virtue of what he/she is in the process of becoming; this is a very short-term anticipation about the future mixed in with actions in the very recent past. The *historical antecedence*, from the near and distance past, constitutes a referential framework, a controlling factor, thanks to the "perception" factor which involves memory power to store and update current knowledge. Adjustment to new knowledge is inevitable. The addition of new knowledge is an update. Comparison of a new piece of knowledge is validation of that piece of knowledge. The process of updating is far more rigid for reasons of preservation, which is prudent behavior. Individuals, like any animals, maintain reliable knowledge about the natural environment which they master and which is useful for their survival; cataclysmic upsets are rare, so updates are always necessary; which leads to behavior of reaction to new knowledge. That said, adaptive behavior facilitates updating of one's knowledge, which will certainly be gauged in a moderate dose. It is difficult to claim that this factor is determining. Associated with the "perception" factor which favors mimicry, the "antecedence" factor can lead to the process of reproduction of behavior thanks to cultural heritage. While certain postures emerge not in continuity but in reaction or in opposition, continuity carries greater weight in a decision-making criterion. We can say that in terms of ease, it is easier to replicate a known state. Risk-taking is minimized or optimized if we add a "cost–benefit" factor to it.

10.11. Ethics

We shall conclude this overview of the factors in control of self-motivation with the notion of **ethics**. This is a factor which conditions acceptance or non-acceptance in accordance with values that are a person's own, but that he/she usually appropriates in line with a doctrine. Doctrines tend to be political or religious, but this is not exclusively so. The existence of paranormal phenomena, animal suffering or a military strategy, although not demonstrated, can be taught, diffused and also considered as non-sectarian – i.e. open to criticism. The aim of ethical standpoints is to ensure immunity of comfort without direct assent from a third party. The rule is a criticism of knowledge which an individual has at his/her disposal and is capable of using. The individual with rules interposes both as an actor and an arbiter. In any sport, the millions of spectators must agree with the referee/umpire of a sporting meeting – otherwise that meeting is no longer acceptable. An ethical code is an arbiter which ensures the rules of conduct are respected. These rules stem from a doctrine, which acts as a charter to which the individual adheres. This activity charter guarantees a certain quality of behavior and serves to produce satisfaction. Thus, we have quality control by the code of ethics which an individual must respect (in a professional context) or which he/she applies to himself/herself in harmony with a politico-religious ideology. Unlike the "environment" or "perception" factors, this "ethical" factor acts indirectly. For instance, a sports club attracts an audience based on its performances in competition and/or its mode of adhesion to democratic or selective practices. Morals and ethics create a space of obligation intended to create a discipline and thus better coalesce the mutual interests of individuals to stay together, to identify a shared acceptance of individual actions. This environment could be qualified as harmony of actions, guaranteeing non-violation of the boundaries between everyone's cognitive territories.

Chapter 11

A Model of Self-Motivation which Associates Language and Physiology

11.1. A new model

In this chapter, we present a new model of motivation which works with a coherence of function, coupling the principles of a neuro-physiological system with those of a psychosocial system.

The presentation of this new model favors a strong link between a monological language system and a self-motivational need system aimed at producing a regular intention to act. This model proposes the idea that motivation is a need – a need which is not massively quantitative. In this model, a hormonal balance is established cyclically when the self-motivational system reaches saturation mode. The cycle is a virtuous cycle, much like the virtuous cycles which exist in society and in relation to an individual's instinctive needs (food, drink, energy, desire and sexual activity) causing satiation and hormonal production which expresses satisfaction, and below a certain threshold, another hormonal production will produce a demand. Similarly as for food and drink, periodicity has a part to play. Assume that the body needs a liter of water per day. After 30 days, an individual's consumption would be 30 liters, but drinking 30 liters of water at once – assuming it is even possible, which is doubtful – would not assuage the function of the cycle for the remaining 29 days. Thus, the requirement is cyclical, with an unavoidable periodicity. A wide variety of ingredients can assuage this requirement, but the important thing is a small amount regularly. For a self-motivational system, little motivation is taken into account. Hence, it is a principle connected to spontaneous motivation/intention which may arise. In the same way as we do not have to be hungry or thirsty in order to eat or drink, spontaneous curiosity may win out over need. Motivation, in the broad sense, may be generated in many situations by curiosity, spontaneously and for short periods of time.

11.2. Architecture of a self-motivation subsystem

Figure 11.1 summarizes the component involved in the *architecture of self-motivation.*

DEFINITION 11.1.– Architecture of the self-motivation subsystem:

– the organization of the language (memory interface system), motor coordination with the sensory organs, the grammatical recognition system, the monological production system);

– the motivational system (physiological control system, self-motivation system, motivation system);

– the controlling factors (seduction, social representation, mass consumption, identity, ethics, historical antecedence, cost–benefit ratio, perception, social environment).

The organization of the language is the object of Chapter 8. The motivational system which manages primitive needs is dealt with in Chapter 7. The external influencing factors are the topic of Chapter 10. The principles of self-organization of such a system are discussed in Chapter 4. These systems present relations which are associated with enzymatic and hormonal balances/imbalances, supported by neural connections. The main relations are defined as follows:

DEFINITION 11.2.– Cerebral relations of the self-motivation subsystem:

– the link between the memory management system (organization of the language) and the memory system;

– the relation between the monological system and the self-motivation system;

– the relation between the self-motivation system and the controlling factors;

– the relation between the control system (motivation system) and the lower region of the brain.

To date, no protein and no connecting link between a monological system and a self-motivational system have been discovered. This is as yet speculation, which modern and confluent works in physiology, developmental psychology and linguistic sciences have led us to formulate.

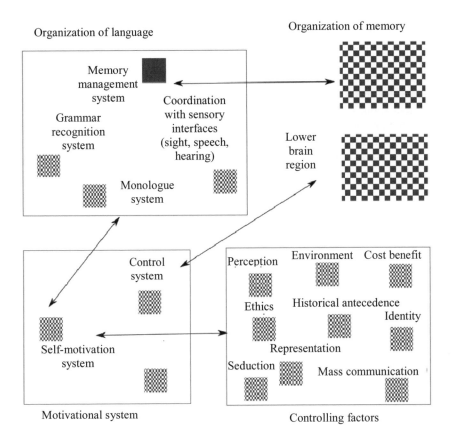

Figure 11.1. *General diagram of a self-motivation system with its dependencies*

Certain concepts are similar to self-motivation: in particular, conviction, *individual belief,* which could be qualified as self-motivation, or knowledge or furtive consciousness. Self-motivation as illustrated in Figure 11.1 may sediment a long-term belief. For instance, having the conviction to pass your driving test is an individual belief. The conviction is often localized in time and responds to a specific question. It is a question of thinking that something is going to turn out right. A form which goes hand-in-hand with this and which complements it is to provoke one's conviction. This is a stimulation which may be exogenous or endogenous. We can speak of conscious autosuggestion which popular tradition has turned into a method, devised in around 1910 by the psychologist Émile Coué de la Châtaigneraie in opposition to hypnosis, which is a suggestion method of the subconscious.

Credulousness is also a form of individual belief marked by guidance of opinion, the economy of which is founded upon the lack of information. In this case, it is also a question of a punctual action – e.g. the credulousness of a lottery player who does not realize that his chance of winning is roughly the same as the likelihood of the earth being hit by an asteroid. He does not know this, and is allowed to believe the contrary, so he continues to play. Over a certain length of time, this may become a self-motivation. Collective belief is a form of individual belief. It is an individual belief that has been maneuvered politically and globally. The control comes in the wake of a want to believe – a want which may be explained by self-motivation and thanks to external controlling factors. For reasons of economic control of resources, and therefore power, we see the emergence of collective beliefs promulgated by political regimes, political ideologies, religions, proverbs and popular myths, or by witchcraft, and which are largely based on the implicit exploitation of self-motivation.

11.3. Level of certainty

The contrary of a state is always possible, even in subjective terms: asleep vs. awake; red vs. yellow; perfumed vs. putrid. The absence of belief is a state of permanent doubt or a *level of certainty*. In this world, nothing is certain; chance plays a very important role. At the very least, a person's life may follow different possible paths, much like a scientific experiment which depends on the initial conditions and the combination of a number of variables. This combination is not always known in advance, or "memorizable". The level of certainty we have, therefore, is a simplified reality. In other words, rare are those who believe in nothing. However, in certain cases, this is possible: e.g. a homeless person whom fate has put on the street by way of an unfortunate series of events, or a retired person who allows themselves to live like a vegetable. In these two examples, there is a common point which is often observed: taking refuge in alcohol so as to forget the boredom. Is it not said that "idleness is the mother of all vices"? Hypothetically speaking, boredom might be a feeling of a need for information, which gives rise to a space of "unprovoked motivation" – just like Konrad Lorenz's bird snapping at imaginary flies. Most people have a level of belief which is variable in practice, and which is very widely exploited.

11.4. Need for self-motivation

A legitimate question naturally springs to mind: that of the *need for self-motivation*. If we look at instinctive needs such as sleep and sex, they do not only provide energy (satisfaction of desire or equilibrium in relationships between couples, or maintenance of cells to redress the body's balances or get rid of damaged elements); the objective is quality of life. Self-motivation also provides a level of quality of life at a cognitive level, and has been doing so for as long as humans have had the capacity for language. It is established in the wake of the other needs, in accordance with the same rules, defined as follows.

DEFINITION 11.3.– *Need*

Need is defined by the following properties:

– cyclical variability;

– psychosomatic symptoms in case of lack;

– universality in individuals;

– an interface with a motivational system which functions with the other needs.

Cognitive need plays an important role, in the same way as physiological need does. Although intentions and reflection account for only 5% of an individual's brain activity, even this is a significant amount of activity. The need for self-motivation results in an innate cognitive demand, which works thanks to the quality of the monological activity, because it is linguistic communication which channels ideas and intentions, no matter what the type of intention: deciding to go to a fair to buy collectible coins, or redoing your kitchen. The intention is formulated in natural language and monologically to begin with. Monological activity produces biological signals which are then detected by the neurotransmitting center situated at the level of the hypothalamus, which transfers the need to activate the search for intentions and beliefs to the motivational system.

The search for intention is performed by way of presentations of semiotic signs exposed by the knowledge of the world around us; here, the controlling factors play a crucial role.

11.5. Notion of motive

DEFINITION 11.4.– *Motive*: We use the term "motive" to denote an objective of an activity and belief performed by self-motivation over a period of time.

A religious doctrine or a sport can be adopted very early on in an individual's development and constitute motives for self-motivation.

Figure 11.2 illustrates the function of balance in two stages. The first stage (A1 and B1) is the formula for seeking a motive.

In this context, the motor center linked to the hypothalamus detects an enzymatic deficiency in relation to a high threshold related to the self-motivation subsystem (Figure 11.2, A1) and triggers a procedure of searching for a motive by the areas of the brain responsible for visual and auditory memory, the language and perception systems which actively consult the field of possibles depending on the controlling factors. Let us return to the principle of enumeration. In view of the availability of information to an individual, a potentiality for attention of 15 hours a day and on average three seconds concretize the mnemonics of a word or an image (it is difficult to deal with both of these at the same time); this gives us $60 \times 60 \times 15/3 = 18,000$ possibilities to concretize an idea in one day, and 126,000 in a week at most. This is supplemented by the inventory of things "already seen" and "already heard". A person's memory retains 50% of what they saw last week, and 10% of what they saw last month. This equates to $7 \times 18000 \times 0.5 + 18000 \times 21 \times 0.05 = 82,000$, which is added to the 126,000. This gives 207,900 possibilities for potential cognitive imprints for acquisition of motives which will be subjected to the constraints of the controlling factors. After the acquisition phase, the first stage involves an application phase, which, in stable balanced mode, tests the comparison with the motives at a low threshold (Figure 11.2, A2). In the case of enzyme deficiency, the self-motivation center interacts further with the monological system (Figure 11.2, B2). The phase (A2, B2) is the second stage, which accounts for the majority of the self-motivation system's stable activity.

This self-motivation system is indifferently and uniformly distributed in any individual on the planet. It is fairly well regulated to make a billion people adhere to a religious doctrine. It seems, in view of what occurs in animals which are close to humans – notably mammals (e.g. pigs, rats, mice, primates) that there is no equivalent – at least not to our knowledge as it currently stands. However, language is a human construction resulting from social living. Self-motivation results from the dialog an individual holds with himself by means of the language and the interrogations it facilitates, in the face of his contemplation to enable him to live in society, which imposes a certain number of requirements and performance. Thus, it is a *de facto* necessity, rather than a desire. This necessity has been reinforced by the technical and daily use of language, rather than the other way round, because humans evolved without language and then appropriated perfected actions. Language made the presence of actions "conventional". This necessity in not biological in nature, but rather is cognitive and cultural. Self-motivation enables us to attain a degree of harmony, which is a judgment of personal satisfaction – e.g. a gambler in a casino who would play even if he won millions, or would try to find a few dollars to play if he had lost his fortune.

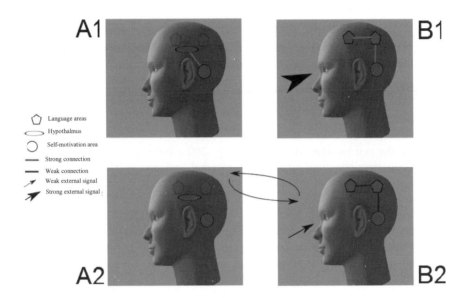

Figure 11.2. *The two stable cycles of function of self-motivation (A1-B1 searching cycle; A2-B2 daily cycle)*

The nature of a motive is probably and *a priori limitless*. Its limits are under constraints from external controlling factors already discussed in the previous chapter. These factors are ventilated depending on the nation in which they evolve, the time-period, the familial, geographical and psychological personality of the individual. The combination is astronomical:

– supposing that the possibilities of social contexts range from 1 to 200, this gives 200 possibilities;

– in terms of culture, if we imagine that the culture depends essentially on the language, this gives 100 possibilities (vehicular languages used by over 90% of humankind);

– in terms of psychological character (see Chapter 3), we have 16 profiles;

– in terms of geographical context, we have three possibilities: towns, cities and countryside;

– in terms of education, we have orphans, strict education with or without fortune, or lax education with or without fortune, so five possibilities;

– in doctrinal terms, we have two political tendencies – progressive and conservative – their extremes, with or without religion, so eight possibilities;

– as regards the level of education we have: no education, manual level, technical level and higher level, so four possibilities;

– finally, regarding the historical era, assume that that era changes approximately every 10 years and that the generations are distributed over the past 70 years. This gives us seven eras.

Finally, the combination of possibilities is: $200 \times 100 \times 16 \times 3 \times 5 \times 8 \times 4 \times 7 =$ 1.075 billion possible configurations of external influences. There are certainly configurations which are in the majority. Of the seven eras, for instance, the last two are certainly the most representative. The technical and higher levels of education are also more representative. Each configuration does not express a possible motive but a domain of emergence of a motive. For instance, if an individual grows up in a non-religious and progressive political environment, it is unlikely that he will express an appetence for the religious fact and hence make it a motive. The ethical factor (and by extension deontology and integrity) is of course variable depending on the configurations, and the sense of whether a motive appeals to the sense of good or evil varies considerably from one configuration to another. Each configuration can accept authorized and unauthorized conducts, which also evolve depending on the eras which are transformed or which are abandoned, only to later do a U-turn and resurface. Ethics is like a chameleon. To a certain extent it is the adjusting variable of the system and which has a minutely detailed impact on what may be acceptable at a given time or place, but it is better to stay abreast of the scope of this acceptation. Essentially, the extent of motives is vaster even that that of socio-psychological configurations, and *a priori*, nothing is impossible.

If we imagine self-motivation, metaphorically, to be a receptacle for basic questioning and activities, ideological micro-groups take over that capacity to adopt questioning and activities in order to manipulate the masses through doctrinal beliefs; the major religions have exploited self-motivation. In France, for instance, ready-made self-motivations, created in the image of the French Revolution, attempted to impose theophilanthropism or the Cult of the Supreme Being in 1796 – banned in 1803, and which finally reemerged from the Third Republic in the guise of a secular or God-free religion, with its rituals and theorists. The Briand Law introduced 9 December 1905 regarding the separation of church and state validates this substitution. These theorists of secularism maintain the doctrine. They teach it in order to consolidate the governing elite which propagate these same ideas and to encourage people to accept them in time.

In terms of daily life, anything can be a pretext to satisfy an individual's self-motivation as long as that "receptacle" is not already occupied by ambient beliefs resulting from the individual's social context. The notion of the judgment of value, connected to the ethical quality, plays a far-from-insignificant role if different actors are at the origin of self-motivation (e.g. in a collective sport). Because nature, in the true sense of the word, knows nothing of good and evil, the notion of the judgment of value is more closely related to positive/negative feelings than to the ethical dilemma of good/evil. The subjective positive–negative ratio is subject to interpretation and aesthetics. The more a situation is interpretable and has an appreciable charm, the more the judgment will lean toward the positive side. This will provide a stronger incentive to adopt a motive. As regards the number of motives, if ethics and judgment do not impose a limit on their numbers but on their adoption, the question remains open-ended, depends on the time needing to be devoted to the motives and is related to the degree of satisfaction, in the same way as one can drink coffee in the morning, water in the afternoon and a glass of wine in the evening, or indeed a liter of water throughout the day. The number of motives is not static, and may depend on an individual's hyperactive dynamism; between 1 and 10 motives are the numbers which enable a compromise to be made between necessity and time spent, acceptable routine and physiological saturation. We can cite some classic and very common motives, some of which may also be combined: professional vocation, education of a child, religious practice, collection of objects, practice of a sport, practice of a graphic art, catharsis with another person or recreation, belief in a philosophical concept, intercultural awakening. If the combinations have few components, the time available is spent mainly on the targeted motives, or in situations of non-action or passive states.

11.6. Age and location

An individual's capacities for written and oral expressions seem to mature at around five years of age (see Table 8.1). Thus, this is a *minimum age* for the acquisition of motives: an age beyond which we can wonder about questions and contemplate our environment with discernment. This continues until the memory is able to function correctly. The robustness of the tissues varies from one individual to another, and can sometimes extend up to the age of 120. *Favorite places* for the acquisition of motives also vary. The urban environment is a great catalyst, because it includes a wide variety of different microcosms and different profiles of local individuals or passers-by. This social and cultural density favors monological activity, and there are as many windows to opportunities.

11.7. Uniqueness

It appears that self-motivation presents properties of *uniqueness*. Self-motivation is a need, but one which tends to favor mimicry because it is heavily constrained by external and particularly social controlling factors. In practice, we very often witness a "follower"-type process, as can be seen, notably, in typical behaviors in buying/selling of stocks and shares, in the domain of fashion, or a process of human crowding. An individual will attach a priority of adhesion to existing situations. Creative people, pioneers and marginal individuals innovate in all domains. These are personalities with a high potential for curiosity, with a will to deliberately model their own personalities, to break away from the norm, with a predilection for taking risks – particularly the risk of being misunderstood and coming under fire from critics. In the image of a bell-shaped statistical distribution, motives are to be found at the center of the bell around an average, but on the outskirts we find cases of less conventional motives.

11.8. Effect of spontaneity

The predisposition to undertake an active search for a motive is proportional to the physiological deficit of proteins generated by the function of the self-motivation system. We cannot speak of *spontaneity* in the true sense, even if a realization based on external factors puts an end to the execution of a motive, more or less suddenly and causes a pathological depressive process and lead to an active search for a new motive. The physiological molecular mechanisms also result in macroscopic signals such as the amount of knowledge available. In parallel, we could imagine any negative signal causing disharmony, such as the lack of some amount of amorous feeling. Overall, the physiological response of the self-motivation system corresponds to a sum of participating signals in the potential for harmony, including the levels of pleasure proteins, such as protein *p11* in mediation with *serotonin*. The greater this potential is, the stronger the self-motivation will be. If we accept that self-motivation is governed by two pieces of information – knowledge and emotion – and assume that these quantities are sufficient (i.e. respond to the current requirements), a very low potential will lead to self-motivation in search mode. If the search is fruitless, the individual will feel no desire to adhere to anything at all.

11.9. Effect of dependence

The long-term motive sheds light on the process of habit-forming and the notion of *dependence*. The process of addiction is a slightly altered variant. It causes a phenomenon of artificial dependence – in other words an "artificial" motive. Otherwise, behavior would be all the more chaotic or even nihilistic. Physical dependence, like the consumption of cocaine or tobacco, leads to energetic stimulation and a quantity of pleasure hormones, and causes a deficit in the wake of a prolonged period of non-consumption. In self-motivation, we again see the notion of a lacuna, in information, and the notion of positive encouragement, in hormones such as *dopamine* and *endorphins*. The oscillatory process between presence and absence of hormones can be deregulated and therefore corrected by an artificial hormone activation mechanism. While self-motivation stems from the cognitive space, we can see similarities with the physical space, which is not entirely unlinked to perception and consequently hormone-producing emotions. Notably, dependence functions by means of biochemical mechanisms which correspond to oscillating balances of over-activation and under-activation.

11.10. Effect of emulation

Emulation between individuals may give rise to personality disorders and self-surpassing. The disorders manifest themselves in anxiety and signs of aggression. Competitiveness must therefore be closely managed, in view of its destructive effects. Its self-surpassing side may stimulate the function of self-motivation into short-term goals to be achieved. In that sense we see a second limiting trait in the absence of a long-term vision of conflict-causing emulation. Surpassing oneself involves enriching one's knowledge by constantly learning new techniques to keep oneself at a good level; it may cause individuals to look for alliances to consolidate actions. The old adage "there is strength in numbers" is thus always to be heard in social interactions, but unions are slow to construct and are based on compatibility and complementation. Learning is also an unwieldy process which requires energy and patience. Emulation makes projections of brighter prospects in the future – a challenge, articulated by self-motivation, the effect of which will be a positive outlook on the future. This is a specific case where the near future plays a part in self-motivation. The final result may be deemed narcissistic, but this is a moral judgment.

11.11. Transition of belief

Chapter 4 explains that modern physics has broken nature down into an infinite number of interlinked systems, interacting with one another, from elementary particles to galactic systems, stopping off at the molecular and cellular components of living beings, which form still more systems when they combine. The initial conditions can alter convergence toward different states of stability, as stated by chaos theory in theoretical physics. In view of an axiomatic which postulates the existence of objects and an operator-based language, this language can be used to express relational properties between these objects. The theories of predicate logic and calculability in theoretical computing show that the relations are no longer calculable within a finite amount of time if the relational expressivity is sufficiently high. This vision confers a weighted point of view on predictability, which does not mask its reality but renders it non-sovereign. It brings a reality to the **uncertainty** of the events – a reality which we believe will likely stem from the possible or the probable. The possibilities of motives generate a complex structure – i.e. a combination of situations giving rise to a macroscopic organization, because globally all the individuals in a large-scale population have motives without having an overall view of all the possible motives, and this distribution guarantees a stability of the balance of the overall function of the social system. Otherwise, we would fall into a situation of social disorder or collective suicide. Chance gives rise to distributions around averages or with one's own groupings. The groups and the averages can be explained by mimicry arising because of controlling factors acting as constraints. Random chance is not so random, and allows perfectly explicable coincidences to transpire. It is simply difficult to predict, at the individual level, the critical motive which overturns self-motivation. Absolutely, we could rightly imagine a random draw which is no more absurd than a choice imposed by external factors – quite the opposite, in fact, as it causes autonomy and a feeling of adult existence than childlike dependence. An individual's consciousness is a complex and multifaceted cognitive system. One facet of the creation of this tool is language, a second is the range of scenarios of action that it can handle, and a third is relation with and within the socio-cultural environment. An individual possesses a biological property, which is universal and which transcends his current physiological state: his lifespan. From a star to a bacterium, from paper to volcanoes, everything evolves through stages of development and then dies (or disappears). Certain periods in the course of the development of life herald moments of transition: e.g. aging or a social integration problem. Between the ages of 15 and 50, an individual will experience at least five or six of these transitions. Add to this the moments of trouble based on politico-historic or professional conjecture. These periods of problems may play a role in self-motivation in one or other direction, and also in accordance with the individual's sensitivities. The influence exerted on two similar individuals therefore remains unpredictable, all things being equal, and at the same time and place. This may also depend on an individual's capacity to react – i.e. to reconsider or to prove conservative. We can identify three possible transitions: the passage from a state of non self-motivation to a state of self-motivation, the passage from a state of self-motivation to a state of non self-motivation and the passage from one state of self-motivation to another state of self-motivation. This leads us to postulate a definition with regard to the nature of the domain of motives.

DEFINITION 11.5.– *Domain of a motive:* a motive M_i will, by definition, be a situation, leading to action, and the occurrence of which is expressed by a set of possibilities in an individual's environment, with a probability p_i weighted by the importance of the set of control factors, for a state of self-motivation $S = \{1,0\}$ dependent on time. The domain of the motives is expressed by: $D(M_i) = \{p_i(t, a \rightarrow b), a \in S, b \in S\}$.

11.12. Effect of individualism

No matter what the structure of the group in which an individual finds himself, life situations are assumed in conflict with oneself. A fundamental reason for this, and one which is certainly crucial in order to understand the phenomenon, relies – as always – primarily on biology. All told, this reason is fairly simple: an individual is made up of a physical and organic body, endowed with mechanical mobility; physiology has demonstrated that most cerebral activity serves to control this motor activity. This physical autonomy is relayed by cognitive autonomy. In addition, each elementary gesture is performed in individualism: going to sleep, eating, drinking, getting up in the morning, washing, going to the toilet, in terms of the simplest of gestures; but also taking public transport, looking for work, travelling to a foreign country, buying clothes, sending a text message, etc. requires more sophisticated individual actions with a very limited context of knowledge and reasoning. An individual is by no means the architect of his own future, but rather affords legitimacy to certain choices which structures his daily life, giving rise to routines, disappointments, successes or other remarkable, memorable moments. Contemporary participative democracy, at the highest level of emancipation, free expression and individual action, honors this assumed *individualism*. The range of possibilities is modulated by social and societal factors. By means of the function of individual decision, we see the emergence of a near necessity to internalize one's motivations. Without these self-stimulated motivations, the individual runs the risk – in extreme cases – of becoming an individual-robot or an unhinged individual, when it is not short-term needs which take priority. The boundaries between personal communication and interpersonal communication are porous. At this level, self-motivation profits greatly from external influence, in the knowledge that the intention comes from the individual and ultimately comes back to the individual regarding his own needs when he is facing himself. The social process around the individual, acting with self-motivation as a controlling factor, is therefore an intermediary path of an initiative which begins with oneself and is ultimately one's own responsibility.

11.13. Modeling of the groups of beliefs

The function and regulation of self-motivation are not neutral in terms of *consequences* for the individual and for his social context.

The "social environment" factor notably reinforces the repetition of acts and therefore forges modes and traditions, previously rural (oral cultures), which have now become urban (written cultures).

The motor center of self-motivation, based on connective communication between the monological system and the self-motivation center, develops and favors individualism. This posture is characterized by freedom to make decisions in accordance with the controlling factors.

The physiological aspects which make the self-motivation motor work are complemented by pleasure hormones which are activated as a reward. It could also be argued that the role of the "cost–benefit" factor also acts in this way. This results in an increase in the feeling of optimism.

Another consequence relates to the public personality of the individual. There are certain judging processes whereby the individual's expression creates a public persona – owing to his professional responsibilities (journalistic publications, scientific publications, technical reports, technological patents, etc.) or his personal acquaintances in less formal media on the Internet (blogs, forums, etc.). His own particular motives reveal salient interests, expressed verbally in written production.

The complexity of the combinations is expressed by means of a representation of the possibilities. The **belief functions** provided by the Dempster-Shafer probabilistic model [DEM 67; SHA 76] can be used to calculate a mass function associated with the sets of attributes and variables. If the sets are singlets, we have to use Bayesian functions [PEA 88]. We define a space Ω, called the frame of discernment – e.g. a list of names of categories – as a set of all the hypotheses in a certain domain. A basic belief assignment (BBA) is a function m which defines the mapping of the power space Ω onto the interval [0, 1] and satisfies:

$$m: 2^\Omega \rightarrow [0,1] \tag{11.1}$$

$$\sum_{A \in 2^\Omega} m(A) = 1 \tag{11.2}$$

The mass function $m(A)$ can be interpreted as a measure of the belief which is associated exactly with A in view of the available evidence. The subset $A \in 2^\Omega$, with $m(A) > 0$, is called the focal element of m. We define the belief function Bel thus:

$$Bel: 2^\Omega \rightarrow [0,1] \tag{11.3}$$

satisfying:

$$\begin{cases} Bel(\emptyset) = 0 \\ Bel(\Omega) = 1 \\ Bel(A) = \sum_{\emptyset \neq B \subseteq A} m(B) \end{cases} \tag{11.4}$$

If we imagine numerous sources of information (e.g. several controlling factors), the theory of belief functions prescribes a combination rule:

$$m_{1-2}(A) = m_1 \oplus m_2 = \begin{cases} \frac{\sum_{\emptyset \neq B \subseteq A} m(B)}{1 - \sum_{\emptyset \neq B \subseteq A} m(B)} & \forall A \subseteq \Omega, A \neq \emptyset \\ 0 & if\ A \neq \emptyset \end{cases} \quad [11.5]$$

It is possible to imagine a distance between masses:

$$d(m_1, m_2) = \sqrt{\frac{1}{2}(m_1 - m_2)^T D(m_1 - m_2)} \quad [11.6]$$

where D is a matrix based on a Jaccard distance, whose elements are:

$$D(A, B) = \begin{cases} 1 & if\ A = B = \emptyset \\ \frac{|A \cap B|}{|A \cup B|} & \forall A, B \in 2^\Omega \end{cases} \quad [11.7]$$

For instance, if s_j denotes the degree of confidence of the category w_j,

$$p(w_j) = \frac{s_j}{\sum_j s_j} \quad [11.8]$$

here is an example of a mass function derived from these probabilities:

$$\begin{cases} m(\{w_1, w_2, \dots, w_i\}) = & i \times [p(w_i) - p(w_{i+1})] \ \forall i < |\Omega| \\ m(\{w_1, w_2, \dots, w_{|\Omega|}\}) = & |\Omega| \times p(w_{|\Omega|}) \\ m(X) \quad = & 0, \forall X \notin 2^\Omega \end{cases} \quad [11.9]$$

Below is another example of a mass function. If we take x^s and x^i to be two samples, d_{si} is the distance between x^s and x^i. The BBA $m_i^{\Omega i}$ on $\Omega i = \{Hi, \overline{Hi}\}$

$$\begin{cases} m_i^{\Omega i}(Hi) = \alpha_i e^{-(\frac{d_{si}}{\sigma})^\beta} \\ m_i^{\Omega i}(\Omega i) = 1 - m_i^{\Omega i}(Hi) \end{cases} \quad [11.10]$$

$$\alpha_i = \alpha_0^{\frac{1}{1-k-k_i}} \quad [11.11]$$

k_i represents the number of neighbors of i, if $k = k_i$ then $\alpha_i = \alpha_0$.

Finally, we can define a conditional mass $m^\Omega(A|B)$ such that if $B \subseteq \Omega$,

$$m^\Omega(A|B) = \begin{cases} \sum_{\{X \subseteq \bar{B}\}} m^\Omega (A \cup X), if\ A \subseteq B \subseteq \Omega \\ 0\ else \end{cases} \quad [11.12]$$

This can be called a Conditional Belief Function (CBF). Figure 11.3 shows the curve for a set of mass functions for an arbitrary abscissa parameter and two values – A (solid line) and B (dotted line).

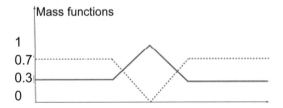

Figure 11.3. *Mass functions with two values of Ω*

There is no "recipe" to define the belief functions for a given problem. This question also arises in the probabilistic domain as regards the *a priori* choice of PDF. The two essential problems with belief functions are:

1) the relevant choice of belief functions for a given problem;

2) the choice of an effective method for combining belief functions.

A great deal of work has been done on the second point – particularly with a view to casting aspersions on the validity of the Dempster–Shafer theory. Yet Dempster's rule of combination is often essential, because it is one of the pillars of the Dempster–Shafer Theory (DST). Unfortunately it poses very serious theoretical problems and it is very risky to employ this rule in applications. There are few serious works to be found on the first point. The choice of the construction of the belief functions is generally made by the designer of the model, based on his own criteria and his own interpretation of the uncertainty that he has or that he wishes to model, of the problem.

Various sources of information may be identified that can be used to associate data with an individual. On the one hand, we find linguistic information (consulted or stated) which defines a space Ω_1, and socio-demographic data which define a second space Ω_2. In the space Ω_1, various sequences may appear which correspond to repeated information, or similar forms of expression, such as:

Nearly 100 **missing** after a **sinking** on the **Volga**

and

A river cruiser **sinks** on the **Volga**: one dead, 88 **missing**.

These two expressions share two phenomena – one based on the length of the sequences, and the other on the existence of certain elements in common (sinks/sinking, Volga, missing). These shared elements may correspond to parameters, or constraints, which can be used to class the two sequences together as belonging to the same subset of linguistic sequences $A \subseteq \Omega_1$. On the other hand, socio-demographic data are described by attributes – e.g. frequency of access to a Website, age group, income bracket, musical taste, etc. Groups of parameters help estimate a belief function for a set of individuals $B \subseteq \Omega_2$. Using equation [11.11] we can estimate a conditional mass function in each of the spaces. We then combine these using equation [11.4] to evaluate a global mass function. This global function models individuals' self-motivation as regards the information available, which is cultural, demographic, social and linguistic in nature.

Chapter 12

Impact of Self-Motivation on Written Information

12.1. Platform for production and consultation of texts

Chapter 11 offered an understanding of the mechanisms of a process of self-motivation. One of the results of this is that such a process provides a cognitive framework upon which an individual relies almost unconditionally once the constraints of the controlling factors are satisfied. Motives are acquired and followed through. They channel salient interests, which are often based not on acquired certainties but rather on consensual acceptances. Following one's motives leaves trails which may be short-lived or long-lasting. The emergence of the Internet and informal social networks is transforming oral and written behavioral practices, and ultimately behavior in general (work, love life, entertainment, etc.). Where in the past, individuals produced written publications in paper format, e.g. in their professional context, the Internet has not transformed their customs but rendered their production highly fluid. The Internet has become a universal library "on the doorstep". On the other hand, individuals who did not previously produce a great deal of written material are now producing far more (text messages, e-mails, blogs, personal pages, etc.). Ultimately, everything is converging toward net-centered and citizen-centered written production. All citizens, in a personal and professional context, are led to consult and produce documents which will be channeled through the Internet (an interconnected physical network on a worldwide scale, including telecom networks). Thus, an individual produces *available digital information.* However, that information may not be available to any and everyone; sometimes we have to obtain usage rights, or we are dealing with hidden databases, or indeed there are no rights being exercised over the content so the database is free for usage. A hidden database does not mean that the information is not available. One simply has to pay in order to gain access to and use it. Databases offer us the opportunity to analyze corpora of information, which is particularly helpful in terms of spotting recurrences in digital documents. The motives are, so to speak, obsessions with activity which tend to give rise to *leitmotifs*. An individual conducts his activity in the same direction as his motives, and produces information in the same conceptual context, which should be found in the form of leitmotifs.

12.2. Informational measure of the motives of self-motivation

Leitmotifs are expressed in a digital document or between several documents by repeated information. These repetitions, which linguists term "paraphrases", serve as an *informational measure of the motives* of self-motivation. In linguistics, Harris has speculated about the importance of analyzing paraphrases. The Internet provides the means to analyze intertextuality and to study repetitions of information from one paragraph to another, and from one document to another, depending on the origin of the document – i.e. heterogeneity of place – and of different times – i.e. heterogeneity of time. Motives appear as background spots which should leave a detectable trace, whose signature is closer to a background than to a detail. In that sense, the leitmotif is distributed by way of heterogeneity of the situations of production.

Chapter 8 showed that language is a system which is divided into interlaced subsystems, which leads to *levels of analysis*. One of these subsystems is lexicology, which is central to semantics and to comprehension. It is through the prism of lexicology that the material and immaterial concepts of the world are viewed – those concepts which anyone can appreciate and at any time in history. The concepts may evolve in accordance with the state of knowledge at a given time. Language is by nature a sequential system, because the physiology of the human body means it is impossible to pronounce multiple words at the same time. The succession of words involves interruption as well, for reasons which are both logical and biological: logical because each group of words (e.g. a phrase) must contain one or two ideas; and biological because the group of words is pronounced in accordance with the rhythm of breathing. The phrase is an analytical marker for the expression of concepts – linguists made that clear over a century ago. However, the phrase is not the only level. Besides the intra-phrastic level, we can also have the inter-phrastic level – between two or more phrases in the same corpus or the same document – and the meta-phrastic level – relating to occurrences between several documents. In reference to Web pages, the intra-phrastic level would correspond to an analysis of the skeleton of a form on a Web page, the inter-phrastic level to an analysis of clicks and the paths they lead the user down on a Website, and the meta-phrastic level to an analysis of hypertext links.

12.2.1. *Intra-phrastic extraction*

Let us examine the mode of analysis in the context of *intra-phrastic extraction*. The MUC (Message Understanding Conference) gatherings, held between 1986 and 2001, popularized types of extraction applied to corpora of documents focused on financial agreements on behalf of insurance companies or technology watch (scenario of groupings of companies, accident scenario). Even in this case, the words extracted are different in nature: the name of an organization, a date, a person's name, a social status, etc. The Achilles' heel of automatic language processing is ambiguity, for reasons of a desire for parsimony, and redundancy of use causing multiple meanings [GAL 92; GRE 94; GRE 96] – e.g. George Washington and the city of Washington. In this particular case, it is not hard to resolve the ambiguity. However, if we wish to disambiguate the words "Taj Mahal" (the landmark in India, the Grammy-winning blues musician, the renowned casino in Atlantic City or innumerable Indian restaurants or hotels), it is less simple. We find use cases such as "Taj Mahal architecture" or "Taj Mahal guitar style" or "Taj Mahal menu" or "Taj Mahal room rates". Analysis of the links in terms of probability and the implication of trigger words (here, "architecture", "guitar", "menu" etc.) may assuage the ambiguity. Sometimes, the ambiguity cannot be assuaged. If we have to deal with the segment "Taj Mahal tours", it is impossible to know whether it is the mausoleum or the musician that is being asked about. Obviously, extraction of named entities is not restricted to the names of people, organizations or establishments. We may imagine extraction of the names of species or names of proteins, to give some examples of extraction drawn only from biology. Automatic extraction of named entities and dates in documents is based on probabilistic language models, regular languages and lexical dictionaries. It is possible to evaluate the system, using a reasonably clear-cut set of entities needing to be extracted. Evaluations to test whether computer programs work use three parameters:

– one called "precision" (in computing) or "specificity" (in statistics), which represents the number of correct results out of those which have been turned up;

– "recall", which is the number of correct extractions over the number of elements which should be extracted;

– the F-score is a combination of recall and precision, to characterize a compromise between the two.

Ideally the values of these parameters would be 1, and in the worst case scenario it would be 0. Current models offer success rates between 90 and 100%, but cannot attain the uppermost limit because of the ambiguities mentioned above.

12.2.2. *Inter-phrastic extraction*

In *inter-phrastic extractions*, the aim is twofold, and could be said to be extremal. The analysis focuses on anaphora – small segments, repeated from one phrase to another, usually in relation to the former. The analysis can look at long segments, which can be broken down into pieces. These long segments can be repeated verbatim after a stage of stabilization. This is similar to plagiarism but not synonymous with it, because in this case it is a question of repeating an expression which symbolizes a concept and its context: this is known as an "idem". A segment is understood in the linguistic sense as a strong collocation. This differs from a fixed expression, which is more representative of a named entity such as "carte bleue" (literally "blue card" – French for credit card) or "château fort" (strong castle, stronghold, fort) – a château fort may be a ruin, and a carte bleue may be green or red. Let us take two examples from Internet news. The first is drawn from news blogs with various sources, speaking about the sinking of the river cruise ship Bulgaria on the River Volga in Russia. The event took place on Sunday 10 July at 13:58 local time (09:58 UTC). The original source of the information was the Russian Ministry of Emergency Situations, which broadcast this message:

По предварительным данным, два человека числятся погибшими на теплоходе "Булгария" – МЧС http://www.itar-tass.com 15:22 10/07/2011 (11 :22 UTC) (MTchS Министерство Российской Федерации по чрезвычайным ситуациям – Ministry of Emergency Situations).

This message was then transmitted and diffused progressively via a number of different channels:

– *Russie: un navire coule au Tatarstan, au moins deux morts* (Russia: a ship sinks in Tatarstan, at least 200 dead) ;
     AFP Fil International http://www.pressedd.com 10/07/11 13:49

– *Un bateau avec plus de 170 personnes fait naufrage sur la Volga* (A boat with more than 170 passangers sinks on the Volga)
     http://lci.tf1.fr/ 10/07/2011 14h08

– *Près de 100 disparus après un naufrage sur la Volga* (Almost 100 people missing after a sinking on the Volga)
     http://www.lexpress.fr/ 10/07/2011 14:23

– *Un bateau de croisière coule sur la Volga, un mort, 88 disparus* (A cruise ship sinks on the Volga, 1 dead, 88 missing)
     http://www.rtl.be 10 July 2011 15h21

– *Naufrage sur la Volga: 167 personnes sauvées (MSU)* (Sinking on the Volga : 167 people rescued)
     http://fr.rian.ru/ 17:40 10/07/2011 (15h40 Paris time)

– *Un bateau de croisière coule sur la Volga, un mort, 88 disparus* (A cruise ship sinks on the Volga, 1 dead, 88 missing)
    http://www.leparisien.fr 10/07/2011 16h09

– *Un bateau de croisière coule sur la Volga* (A cruise ship sinks on the Volga)
    http://www.lefigaro.fr 10/07/2011 | updated : 16:12

– *Un bateau de croisière coule sur la Volga, un mort, 88 disparus* (A cruise ship sinks on the Volga, 1 dead, 88 missing)
    http://www.la-croix.com 10/7/11 16 h 30

– *Un bateau de croisière coule sur la Volga, 111 disparus* (A cruise ship sinks on the Volga, 111 missing)
    http://www.liberation.fr 10/07/2011 16h32

We note that the formula "*Un bateau de croisière coule sur la Volga*" ("A cruise ship sinks on the Volga") marks the idem repeated by the multiple broadcasters, who will repeat the information dozens of times after a certain date. Once the spark has been struck, the political wildfire waits for no-one. On Monday 11 July 2011 at 12:30 the Russian President Medvedev ordered "a complete check on all means of passenger transport" in Russia. Tuesday 12 was declared a national day of mourning.

Another example is drawn from scientific publications from an embryology corpus containing 30,000 notices, broken down into 339,764 phrases and 263,684 unique phrases (without noise). These digital documents are hosted on PubMed. We note 71 phrases which occur more than three times (after noise removal). Two examples are:

– amyotrophic lateral sclerosis (ALS) is a progressive neurodegenerative disorder characterized by:

- Mawal-Dewan M. *et al.* [MAW 96]	1996
- Shibata N. *et al.* [SHI 00]	2000
- Lee K.W. *et al.* [LEE 02]	2002
- Portera-Cailliau C. *et al.* [POR 07]	2007
- Laird F.M. *et al.* [LAI 08]	2008
- An J.J. *et al.* [AN 08]	2008
- Kalmar B. [KAL 08]	2008
- Forostyak S. *et al.* [FOR 11]	2011

– heat shock protein 90 (HSP90) is a highly conserved molecular chaperone

- Picard D. [PIC 02]	2002
- Gao Q. *et al.* [GAO 07]	2007
- Gao Q. *et al.*[GAO 08]	2008

- Prassinos C. *et al.* [PRA 08]	2008
- Sidera K. *et al.* [SID 08]	2008
- Kim M. *et al.* [KIM 09]	2009
- Millson S.H. *et al.* [MIL 10]	2010
- Taipale M. *et al.* [TAI 10]	2010
- Reddy P.S. *et al.* [RED 11]	2011

In interphrastic studies, just as in intra-phrastic studies, we also find traditional analyses called co-occurrence analyses. A co-occurrence is a co-apparition of two given entities (specific or generic words) in a word window – the window being the maximum number of words separating these two entities or their co-apparition in a unit (phrase, field, paragraph or document). These co-occurrences may arise in different contexts and therefore different documents. Innumerable classification studies have been done on the basis of co-occurrences. Indeed, once a co-occurrence matrix has been drawn up, based on the data, we can apply all so-called distance or similarity calculation techniques in order to establish groupings.

These groupings will either be hierarchies or partitions, and a hierarchy can be broken down into multiple stages to establish a partition. Finally we obtain a partition of classes of entities which can be assimilated to themes or semantic classes. An example of a hierarchical classification is an ascending agglomerative similarity method based on a Jaccard coefficient, where the elements are grouped two-by-two; the classes obtained form new classes, between which the similarities are calculated, and so on until a single class is obtained. Thus, the inter-class links form branches of the hierarchical classification tree. An example of a partitioning method is the frequent pattern technique which estimates all the possible combinations by adding a new element to the existing classes in order to estimate the classes with most cardinality in reference to a threshold of occurrence.

There are dozens of calculatory variants of grouping, and just as many means of estimating the similarities; the efficacy of the calculations depends on a number of elements: specialist language (electronic messaging, biomedical scientific discourse), noise tolerance (form, main text), heterogeneity of types of digital documents (just text or image and text), and so on. For this reason, a classification-based analysis may have difficulty in coping with the complex issue of the study of self-motivation, but it can provide some relevant indicators.

12.2.3. *Meta-phrastic extraction*

A **meta-phrastic extraction** gathers non-textual elements of information which relate to textual information. Typically a segment of text (a named entity or part of a phrase) will be studied through the lens of several documentary units. The segment will also have a confirmed presence in a database, semantic descriptions of which will provide a nuanced interpretation about the context. This kind of analysis is tricky, in that we have to use a robust, unambiguous pivot language in order to be able to align the pieces of knowledge developed in the text and the structured pieces of knowledge.

12.3. The information market

In 2012, the production of digital information has become extremely prolific. We even speak of the phenomenon of "big data". According to certain sources, 80% of the data available today have been produced in the past three years. It is estimated that 85% of all data existing in the world are unstructured [ALS 10]. The unrelenting progression of low-cost computer technologies in society, both at home and at work, tends to produce massive amounts of digital information. Globally, this information production gives rise to economic markets (news, legal information, financial information, scientific information), which account for transactions totaling over a billion Euro a year in France alone. Simba Information Consulting assesses global markets to be worth around $53 billion, 54% of which is marketing and financial information. Furthermore, the true size of the Web is difficult to estimate. The volume of data available is growing at a very fast rate: around seven million additional pages per day in 2002, and probably 100 million in 2012. This increase is occurring alongside a high mortality rate of Web pages. Indeed, their lifespan is limited. Google probably has over 400 million sites indexed and 100 billion Web pages. Also, there is a "hidden Web" available – more commonly referred to as the "Deep Web" – available via pages generated dynamically – i.e. upon the request of a user at a given time and in accordance with precise criteria.

Information overload is part of the human condition: we are faced with too many possibilities, and too much complexity. This feeling of overload also expresses an insatiable curiosity and a need for innovation. This leads us to constantly sort, search, find, arrange, classify and understand. It is unsurprising therefore that Google has become so important – the word itself has become an expression of the instantaneous need for digital information. In fact, information overload is a force which generates innovation. It enables us to identify new needs, to create new forms of information. Thus, the writer Théophraste Renaudot invented two forms to deal with such information overload. He was the creator of the "Conference", which he termed the "commerce of souls" in his eponymous work from 1641 [REN 41]. He offered a public occasion to talk about the social or scientific issues of the world. His conferences were a format which would spread throughout France and Europe and continue to enjoy success right up to the present day. Today we are more interconnected, and we are witnessing information acceleration. However, this does not mean that the information overload is any greater today than previously. Finally, we should also look at how our lives can be made easier by such overloads. They do not only have negative aspects. They also allow us to access information, communicate, exchange, and coordinate. This feeling is known as FOMO (Fear Of Missing Out), the term coined to express the anxiety caused by the impression of always missing out on something. This describes the tyrannical feeling of being on the sidelines. Hence, it is clear that if free time serves only to describe our free time and the way in which we fill it, we are merely distorting the image of what the world really is. FOMO blights our every move.

Information overload is not a recent phenomenon. This feeling of being left out, of overload, is in fact to be found in all ages of humanity, from Ancient Greece to the present day. In every era, people have felt it was something new, something peculiar to their own epoch. In the Phaedrus, Plato criticizes writing as something which makes us lose our memory. For Seneca, the abundance of books is a distraction. Descartes explains that we spend more time choosing books than reading them. Every generation reacts differently to overload. Descartes explained that we need to trust our own good judgment. Others have opted for simplicity. Everyone adapts differently to this complexity. Noone has ever read every single book. We have always abused rapid "skim" reading and turned several pages at a time.

Attention – the attention paid to the environment of the data and information in which the "knowledge worker" is immersed – is an element of the ecosystem of knowledge management. Information-sharing to favor learning is only effective if the addressee of the information pays attention to it. Information overload disturbs attention. Knowledge management support devices therefore must take account of the capacity of a piece of information to capture the attention. This underlies a relation between attention and emotion, or attention and perception. We pay greater attention to information which arouses emotion – e.g. by telling a story.

12.4. Types of data

In 2007, the highly prestigious American organization National Science Foundation published a strategic report on cyber-infrastructure, which is now used as a point of reference, with points about the nature of the technical data from a general point of view (*Cyberinfrastructure Vision for 21st Century Discovery*). The report proposes the following categories:

1) Observational data include weather measurements and behavioral studies, which may be associated with specific eras and places or may involve several places and periods (i.e. longitudinal or transversal studies).

2) Computational data, for their part, result from a computerized model or a simulation, either for virtual reality or physics. Reproducing the model of the simulation also requires us to write documentation on the hardware, the software and the data. In certain cases, only the output from the model can be preserved.

3) Experimental data include results of lab studies such as measurements of chemical reactions, or experiments in a domain such as controlled behavioral studies. The capacity to conserve enough data and documentation varies depending on the cost and reproducibility of the experiment.

4) Notices drawn from public services, the world of business and private life also provide useful data for research in human and social sciences, and in science in general.

Language is the main phenomenon observable on the Web. On this medium, language is not produced by certain people and consumed by others: anyone and everyone is a producer and a consumer of information at the same time. In fact, there are no producers or customers, and what is established is generally an equivalence of individuals in terms of language, but immediate reciprocality of exchanges through the medium of the language. This reciprocality is found in oral language, which is the primary linguistic practice. A company such as EDF employs 8,000 telephone advisors who deal with 25 million calls a year for the residential market alone. This is a goldmine of potential oral data to exploit. It is possible to switch to written analysis, but the process is fraught with pitfalls. The production of oral discourse is subject to the time factor. Indeed, an oration is produced at the same time as it is being constructed by the speaker. This process is similar to that of drafting, in written form. In oral language, the modifications and corrections present in the statement are re-transcribed during automatic speech-to-text conversion, and consequently a great many errors are present (Stöber *et al.* [STÖ 00], Adda-Decker [ADD 06]). Spoken language, or more precisely, spontaneously language, contains numerous disfluences, whose weight is therefore considerable. Linguists have not yet reached agreement as to the precise definition of the term "disfluence", but there is one definition which surfaces frequently. According to Blanche-Benveniste and Jeanjean [BLA 87], it is a place in a statement where the "syntagmatic flow is broken". Transcription from oral into written language is an extremely difficult exercise. The language is characterized by a great many homophones which cause recognition errors. For instance, in an example taken from French, "…pour *le papa, c'est* une surprise …" ("…for my dad, it's a surprise…", spoken message) is mis-transcribed as *pour le pas passé une surprise* ("for the past step a surprise", automated transliteration), and "c'est cool" ([it's/that's] cool) as *s'écoule* (passes/slips by/runs out [as in time]). One artificial example from English would be the rendering of "…whether they can bear their son's hair" as "…weather they can bare they're suns hare"; another is the indistinguishability of "Overreaction" from "Ovary action". Disfluences, like false starts and truncations, cause homophones.

Hesitations can be defined as a behavior of indecision, and they also cause recognition errors. Emotions and background noises also disturb conversation or even the speech of an individual. An emotion of greater or lesser intensity may change the tone of voice, accelerate oral production and therefore cause further recognition errors. Filmed data making up an audiovisual stream may be transcribed. Also, technology has been developed by the company Vecsys and the laboratory Limsi (University of Paris 11) to automatically index audiovisual corpora.

An academic publication (legal text, expert report, natural science journal article) communicates a piece of information. This is also done by social networks, discussion forums, tacit knowledge, informal knowledge and everything that is relevant to the sociology of sciences and from the cognitive point of view as regards science. In bioinformatics, or the use of intensive computer technology applied to highly complex biological models, publications are beginning to be considered as morsels of scientific information. Thanks to knowledge extraction and particularly identification of biological entities and logical relations established in the publications, bioinformatics uses the publication as an entity of information, so its role becomes far greater than that of a tool for discourse within a scientific activity community.

On the Internet and on a less formal level than scientific publications, a number of current tools offer a means of information processing at a personal level (information on the scale of an individual):

– blogs, sources of conversation streams and narrative streams;

– social tagging (bookmarks, tags…), which is a source of metadata;

– Wiki pages, denoting shared workspaces.

Beyond "facilitation" in knowledge extraction, a global approach to information on the Web is also being seen in the dynamic of digital humanities, which constitute those sets of communities of practices making use of digital techniques. One challenge of the architecture of information is to properly make it understood that there is a genuine need to take account of the totality of the processes of production, search and diffusion of knowledge. Taking care of the design of information is understanding that it is possible and necessary to sculpt the way in which we learn, teach, communicate; that these new humanities transcend traditional disciplines and ways of learning. The example of the social network Twitter is emblematic. Using a hashtag (from hash, #, using which you can turn any word into a hashtag) or "click word", is a procedure to link the "tweet" containing that hashtag to a category of tweets. A hashtag is a means of grouping together tweets about the same given subject. Thus, it enables users to classify certain pieces of information "to find and follow them more easily", according to a Twitter guide. The reality is more complicated than this: it appears the hashtag has become a discursive element that obeys laws which render its usage subtle and make it a social marker throughout a Twitter community. On a lexical level, hashtags are accepted in the community of "geeks" that is Twitter: thus, to group together cat lovers, the hashtag *#catlovers* would be chosen, which is easily identifiable and serves to tip the wink to cat lovers the World Wide Web over.

12.5. The outlines of text mining

Text mining, and in particular the extraction of knowledge based on texts, has in the past ten years become a true discipline, based on statistical methods and machine learning, which is widely used [HAH 97; KOD 99; HEA 99; BLE 09; MIN 12]. The abundance of information available necessitates an exploitation of the data based on models, by and for the users. In some rare cases, deterministic and classical models may offer a certain degree of satisfaction in certain fields, such as meteorology for instance, with relative efficiency. In other cases, it is impossible to predict anything precisely. This requires us to draw upon exploration in the data, which is known as data mining [FAY 96; HAN 01; WIT 05]. Artificial intelligence (AI) is a term coined by John McCarthy, and defined by another of the pioneers of the discipline, Marvin Minsky, as the construction of computer programs which are devoted to tasks which, hitherto, have been performed more satisfactorily by human beings, because they require high-level mental processes such as: perceptual learning, organization of memory and critical reasoning. In that sense, text mining is artificial intelligence, because it involves extracting the useful information and sorting that information, in a mass of (real-world) data, using computer programs which operate intensive processing techniques based on the notion of knowledge. It is a question of going from a piece of data (a perceived signal) to a piece of information (that datum stored and incompressible) and then to knowledge (information interpreted and stored).

Text mining or the extraction of knowledge from texts is a specialization of data mining. It is a set of computer treatments which consists of extracting knowledge based on a criterion of novelty or similarity from texts produced by humans for humans. In practice, this involves constructing an algorithmic form of a simplified model of linguistic theories in statistical and learning computer systems. Thus, the disciplines involved are computational linguistics, language engineering, artificial learning, statistics and of course, computing.

Text mining involves processes of structuring an input text presented as a digital document, processes of acquisition of invariant schemas in the form of structured data, and finally processes of evaluation and interpretation of the output. A "high quality" in text mining usually refers to a certain combination of relevance, novelty and interest. Textual data mining is presented as an ecosystem of systems, including standards for metadata, ontologies, syntactical and semantic analysis of the features of search objects, workflows, annotations, means of storage of various digital contents (tables, texts, images) of different origins (e-books, technical reports, SMS messages, etc.). The main functions of such an ecosystem are:

– detection of named entities. A named entity is a "real-world" object, the linguistic form of which is a direct and unambiguous representation;

– documentary searching. In this case, the information in materialized and processed in the form of documents in one or more modalities;

– theme tracking. This involves detecting thematic turning points or breaks using the linguistic content;

– categorization or classification of texts;

– production of taxonomies. This is the extraction of concepts positioned in accordance with certain hierarchical relations;

– sentiment analysis or judgment. Also known as opinion mining, this relates to the extraction of an opinion from forums or questions/answers;

– modeling of the relationships between entities. This involves learning the semantic relations between named entities.

Thus, data-mining methods are able to extract sense from a dataset which, *a priori*, is disparate in form, and thereby these methods create semantics [HAB 96; HAH 99]. The semantics created tends to take one or both of two forms (the expression of formal signifiers), drawn from artificial intelligence: a table (row/column format) and a graph (a meshed network of objects). These are signifiers, in the sense that they represent knowledge. Such structures can then be annotated with the raw data: each piece of information (document, phrase, etc.) is attached to a node on the graph or a cell in the table. Analysis then takes place at a more complex level of comprehension. However, since the process only manipulates signifiers, the technique of data-mining requires input from a human expert in the domain. That expert will reconstruct the semantics extracted and lend meaning and value to it in accordance with three criteria: is this known? Is this explicable? Is this useful?

DEFINITION 12.1.– Data mining is the search for useful information without knowing exactly what we are looking for in a digital dataset.

This enables us to change direction and give the definition for non-numerical (qualitative) – particularly textual – data.

DEFINITION 12.2.– Text mining is the search for useful information without knowing exactly what we are looking for in data containing textual information.

From the epistemological point of view, reasoning takes a number of forms. There is no one, unique way of constructing knowledge: rather, there are many. Philosophy and particularly logic enumerated them over a century ago:

– abduction: "It's cold in here" interpreted as a request to close the window. If we have the fact b and we know that $a => b$ (a implies b) then we can infer a;

– induction: "There's no smoke without fire";

– deduction: the "red light" is part of the Highway Code in many countries;

– analogy: two variables a and b are analogous, $a = b$, if a and b share the same property, such as two genes between two species have the same DNA sequence;

– paradox: e.g. the populace will not accept a single death when a new epidemic breaks out (such as the BSE/CJD crisis or the blue-green algae crisis), but accepts 5,000 deaths a year on the transport networks;

– intuition: intuition is the capacity to spontaneously and mentally combine two or more experiences to solve a problem which has never been posed;

– probability: an event is probable when it is neither certain to occur (probability 1, the maximum) nor certain not to occur (probability 0, the minimum).

Reasoning may be composite. For instance, the visualization of clusters of terms based on documents would be a chain such as "induction => analogy => deduction". Text mining, and particularly the knowledge extraction facet of it, is an algorithmic induction procedure. In digital analysis, the induction procedures stem from inverse problem methods which consist of identifying a model based on numerical experimental data. The least squares method is one example of this: this involves identifying a linear relation between a target variable and one or more parameters. The spectral methods which are widely used in signal processing, such as the wavelet transform or so-called Fourier Transform, also belong to this family. As regards the information reconstruction facet, text mining is a procedure of deduction (keyword search) or analogy (categorization of documents, for instance).

Hence, in terms of the "knowledge discovery" facet, text mining differs from traditional tools which deal with linguistic phenomena, so-called natural language processing (NLP) tools [WAT 96; IND 10]. That said, a growing number of NLP tools use automatic learning, so they take account of induction as a means of computation. The treatments these tools implement are syntactic and morphological analyses. On a larger scale, treatments are carried out to model the relations between terminological units and documents: this is information retrieval or document retrieval [NEE 61; SPA 87; MIN 72; SAL 83; HEA 94; SCH 97; TUR 98b; SPA 99]. Alternatively, the process of associating units by way of stereotypical relations between terminological units based on a pattern is called information extraction. Information extraction and information searching, at the heart, are deductive processes but can also integrate inductive learning procedures. Text mining is not linguistic. The distinction is based on the nuances of the analysis. Text mining aims to extract regularities in a set of texts in order to advance the overall comprehension of a problem; linguists use the technique to extract information that can be used to define linguistic models of general language. The archaic model of text mining is keyword indexing [CHE 98]; the issue for text mining is a "post-Google" step to extract meaning from the results.

The academic objectives of text mining are the honing of new techniques of information extraction from texts, network analysis and knowledge management, the marriage of which proves interesting for users. Users may have the intention of exploring corpora of documents from a thematic domain or digital information files containing text:

– data are a pillar of such objectives. They are digital, contain textual information, and are often heterogeneous and voluminous. A degree of thought is necessary as regards their storage, structuring of the metadata, and their possible fusion;

– techniques for algorithmic treatment of voluminous datasets require innovation. Such techniques involve very varied treatments: conceptual navigation and visualization of knowledge, distributional analyses, linguistic and terminological analyses and human/computer interfaces, involving the user in the process;

– the problems and issues are the object of heuristic and constructivist prototyping. They lead to continual developments and co-construction of new methodologies to help answer a user's questions.

The technical skills required are closely linked to computer programming, integrative technologies devoted to software platforms, and the types of algorithms which are found in the scientific domains of network analysis, knowledge extraction and knowledge management. Later on, a word cloud is used to demonstrate the diversity of activities linked to the skills sought. These will, of course, change over the course of the next few years, given that Web technologies and mobile telephony greatly impact computational engineering activities.

The activity relating to "knowledge" – extraction, storage and access – is targeted at users whose reflections guide the construction of a generalist corpus, or whose reflections are based on the construction of a problem-oriented corpus. In the first case, the users are qualified as "corpus-based". They assume the existence of linguistic theories and use corpora to observe the way in which they apply, in order to validate them. The extraction of keywords on the basis of nominal patterns is a corpus-based activity [BOU 94]. In the second case, we have "corpus-driven" users – specialists in a given domain, who believe that linguistic constructions will emerge from analysis of corpora: this analysis enables the users to uncover patterns of co-occurrent words which will then serve as a basis for linguistic analyses in the true sense. One of the earliest corpus-driven approaches was put forward in [REN 91].

The texts are rarely used as blocks but rather are transformed into one (or several) formal representation(s) which are then exploited by data analysis algorithms to extract a global structure, e.g. an index or a visualization [BEN 73]. The following are the different levels of unitary representations:

– the character, forming a sequence such as an n-gram;

– the word, drawn from a dictionary, and which can be a raw word, a lemma, a useful word;

– the term, formed by a nominal group or collocations;

– the named entity, constituting a nominal group which is a material thing in reality;

– the grammatical label, drawn from a set of syntactic labels;

– the semantic label, taken from a thesaurus;

– the ontological relation, which symbolizes a relation between concepts.

Once a dataset has been broken down in accordance with the levels of unitary representation, we can use medium-level representation models to connect the low-level representations. We find a number of models:

– formal language models, a classic example of which is the "fingerprint" or "hashing" approach;

– relational models, which allow the application of patterns or standardized schemas;

– tree models, using properties of navigation of an n-area tree;

– vectorial models, largely based on matrix algebraic calculus;

– probabilistic models, involving estimations of conditional probabilities (Markov random fields, Bayesian analysis, belief functions);

– "cross-mapping" models, being methods which jointly associate several representations or passages from one representation to another (KCCA – Kernel Canonical Correlation Analysis).

In terms of involvement of a user in iterative considerations, we find structural representations based on:

– frames and templates, these being visual frameworks associating properties and relations;

– ontologies, first-order logic theories offering both visual and capacities of inferential computation to ensure coherence or make deductions (subsumption);

– collaborative labeling (Web 2.0) by users, or a mass of users ("crowdsourcing");

Mohamed Merah, « le tueur au scooter »_*_ who killed seven people in March in the south of France, learned just before he died that one of his friends, whom he thought was a jihadist, was in fact an agent of the French Intelligence Agency, claims an Algerian newspaper, which has apparently seen video-testaments.	
Person	Mohammed Merah
Vehicle	scooter
Country	south of France
Organisation	French Intelligence Agency
Date	March
Event	killed seven people
Person attribute	jihadist
Material	Algerian newspaper
Material	video-testaments

Table 12.1. *Facts observed in a segment of text*

In Figure 12.1, a segment of a passage on terrorism reveals (highlighted) a number of categories annotated by an information extraction system. Only some of the attributes extracted will be exploited by a user, depending on the information they contribute when dealing with a particular problem, to help perform a more precise pattern-based analysis, as shown in Figure 12.2.

Regular expressions to be applied	Results found in data corresponding to the regular expressions
PROTEIN activates PROTEIN	in *Bacillus subtilis*, HlyD, also anchored in the internal membrane, *interacts with* HlyB and TolC
BIOAGGRESSOR attacks PLANT	In *spring peas*, the very first *aphids* have been *detected* in the Ardennes
PERSON telephones PERSON	around twenty employees are demanding that *Dominique Bernard telephone Philippe Hersant*
ORGANIZATION invests MONEY	The *Gabonese government* is to *invest* over *13 billion dollars* in roads, railways and ports

Figure 12.2. *Phrases coinciding with the application of patterns*

12.6. Software economy

The subject is not confined to conceptual and exploratory lab projects but is also anchored in the day-to-day economy for the world of business – at least, business relating to industry and services. Commercial toolboxes for text mining have been released, both by established actors in the software economy and by startup actors on the Internet: Text Miner and Teragram from SAS; ManyEyes and UIMA from IBM; TextAnalyst from Megaputer Intelligence; Books Ngram Viewer from Google. The main platforms for statistical tools – SPSS (SPSS Clementine), SAS (SAS Enterprise Miner), Statsoft (STATISTICA data miner), R-Temis (Temis), Rapid-I (RapidMiner) and the platforms offered by computer groups IBM (IBM Intelligent Miner), Oracle (Oracle Data Mining), Microsoft (Microsoft SQL Data Mining) and Google (Google Analytics) offer effective solutions to deal with the question of data exploration. In France, in the domain of language engineering, the *association des professionnels de l'industrie de la langue* (APIL – Association of Professionals of the Language Industry) includes 82 financial actors in domains such as language consulting, technical writing support, decisional computing, customer relations management, knowledge management, language learning tools, electronic dictionaries, research in natural language processing, e-document management, voice recognition and synthesis, machine translation (MT), optical character recognition (OCR), text mining and semantic Web applications and ontologies. The Website LT World (http://www.lt-world.org) lists 2,800 such associations the world over, including 901 in the United States, 298 in Germany, 266 in Great Britain, 115 in Canada, 122 in Spain, 118 in Italy and 101 in France. Laboratory platforms have risen to a degree of sophisticated development of user access which performs as well as do commercial platforms. We can also cite the TXM platform [HEI 04] and the Cortext platform at the University of Paris Est Marne la Vallée. The semantic annotation project "Generic Architecture for Text Engineering" (GATE) is founded on the software package "Semantic Annotation Factory Environment" (SAFE). While it does not substitute the manual process of annotation, this software performs part of that task automatically, using automatons. It is used in other projects about the semantic Web and knowledge management such as Ontotext KIM or the MUSING Project (EU, 2006). While it is particularly well adapted to commercial annotation services, it also serves the needs of researchers in linguistic computing or social sciences.

12.7. Standards and metadata

Metadata and standards facilitate better communication between tools. It is a technique of formatting and annotation, and therefore enrichment of the digital resources. These metadata define descriptions of the "content" according to a model or schema and responding to use contexts. For instance, the LOM (Learning Object

Modeling) scheme is a scheme for the context of teaching/learning; the DC (Dublin Core) scheme acts in a library context; the MPEG 7 (Moving Picture Experts Group 7) scheme applies to the context of use, storage, management and exploitation of audiovisual data. The TEI (Text Encoding Initiative) standard emerged in 1999 as a group of initiatives for standardized tagging of texts. It is a standard of tagging, notation and exchange of corpora of electronic documents based on SGML (Standard Generalized Markup Language). It was elaborated pragmatically based on the needs for structuration, conceptualization and networking of texts. There is no other system of norms for the semiotic structure of the text – this is also part of the justification for the use of algorithms for knowledge management and extraction enabling us to automate certain aspects of the thematic description (segmentation, indexing, etc.) of the content of a corpus.

12.8. Open-ended questions and challenges for text-mining methods

At present, there are several avenues for development which appear promising, and exploration of these avenues requires innovations, which will converge to offer greater effectiveness in text-mining tools:

– trend analysis with an adjustment between historical data and models of several linear equations;

– cross impact analyses, which focus on the interactions between pairs of events. As yet, this type of study remains too heavily based on probabilities of judgment by experts;

– selection of variables to identify the right variables, and weight them properly;

– scenario extraction is certainly one of the most promising directions. We devise experiments on the boundary of the scenario which will offer the most flexibility and utility of the approaches. Today, interactive scenarios only exist in an as-yet primitive form;

– simulation and games are gaining ground in today's world and that of the future as digital tools are improved and diffused;

– participative methods should benefit from future forms of collective intelligence;

– visualization methods are more important now than in the past. The techniques for elaborating and implementing shared visualizations will evolve in the future. Social networks, the Web and finally, virtual worlds will enable us to develop a common and global vision. We imagine multicriterion navigation, coupled with multi-timeline visualization;

– modeling by agents will benefit from massive computers (networked computing) which are faster, enabling us to simulate more numerous communities of agents interacting with one another and their environment in accordance with more complex rules;

– finally, in the near future, we can hope to see a greater integration of varied sources of data, where text and graphs are only two of many modalities.

The word cloud shown below represents the domain of text mining:

data mining – text mining – textual data mining – textual analysis – information searching – OLAP (online analytical processing) – discovery of knowledge in databases – knowledge base – datawarehouse – information extraction – knowlege extraction – selection of variables – spelling analysis – morphological analysis – syntactic analysis – semantic analysis – documentary searching – close neighbors – k-means – automatic classification – relational learning – link analysis – linear regression – decision tree – neural network – similarity – distance – belief – probabilistic analysis – score calculation – classification method – lattice – class – motive – pattern – hierarchy – sequence mining – rule extraction – nonlinear regression analysis – bioinformatics – social networks – semantic networks – parser – crawler – indexer – workflow – socio-semantic network – lexicometry – webometry – Web mining - bibliometry – watch – infometry - Markov models - data aggregation – data cleansing - data collection – pattern recognition – interpretation – user experience – interface design – information management – iterative processes – software development – information fusion – explanation – argumentation – decisional risk – automatic language processing – ARP – semi-supervised learning – unsupervised learning – supervised learning – automatic indexing – automatic identification of themes – categorization – taxinomy – ontology – conceptual structure – cognitive process – Human and Social Sciences (HSS) – statistical processing – digital library – digital archives – linguistics – statistics – computational sciences – visualization of knowledge – knowledge extraction – scenario analysis – terminology – dictionary – token – lemma – term – named entity – lexicon – simulation – language modeling – modeling of complex systems – opinion mining – algorithmics of semantic spaces – descriptive analysis – predictive analysis – qualitative analysis – dynamic structuring – interactive knowledge interfaces – individual consciousness – collective consciousness – script – software platform.

12.9. Notion of lexical noise

In Chapter 8 we introduced textual statistics. Textual statistics uses the lexical distributions to create a snapshot of the state of usage of words in a corpus. Using Zipf's Law, it appears that a small number of words, otherwise qualified as useful words, present distributional over-representation in any corpus [BAA 08]. It also appears that over 70% of occurrences of lexical forms are unique. Over-representation and under-representation are sources of lexical noise; or lexical background noise, which prevents identification of regularity and relations.

With a variety of possible motivations, the actors in knowledge productions engage in obfuscation by producing ambiguous, false or erroneous data with the intention of causing confusion in the face of adversity, or simply by adding time and cost to the process of extraction of the correct data from the false ones.

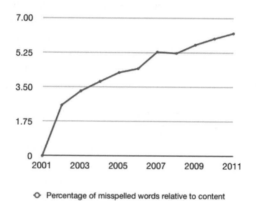

○ Percentage of misspelled words relative to content

Figure 12.3. *Source of errors on Wikipedia [STA 11]*

Figure 12.3 shows the increase in spelling errors noted on Wikipedia pages.

The momentary and massive interest shown in a relation or a named entity is not a source of intensity of its existence but revealing of an event that concentrates means and therefore enthusiasm; this is the principle of "looking next to the lamp because there is light". The phenomena of buzz, memes and viral videos are intrinsically linked to the advent of the Internet and of a world where information is instantaneous, and where anyone can – with a little luck – display their creations to the entire world. However, very few of these original, amusing, irritating or more usually absurd creations ever manage to break free of the Web and create an identity for themselves in the real world. We note that there are three types of phenomena that create a buzz on the Internet:

– the meme: an image, text, a .gif, generally but not always drawn from pop culture, which people modify to their own tastes using Photoshop or Paint, generally with a humorous aim. This gives rise to a plethora of images with the same basis that are to be found everywhere on the Internet, from forums to blogs. This type of buzz never reaches other media, and remains confined to underground surfers.

– the viral video: a poor-quality amateur video, often filmed at the expense of the protagonists, it usually depicts something amusing or mocking. If this type of video is shown on television, it is often because those behind it have been taken to court (as was the case with the Star Wars Kid), or because it has been so successful that it is thought that it would make the average Joe laugh. This type of video can also become a meme, by being taken up and remixed or improved in all manner of ways by surfers. These memes represent a large percentage of YouTube content;

– the original video, which deliberately aims to create a buzz: created by people producing a genuine piece of original content, these videos sometimes become veritable series whose episodes are eagerly awaited, and their originators can attain a degree of celebrity which goes far beyond the Internet (e.g. Justin Bieber, Rémi Gaillard, etc.). In this category are also commercial-type buzzes, created by companies or communication agencies.

12.10. Web mining

All information is connected, however tenuously, to the Web. SMSs send via the Web (voice over IP or VOIP), intranets are private and isolated parts of the Internet, hidden databases require paying accounts to be set up. The databases *Web of Science* and *PubMed*, which are archetypes of textual data mining, are Internet databases; thus they involve Web mining approaches. At the root of Web mining, we find social network analysis techniques, because the Web, by its very nature, arranges pages and users in a network. Thus, Web mining was one of the first instruments to test extraction from social networks, particularly with the project "Referral Web" conducted by Kautz *et al.* [KAU 97]. The aim of this project was not to conduct sociological experiments but to create an interactive tool to search for referral chains. It identifies the names of experts which co-occur in documents, on the basis of the name of a particular expert. This social network then serves as a request to obtain pertinent documents about that expert's field. The information which is extractible from a network should be visible on the Web in the sense of what Matsuo *et al.* [MAT 06] do, with certain underlying problems to be taken into account, such as the duplication of co-occurrences of names and the lexical ambiguity of certain names. In Web mining, we can also identify co-occurrences of terms [BRO 97; DIN 03]. Mika [MIK 05] explains a convergence between the co-occurrence of terms and the uses of an ontology by a community. Information on practices indicating visit routes, as explained by [STO 05], are also part of Web mining. Enormous quantities of data such as users' IP addresses and the URLs consulted are automatically recovered by servers in "access log" files.

Web mining can be broken down into three sub-categories of information analysis: Web content mining, Web usage mining and social network mining [KOS 00; LEV 02; HAN 01; VEL 11; TIN 12]. Web content mining is searching for and organizing information extracted from the Web; Web usage mining relates to classification of users' behavior [SRI 00]. Web mining possesses certain peculiarities in relation to the search for information in a relational database (a relational database management system – RDBMS). In an RDBMS, the basic scheme is known in advance. It is established in accordance with the relations and concepts inherent to the domain (i.e. the profession) of the users. On the Internet, the equivalent would be to establish requests about the structure of the document. This structure is not always stable, and requires specific types of treatment. We find HTML (general tags, frames and tables), XML (general or specific tags), blog posts (specific schema of paragraphs), information bulletins (specific schema of paragraphs), semi-structured scientific bases (specific value fields), and so on. It is prudent to think that a request about the structure of the document may be just as advantageous as a request about the data themselves [WAN 99; KRA 02]. The analysis of implicit structures enables us to obtain general information about the content. In addition, the search for and identification of information simultaneously involves automatic strolling around servers and sites with certain choices to target those sites which are interesting depending on keywords or a predefined list; this type of module, which at a certain time was pretentiously called an *agent*, is sometimes called a *spider* or *crawler* module. Other analyzers which we find for "plain text" documents, called *parsers*, take up the baton to study the basic syntactical structure and possibly position annotative tags. Extractors then exploit these tags – either sophisticated, such as the start or end of a named entity, or more basic such as the start or end of a title – to extract information with finer semantic granularity such as the date of a Web page, for instance [KOT 10]. Finally, semantic analyzers study the relations between pieces of information and possibly display them using a visualization tool or store them in tables. Web usage mining has long focused, for commercial reasons, on access and history of link usage to create systems of recommendations based on a user's profile. For instance, a user who buys book *A* will receive a recommendation of another book *B* because a rule has been deduced from purchase lists, whereby 60% of buyers who buy book *A* also buy book B. This is not the only use context. Computer-aided mining, aggregation and collection of data have dramatically changed the nature of contemporary surveillance. The traces of daily life, logs and access histories are becoming analyzable by an ever-growing number of sophisticated analytical tools developed for commerce and governance. This may become a key to iron out disparate databases and bring them together in new sets. Simply refusing to contribute to these profiles and these collections is not a practical option, because data collections are an inherent condition of most societal transactions, from connections between friends on online social networks to online business and travel involving a variety of public and private institutions. Recommendation systems are mining tools which analyze clicks and logs to extract a profile based on past activity in order to suggest new things which might be of interest [BAD 01; PAZ 07].

Popular uses are also very much oriented toward connection to networks (meeting sites, professional networks), viewing of videos (sport, films, etc.), consultation of the press (news), interaction in forums (blogs) with one or more pseudonyms. Mining of social networks includes different kinds of analysis. In particular, this involves the detection and mining of communities of social networks, social recommendation systems and social sentiment analysis. In terms of community detection, the objective is to identify groups and elements outside those groups (which may be harmful). The dynamic nature of the networks often needs to be taken into consideration here. In recommendation systems, the objective is to model social behavior with a sufficient degree of precision to be able to predict the users' preferences. These models often have to consider data with similar users to deal with the problem of the hollow nature in the typical configuration of a social network. Collaborative filtering and other techniques based on network vicinity are often employed. As regards sentiment analysis, an important question relates to summarizing the opinions of numerous users on a network and analyzing the distribution and the tendencies of those opinions.

Mining can facilitate the **learning of concepts** in a hierarchical and relational format, or the simultaneous mining of a thesaurus and documents [MOT 07]. An ontology defines a common vocabulary for researchers who need to share information in a domain. It includes machine-readable definitions of the basic concepts in that domain and the relations between those concepts. Sharing the common understanding of the structure of the information between the people or software manufacturers is one of the most common reasons that lead to the development of ontologies [MUS 92; GRU 93]. Here are the reasons for which an ontology might be developed:

– for a shared understanding of the structure of the information between the people or software manufacturers;

– to facilitate the reuse of knowledge about a domain;

– to make explicit what is considered implicit in a domain;

– to distinguish knowledge about a domain from operational knowledge;

– to analyze the knowledge about a domain.

12.11. Mining approach

We can distinguish different stages common to most methods for learning an ontology based on texts (Figure 12.4):

– collection, selection and preprocessing of an appropriate corpus;

– discovery of sets of equivalent words and expressions;

– validation of the sets by establishing the concepts, with the help of an expert in the field;

– discovery of sets of semantic relations and extension of the sets of equivalent expressions and words;

– validation of the relations and the extended definitions of concepts, with the help of an expert in the field;

– creation of a formal representation, in which not only the terms, concepts and relations are important, but also the circumstances of their exploitation.

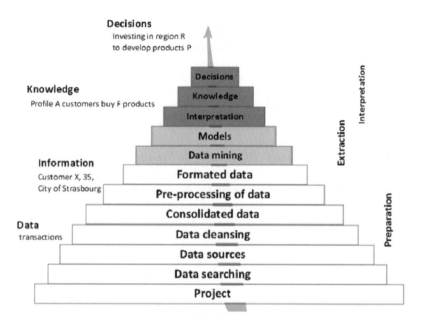

Figure 12.4. *General process of knowledge extraction*

An analyst, an expert in a technico-scientific domain, is in charge of guiding the process of extraction from a large quantity of texts. The first stages are devoted to the acquisition of linguistic knowledge: lexicon, terminology, semantic relation markers, discourse markers, specific markers [DES 03]. The next stages are aimed at identifying or structuring the basic knowledge with a view to extracting new units of knowledge.

Chapter 13

Non-Transversal Text Mining Techniques

13.1. Constructivist activity

Text mining is a rigorous activity which is based on electronic formatted data, with reproducible and validated methods. The overall philosophical environment stems from two antecedents, which are not mutually exclusive. The first is Gödel's theorem; the other is mathematical constructivism. Constructivism [BIS 67] is a stance toward mathematics which holds that we can only prove the existence of mathematical objects by *constructing* them. In reality, deductive arguments from absurdist reasoning prove nothing.

Gödel's argument [GÖD 30] holds that any theory (or language) accepts non-deductible (non-demonstrable) propositions, considering only the intrinsic properties of the language. In other words, a theory is consistent if no contradiction can be proven from its axioms. The theorem is stated as follows:

> "If T is a recursively axiomatizable, consistent theory which proves all the formulae Σ_0 true in N, there is a formula G, the negation of a formula Σ_1, which is true in N but is not demonstrable in T."

The process of prototyping developed in [TUR 00; TUR 04; TUR 12] involves the design of computer systems whose functions are developed in co-construction with users, with the aim of solving problems using computational models. The process is often but not exclusively iterative, and leads to an architecture that expresses an information-processing workflow equivalent to an approach of feasibility demonstration or concept proof of research objects. In this context, the theory is pragmatic, applying the test of demonstration and effectiveness, in the loop of information processing, of the users and models with testing procedures [ROC 07; BIL 08; MCC 08].

13.2. Typicality associated with the data

The objective of knowledge extraction from texts is to identify new units of useful knowledge in large collections of texts. While this relies upon principles of knowledge extraction and discovery from databases, it also turns up peculiarities of that knowledge due to the structure of the format of the text files written in natural language. The information in a text is expressed informally, in accordance with linguistic rules, which renders the process of discovery more complex. In order to avoid dispersion of the information (i.e. informational silence), a process of text mining must take account of paraphrases, ambiguities, specialist vocabulary and terminology [ZER 91; YAR 92]. Furthermore, the interpretation of a text relies on shared knowledge between the authors and the supposed readers. Some of this basic knowledge is expressed in the texts and cannot be extracted as a new piece of knowledge. Another part of it is not expressed but could be useful to link the concepts in a text which, at first glance, appear to be unconnected. Text mining focuses on the linguistic resources of the current texts in the contemporary use contexts and with robust tools. The language is considered as a way of accessing the information, rather than an object to be studied in itself. Thus, the process of text mining is involved in a loop, in which this process can be used to improve linguistic resources, and in which the linguistic resources, in turn, can be used to improve the process of information extraction to guide a certain type of process of text mining based on a model; this model refers to the knowledge available in the domain of the texts.

1.3. Specific character of text mining

As specified at the start of this chapter, techniques can be categorized into two main families: supervised and unsupervised techniques, depending on their intrinsic algorithmic nature – i.e. their optimization function. It is also worth mentioning the fact that there is another division of techniques into techniques peculiar to text mining and transcendent techniques which apply to all "mining" methods, given the nature of the input provided to the system. Methods specific to text mining will of course depend on the nature of the content of a document which has a structure: a document format (e.g. a font size, a particular system of bibliographical referencing, etc.). The elements of the document must be broken down into simple elements. These two aspects – format and division – lead us to construct analyzers which would not be found in other fields of data mining dealing with digital data such as: patterns over time in the domain of stock exchange, or extraction of logos from a database of pixilated images. Different typical levels of treatment must therefore be envisaged: morphological preprocessing, selection and weighting of terms, properties of statistical distribution, sub-lexical units, surface analyzers and certain techniques for extraction of named entities.

13.4. Supervised, unsupervised and semi-supervised techniques

Data-mining methods can be used to elaborate a model which will then be exploited in accordance with given parameters or new data. This model is often computed based on the data input into a system. From this, we can distinguish two main categories of algorithms for computing the model. Drawing inspiration from the domain of learning, the terminology imposed the denomination of "supervised" and "unsupervised" models. Machine learning may play a role in the processing of textual data. This topic is discussed in the next chapter, about transversal techniques.

13.5. Quality of a model

The quality of a text-mining model is important, just like for any knowledge extraction process. The evaluation is a recurrent and well-formalized process for testing computational models in general, although sometimes a cohort of users is engaged for this purpose. The next chapter explains the main concepts of evaluation of a model.

13.6. The scenario

Text mining offers a whole range of approaches aimed at identifying the primary elements of information: the data. These approaches are able to filter these data in order to classify them, and then group the data together in different classes. Finally, they enable us to identify relations between these classes or between the different pieces of data. This requires techniques specific to text mining (e.g. algorithm to divide a text into words), or algorithms transversal to data mining (e.g. classification algorithm using k-means clustering).

The use of text mining relies on a set of treatments which can be qualified as a scenario. The scenarios are elementary (in three stages: division, computation and restitution/evaluation) or more complex – which, at various moments along the line, involve partial classifications and interactions between the user and intermediary results. The aspects of division and computation involve a representation of the data. Computation requires us to integrate an optimization which will enable the computation to converge towards a solution in a reasonable space of time.

Restitution requires techniques of display and/or data labeling to estimate the precision of the results, or select a model when several models are computed.

13.7. Representation of a datum

The data are not uniform in text mining. It is not a case – as with digital data – of character strings denoting numerical variables. It may be a question of documents, parts of documents or different kinds of character strings.

The nature of a character string may be intuitive, like a word in a dictionary. Sometimes it becomes more complex: certain words assume a different meaning when they are associated to form nominal groups – e.g. "credit card" or "General de Gaulle". This representation is called an n-gram of words or a multi-term. This may be counter-intuitive when it is a question of consecutive strings of characters [BRO 92]. A bigram of characters would be "ab"; a trigram "rty". In the word "example", we find five trigrams: "exa", "xam", "amp", "mpl" and "ple".

The next level of granularity above the character string is the phrase. Then we have the document, which is a composition of phrases. A phrase and a document can in turn be broken down into character strings.

A character string found in a dictionary may have several functions: it may act as a signifier of a real-world object – e.g. "credit card"; a date such as "25 January" or a person: "President Obama", but this is not the only use. We also find locutions such as "there are"; tool words such as "everyone"; symbolic expressions such as a metaphor: "pigs might fly"; a sentiment: "sadness"; or argumentative elements such as "I am in favor of" or "the hypothesis demonstrates that".

Division is the first level of representation. A second level of representation is the combination of the elements. Four main types of representation are used: the predicate, the collection, the vector and the tree. In text mining, vectorial representation is most common [SAL 83]. It enables us to exploit the properties of the formalism of linear algebra and matrix calculus. For instance, a graph finds an equivalent by way of an incidence matrix. A number of hypotheses can be used to calculate the value of a matrix element. This also forms part of the considerations when choosing a model to represent the data. The three classic values are calculated in the following manner:

– a binary value (occurrence or non-occurrence between the row element and the column element);

– a number of occurrences between the row element and the column element;

– a relative weight, which might for instance use the classic weighting scheme TF–IDF (term frequency–inverse document frequency):

$$\text{TF–IDF} = n.\ \log(M/m) \tag{13.1}$$

where n is the number of occurrences in an element of information, m is the number of occurrences in the collection of elements of information, M is the size of the collection. The dimensionality of the variables sometimes makes the size of the vectors significant with non-informative attributes, and the processing of the matrices costly in terms of computation time. One of the main problems is the large dimensionality of these vectors.

Representation by sets in natural language processing uses "w-shingling", which is a set of unique "shingles". A "shingle" is a contiguous sequence of lexical forms that can be used to gauge the similarity of two documents. The w denotes the number of lexical forms, or tokens, in each "shingle" in the set. The extraction of 4-shingling in the sequence "a rose is a rose is a rose" would give the following set: { (*a,rose,is,a*), (*rose,is,a,rose*), (*is,a,rose,is*) } where duplicate shingles have been deleted.

Statistical approaches which use vectorial-type representations have been christened "bag of words" techniques (or BoW), because they take no account of syntactical dependencies. For instance "the man bites the dog" or "the dog bites the man" lead to a representation of four words in the "bag".

13.8. Standardization

One of the issues raised by automatic processing is the presence of redundancy. Redundancy in terminology is related to synonymy which is very difficult to detect automatically. Certain standards have been developed, such as the DOI (digital object identifier) which gives a unique identifier for a document. Sometimes the same document is to be found in more than one database; the DOI is a useful tool to test for the repeated presence of a document. The DOI system has only been in existence since 1998. For the names of the authors of a publication, an identifier is currently being created, which can distinguish between "L. Lee" and "Lin Lee", for instance. Such ambiguities exist for names of organizations (e.g. "Univ. of Strasbourg" and "Strasbourg University"), the representation of dates (e.g. "25 January" and "25/01") and a great many other categories, so we have to standardize the result of an extraction in order to compare the entities from one document to another. Some people have also studied this question as regards terminological variation and combine several forms of multi-terms into one, such as "mass spectrometer", "mass spectrometry" and "mass spectra", brought together under the umbrella of "mass spectrum".

Specific standardization algorithms can serve to calculate the proximity emanating from a clustering method based on a weighted local alignment metric and learning of connected components [JON 10].

13.9. Morphological preprocessing

Preprocessing relates to the elimination of pieces of textual information which are irrelevant or are sources of errors for the resolution of the subsequent tasks of mining [MOE 04]. A golden rule holds that more than 50% of the words will appear only once in a large corpus comprising several millions of lexical forms: these words are known as *hapax legomena*. These words cannot appear in training corpora and test corpora. Hence they are ignored. Stemming is another stage in preprocessing, whereby the words that appear in the corpus are associated with a canonic form. The Porter stemming algorithm [POR 80], which implements a cascade of regular expressions, is often used for texts in English, removing the more common morphological and inflectional word endings [KAR 97]. Stemming can be a more complex process to implement in certain languages which are highly productive in terms of morphosyntactical variation. Stemming can be performed at different levels of depth and in great detail. The resolution of each morpho-syntactic rule inevitably leads to a loss of information. Even the reduction of a plural form to a singular form leads to a loss of semantic information: one crude, decontextualized example drawn from French is the difference between "*la page jaune*" (the yellow page/sheet) and "*les pages jaunes*" (the Yellow Pages [phone directory]). Stricker *et al.* [STR 00] give a more subtle example for French with the term "*action*" in the sentence "*Le jugement est plus nuancé selon le domaine d'*action *du gouvernement*". Here, the term can be translated by the English word "action" – "The judgment is more nuanced depending on the area of the government's action". However, in the sentence "*Den Danske Bank a acquis en décembre dernier 90% des actions de Fokus Bank*", the lexical token « actions » can be translated as "shares" – "Last December, Danske Bank purchased 90% of the shares of Fokus Bank", and this meaning is clearly indicated by the plural ending. In some languages it is useful to split complex words, e.g. compound words, into their simple elements, and preserve them for subsequent processing. The resulting features can be further reduced by applying other feature selection. Compound splitting can thus be considered as a sub-task of stemming, where compounds are split into their components. This is less necessary for the English language, but compound splitting is usually beneficial when applied to compounding languages like Danish or German.

13.10. Selection and weighting of terminological units

Certain words in the vocabulary of a language are very frequent and are uniformly distributed throughout the documents in a corpus. In some cases, these words are superfluous from a statistical point of view and can be eliminated depending on the application of the data mining algorithms. There are many techniques to carry out this task. The simplest method to eliminate these non-informative words is to use a pre-defined *stop list* and eliminate all words in the text which are on that list. The stop list is, in principle, made up of functional words (articles, pronouns and conjunctions). The problem with stop lists is that they may not be appropriate for the specific corpus or task in question. In a corpus of texts on computers, the word "computer" will probably be equally distributed amongst the documents and thus fairly uninformative. In such a case, the word "computer" could be included in a list of stop words. When the task is authorship recognition, function words may be important cues for recognition of the attribution of a text to an author, though useless for content classification. Other methods of identification of uninformative terms make direct use of their statistical distribution among the texts of a corpus. When pre-processing is performed prior to classification, the distributions of terms in different classes in a training set can be compared against each other. Terms are omitted when a statistical test suggests that they are equally distributed in different classes. Pearson's chi-squared test, for instance, has been applied successfully [PAA 02] prior to text classification based on sequences of syllables. Similar techniques such as information gain, mutual information, cross entropy or odds ratio are described in [MLA 99]. Term weighting is another way of exploiting the direction of terms in order to take account of their influence in their context. Equation [13.1], expressing the well-known TF–IDF relative frequency is a good example of this. Other term weighting schemes are widely used, such as redundancy [LEO 02] or more probabilistic techniques [GÖV 99]. These weighting schemes are especially useful when the length of the documents exceeds some 1,000 words. Eigenvalue computation methods take account of the frequency and their associativity. By transforming a space in a linear fashion, we can select a limited number of dimensions (causing a reduction of dimensionality), retaining only those dimensions which harbor a maximum amount of information with a minimum of initial dimensions. The principal component analysis method, which in information searching is known as "latent semantic indexing" contributes to this type of reduction. Other methods can cause selection based on a measure of influence – e.g. with Information Gain (IG). This method is aimed at measuring the number of bits of information obtained for a given task, as the document classification in the knowledge of the presence or absence of a word in the document [MOE 04].

13.11. Statistical properties of textual units: lexical laws

The skewness of frequency distribution makes linguistic data a special challenge for any linguistic method. We can list officially at least 19 laws for textual statistics: Lotka [LOT 26], Behaghel [BEH 32], Bradford [BRA 34], Zipf [ZIP 35], Yule [YUL 44], Mizutani [MIT 82], Kabashima [KAB 55], Oono [OON 56], Frumkina [FRU 62], Alekseev [ALE 63], Herdan [HER 64], Arens [ARE 65], Piotrowski [PIO 68], Shibuya [SHI 79], Menzerath-Altmann [ALT 80], Krylov [KRY 82], Beöthy [BEO 84], Goebl [GOE 84] and Martin [MAR 92][1]. The laws describe different types of dependencies. The most popular are rank-frequency laws on the number of word associations, the number of words and unit size. We can also find diachronic laws.

Martin's law relates to lexical chains which are obtained by looking up the definition of a word in a dictionary, and then looking up the definition of the definition and so on. Finally, all these definitions form a hierarchy of increasingly general meaning, in which the number of definitions decreases with decreasing generality. Among the levels of this type of hierarchy, there are a number of equations dependent on a law.

Menzerath's law, also known as the Menzerath-Altmann law, establishes that the sizes of the constituents of a construction decreases with increasing size of that construction. The longer a sentence is (measured in terms of the number of clauses), the shorter those clauses will be (measured in terms of words); or the longer a word is (in syllables or morphemes), the shorter the words or syllables are in terms of sounds.

Rank-frequency laws apply to any and every type of linguistic unit. The following are some illustrations. The words in a text are arranged as a function of their frequency in the text and with a rank number assigned and the corresponding frequency or number of words with that rank. This is Zipf's law, which is empirically confirmed and historically the best known, and has birthed a number of derivative laws. A similar distribution between the rank and frequency of sounds, phonemes and letters can be seen. Coming back to the classic law, it specifies precisely that the r most frequent words occur $f(r)$ times with $f(r)$ defined by:

$$f(r) = \frac{a}{(c+r)^g}, \text{ where } a, c \text{ and } g \text{ are parameters} \qquad [13.2]$$

g varies from 1, corresponding to normal language use, to 2, corresponding to a more specialized or restricted use, such as in the PubMed corpus of biomedical publications. As a rule of thumb, the parameter g decreases with increasing unit size.

---

1 www.glottopedia.de.

Note that the double logarithm of the law displays a linear, negative slope. One consequence of Zipf's law is that the word frequency distribution is very skewed, i.e. some few words are very frequent (around 10^5 occurrences) whereas the frequency of most of the words is several orders of magnitude smaller (<10). It is known that the majority of words appear very rarely, and that the rare words are particularly informative about the content of a document; therefore they cannot be omitted in a text-mining approach. A further consequence of Zipf's law is that most of the words in a document will not be found in the other documents in the corpus. When we adopt vector representation, we are led to handle a hollow (or sparse) matrix format where most values are null, in the knowledge that the dimensionality is high; hundreds of thousands of forms for a few dozen non-null values of a vector.

The laws of change in the language express processes of growth in the language such as the expansion of vocabulary, the dispersion of foreign words or neologisms, and change in the declination systems. These laws are marked notably by the Piotrowski law, which corresponds to models of increase in other disciplines. The Piotrowski law is a case of a model better known as the logistic model [PIO 68]. It also covers language acquisition processes. The distribution of neologisms from a given source in a time period $[t_1, t_2]$ in the lexicon varies with the difference in the number of inherited or borrowed words, given by:

$$v_i(t_1, t_2) = e^{-\eta_1 t_1} - e^{-\eta_2 t_2} \qquad [13.3]$$

where i denotes the ith rank-frequency class.

Finally, the Piotrowski law represents the development (increase and/or decrease) in the proportion of new units or tokens over time. In a different but very similar register, we find the Pawlowski law, which predicts auto-correlation of phonemes when a text segment is interpreted as a time-series of units with a time-step [PAW 97]. Still in this category associated with a change, although this is not common, certain laws have a linear form – thus, the Oono law establishes that the proportion between the number of all the parts of the discourse remains the same over time in the lexicon of a language, although the size of that lexicon typically tends to increase [OON 56].

The text block law specifies that the linguistic units (words, letters, syntactic functions and constructions) exhibit a specific frequency distribution in large blocks of text of similar size.

13.12. Sub-lexical units

In order to deal with the issue of sparse matrices, we use a different linguistic model, breaking the text down into "interpretable" lexical units. Such units must necessarily be smaller than words: thus they are sub-lexical units which are commonly called n-grams (sequences of letters, syllables or phonemes). These units yield good results particularly when small corpora are considered. A fairly high-performance application is that of corpus cleansing when fusing documents from several bases [MAN 93]. The SSF (socio-semantic fingerprint) method constructs a unique key for each document based on the bigrams in it. The method proceeds as follows. Firstly, the title and the surname of the primary author are concatenated into a single character string S. Secondly, S is reduced to lowercase lettering. Finally, we preserve only the first bigram of each word in the same order of occurrence as the words, within the limit of the N first bigrams of the title. In practice we choose $N = 8$. Here is an example of the creation of a key K_{SSF} based on two strings from a document (AU: author field and TI: title field):

AU – S **Ay**ral-Kaloustian, **J** Gu, **J** Lucas, **M** Cinque, **C** Gaydos, **A** Zask, I Chaudhary, J Wang, L Di, M Young, M Ruppen, TS Mansour, JJ Gibbons, K Yu.

TI – **Hy**brid **In**hibitors **of** **Ph**osphatidylinositol **3-**Kinase (**PI**3K) **and** **the** **Ma**mmalian **Ta**rget of Rapamycin (mTOR): Design, Synthesis, and Superior Antitumor Activity of Novel Wortmannin-Rapamycin Conjugates.

The K_{SSF} key generated is:

K_{SSF} = hy in of ph 3- (p an th ma ta ay).

The first 10 parts of K_{SSF} are shown in bold in the title field; the last part is drawn from the author field, also highlighted in bold. The following algorithm presents the process in two stages to select the duplicates.

Socio-Semantic Fingerprinting Algorithm

Require: Databases files first step {key s building};

1: N <- 8

2: for each document D from the databases do

3: select title (T) and first author name (A)

4: transform T and A in lower case

5: split T into words; store in LW

6: for each words W i from the LW; and i < = N do

7: select the first bigram of W; store in K

8: end for

9: select the first bigram of A; store in K

10: end for

11: K is stored in a hash table HT

Require: given hash key of test document D(c), hash table HT of target

databases find step; comparison g;

12: if HT (K D (c)) return d then

13: set D (c) as duplicate of D (d)

14: end if

A compromise between the length of the linguistic units and their frequency (see the above section about the laws) accounts, at least in part, for the quality of the results of algorithms using sub-lexical units for certain processing tasks. This has been proven for words [GUI 74], but has also been applied for syllables. This means that the smaller the categories, the larger the units (types). The largest types become improbable so that they appear exclusively in training sets or in the test set. Thus, the units must be shorter in order to compensate for the small size of the categories.

13.14. Shallow parsing or superficial syntactic analysis

Surface or "superficial syntactic analysis" is a syntactic analysis which identifies the constituents of a sentence (nominal groups, verbs, etc.) without specifying the dependency links between them. Hence they do not produce a complete syntax tree [BRI 93; CHA 93]. We can imagine that extracting all the linguistic information about dependencies will be beneficial for the comprehension of a sentence. However, assuming it is possible to formalize and represent the lexico-grammatical structure of the language, this would necessitate a high degree of robustness and efficacy. It would not be conceivable, within a reasonable amount of time, to create such a system for large quantities of text. This explains the success of vector representations. However, this led to the development of so-called "shallow parsing" approaches, which manifest regularities of the language, posing questions about the complexity of the language and established pragmatically [NEU 02a]. Neumann and Schmeier [NEU 02b] showed, for instance, that the morphological analysis of short texts in German worked better with tri-gramming. However, for longer texts (average length 578 words) there was no significant difference in the quality of the results of classification between words and trigrams. Light syntactic analysis or parsing can usually greatly benefit procedures of extraction of named entities.

13.15. Argumentation models

Beyond surface analysis, certain works offer discourse analysis to capture an organization of discursive elements related to argumentation (e.g. alternative approach, authority argument). Such models can be associated with the exploration in the texts [SIL 92]. Angosh [ANG 10] presents a framework of categories of argumentation to identify contexts associated with sentences in scientific publications. His aim was to use these categories to give added value to information services (Table 13.1).

Category	Label	Description	Category	Label	Description
Background/Introduction			Sentences comparing research efforts		
Background	BG	Sentence describing the background in the research area	Background	RWSC	Sentence describing the background in the research area
Citation sentences			Contrasting work for a related work	RWD_CS	Sentence describing a contrasting work for a related work
Related work description - citation sentence	RWD_CS	Citation sentence describing related work			
Related work outcome - citation	RWO_CS	Citation sentence describing the outcomes	Alternative styles		
Related work strength - citation sentence	RWS_CS	Citation sentence describing the positive points of the related work	Alternative style for a related work - citation sentence	ASRW_CS	Citation sentence describing an alternative style for a related work
Descriptive sentences			Alternative style for a related work	ASRW	Sentence describing alternative styles for a related work
Related work description	RWD	Sentence describing a related work	Current work		
Related work outcome	RWO	Sentence describing the outcomes of a related work	Current work outcomes	CWO	Sentence describing the outcomes of current work
Related work strength	RWS	Sentence describing the strength of a related work	Current work shortcomings	CWSC	Sentence describing the shortcomings of current work

Table 13.1. *Judgment of the expert and choice of classifier [ANG 10]*

Chapter 14

Transversal Text Mining Techniques

14.1. Mixed and interdisciplinary text mining techniques

Levels of analysis of the relations can benefit generic methods, particularly on aspects of matrix analysis or statistical learning analysis [BEN 73; HAR 75; TUK 77; MUR 87; JAI 88; GOV 09]. Such is the case of latent semantic indexing and approaches to extraction of named entities.

14.1.1. *Supervised, unsupervised and semi-supervised techniques*

Data mining methods can be used to elaborate a model which will then be exploited in accordance with given parameters or new data. This model is often computed based on the data input into a system. From this, we can distinguish two main categories of algorithms for computing the model. Drawing inspiration from the domain of learning, the terminology imposed the denomination of "supervised" and "unsupervised" models. Models in the supervised category suppose that knowledge about the data exists. This knowledge can be found in the form of metadata in the data or as an external knowledge base connected to the data. Unsupervised models, for their part, suppose that only the data input into the system are available; this is more economic and sometimes more robust; however, this assumes a less intense level of interpretation. Other denominations speak of "knowledge rich" or "knowledge poor" methods. There is an intermediary family: "semi-supervised" models, which suppose that little information/knowledge is available to us, on a reduced sample [BAS 96; BAK 98; MAN 99].

Unsupervised methods take account of indicators such as metrics or standardized similarity coefficients acting on an input space. Automatic classification (or clustering) techniques are representative of this family [TUR 98a]. Clustering seeks to identify a finite set of abstract categories which describes the data by determining natural affinities in the data, based on a pre-defined distance or a measure of similarity. Clustering can use varying types of categories, which ultimately are distributed into a partition of clusters. The properties are the granularity of the partition (hierarchy), exclusivity of belonging (overlap between clusters), stability of a cluster (centrality) and distance between clusters (density). The mode of construction is elaborated either by agglomeration, whereby the instances of a cluster are initially aggregated to form small clusters and gradually brought together to form larger ones, or by successive division, beginning with the dataset and forming large clusters which are then broken down into smaller ones.

Unsupervised methods extract regularities directly from the data. Over a hundred metrics and coefficients are available. The most popular of these are the Euclidean distance and the Jaccard coefficient. If certain data require an adaptation of an existing metric, it is difficult to prove the qualitative superiority of one metric over another.

Supervised methods, for their part, require additional information to the raw data. Most of the time, the models are learned from training data and then evaluated on test data which serve to adjust the parameters of the model, and to obtain the final measure of the validation score. Supervised methods pre-suppose the existence of pre-defined classes; and therefore the computed model is exploited in order to classify any piece of data presented in one of the known classes – typically applied to a set of instances (textual documents) which have been assigned a categorial label, to affirm their belonging to that category ("sport" or "politics", for instance). In view of the representation and the elements of information chosen, the objective then becomes to decide which category a new document belongs to. There are a variety of popular techniques which use particular algorithms to act as a supervised classifier – e.g. decision trees, Bayesian classifiers, the support vector machine (SVM) or the nearest neighbor method.

A related notion is that of the degree of similarity. The methods usually consider similarities of order 1 – i.e. two elements share contexts. One might also come across higher-order similarities (second order, third order, etc.).

14.2. Techniques for extraction of named entities

Documents, whether or not they contain text, are formed by a structure of metadata. In the minimal scenario, such metadata include the date of the file's creation, its size in bytes and its filename. In a less minimal and semi-structured case, we find labels equivalent to fields, followed by certain values. In this case, for instance, we typically find a field describing one or more organizations containing the name of an establishment and its postal address. The following is an example of this: "C1: Stanford University, 353 Serra Mall, Stanford, CA 94305, USA." In both these cases, processing does not require a huge amount of effort to extract the information. For instance, it might suffice to know a value separator for each field. Labeling languages are available; sometimes the granularity of the labels is very fine and depends on a domain (ontological labels). When the words of the text are surrounded by such labels, their extraction is immediate and practical in terms of reconstruction of information. We can imagine such labels for the name of an object ("credit card"), the name of a species ("vinegar fly"), the name of a person ("General de Gaulle"), the name of a place ("East Germany"), a date ("24 January 1973"), a technique ("Fast Fourier Transform (FFT)"), an institution ("Smithsonian"), an event ("G8 Summit") and so on. When a user has a set of labels to create a document and uses that set in his text editor, consultation and identification tools can take advantage of the labels and reconstruct the content with a very fine granularity, quickly and for any usage. In practice, unfortunately, this case is rare; it is to be found for fields of keywords in databases of academic literature but which only have the status of "keywords" – a label which is very generic. Thus, we use specialized algorithms which will process documents whose internal structure is not clearly known in order to correctly detect named entities such as the examples cited above. In the early 1990s, popular algorithms used for this purpose were based on purely linguistic and generalist rules intended to identify nominal groups [AUS 95]:

– the dictionary-based technique. The user has to store the nominal groups he wishes to identify in a file called a dictionary; then "pattern matching" is performed to identify where in which document an entry in the dictionary appears. The dictionary has a flat, list-type structure of character strings;

– the repeated segments technique. Without external resources and without syntactic analysis, we identify all the repeated forms, with certain heuristics at the beginning of the strings to avoid their starting with functional words;

– the so-called boundary technique. A preliminary phase, based on a "syntactic lexical-category form" dictionary, intended to label each form in a text with a grammatical label. The subsequent phase runs linearly from start to end, through the whole text to conserve the sequences of lexical forms which are not associated with authorized labels (morpho-syntactic wildcard or joker pattern);

– the pattern technique. A preliminary phase is identical to that of the boundary technique. A second phase runs through the text from beginning to end and identifies sequences of forms which correspond to series of sequences of specific categories such as Noun+Noun, Noun+of+Noun or Adjective+Noun.

There are evaluation corpora for such automatic methods; a corpus created in 2004 by Chantal Enguehard [ENG 92] (University of Nantes) about metal chemistry contains 1,280 documents (titles + summaries) with a list of 1,100 nominal groups established by experts and anchored by labels in the corpus. Pattern techniques applied to this corpus throw up between 10,000 and 20,000 nominal groups depending on the patterns used. The rate of recall is between 45 and 55%, and the degree of precision is between 2 and 6% (for details about the method of evaluation, see the later part of this chapter). Some fairly heavy-duty cleansing engineering is necessary. The ATRACT workbench [MIM 01] is an example of a toolbox (or framework) for terminology management, incorporating term extraction and terminology management modules.

Heuristic approaches consider dictionaries and "manually-defined" rules for specific datasets. For instance, "January" and "February" are months, whichever word comes directly after "Mrs" is the name of a person, and so on. These rules can basically be compiled in the form of deterministic robots, and programmed as regular expressions.

Figure 12.2 shows rules of high granularity and which cannot be known in advance by an extraction system. They can be learnt on the basis of the syntactic combinations present in the data, as long as at least a few elements of the rule are known. For instance, in rules such as "protein 1 activates protein 2", we must specify the presence of protein 1 and protein 2 in the rule, which requires some degree of knowledge of molecular biology. When patterns of rules are not clearly specified, we have to resort to extraction of linguistic elements, which must belong to a category. This is what is seen in Figure 12.1 for instance, with the categories "vehicle" and "person". They account for a capacity to extract elements of language attached to these categories, but to have to specify rules combining vehicles and people. In summary the specification of categories is a preliminary stage that is necessary for the specification of rules which combine these categories.

The rules are empirical and costly in terms of time taken by an expert to establish, but the more rules there are, the better the system responds. The advantage to having rules is that they increase the precision. The difficulty lies in combining and ordering the rules if need be. When there is a sufficient quantity of data, supervised learning algorithms may serve as a support. These programs detect morpho-syntactic regularities and can help increase recall because they are exhaustive. They often need to be carefully considered because they are riddled with errors and therefore the raw results may propagate errors into the databases which will serve as sources of data for other systems. Two main types of learning are used: inductive logic programming (ILP) and probabilistic automatons (Hidden Markov Models or HMM, and Conditional Random Fields or CRF) [KAN 95; LAF 01]. Semantic annotation assuages the difficult in finely resolving ambiguities. In this vein, learning methods may be based on annotated texts, using this annotation metalanguage to compute a pinpointing model. An illustration of this approach is Reuters' OpenCalais system – a free annotation service which annotates names of people and place names. This system is trained using an annotated model, which accounts for the restrictiveness of its automatic annotation in categorical terms, particularly of scientific knowledge. Ciccarcse *et al.* [CIC 11] put forward an ontology to annotate scientific documents on the Web, because they observed a gap between a rich and expressive collection of published biomedical ontologies and natural-language expression. Annotation can also aid elucidation of documents – i.e. a critical interpretative dialog between an author and his reader in order to anchor the categories in a document. The distribution of these anchoring points gives rise to distributional analyses to illustrate a point of view about the text or reveal an idea of its content by means of dynamic elaboration of the metalanguage of annotation as the document is read. In a manner of speaking, the annotation model and the distribution of the categories throughout the text reflect the genuine value of the knowledge far more accurately than do the individual syntagmatic elements which result from it.

14.3. Inverse methods

"Inverse methods" provide invaluable mathematical tools which allow us to work back from observations to models. We can see that inductive, data-guided learning methods share this type of analysis no matter what the domain – social sciences or life sciences – from which the data are drawn. The adjustment of a simple "least squares" plot, or the obtention of a three-dimensional image of the distribution of the velocity of seismic waves below the surface of the planet, are reasonably simple applications of inverse methods. Linear and discrete problems or easily linearizable problems can be examined by being broken down into singular vectors, yielding solution or information matrices which overdimensioning or underdimensioning effects. Thus, spectral methods, which are very widely used in signal processing, represent an advantage, as do the Fourier or wavelet transforms. Probabilistic approaches are used to solve nonlinear problems. The space defined by a model's parameters is often vast, which leads us to use methods for systematic exploration of that space, such as simulated annealing or genetic algorithms. Inverse methods are sensitive to the updating of data with new measurements or pieces of information. Linear and Gaussian problems are dealt with by the "stochastic generalized inverse", which facilitates the introduction of the notion of *a priori* into the model.

14.4. Latent Semantic Analysis

Latent semantic analysis (LSA) is a statistical technique intended to estimate the hidden structure of content in documents [DEE 90]. LSA uses a fairly old technique drawn from linear algebra: singular value decomposition. This decomposition is able to uncover the most meaningful co-occurrences of terms. If we are dealing with very large quantity of data, it is possible to use data sampling techniques to generate manageable sets of relevant documents [WEI 99; WEI 05; WEI 10]. This approach is widely used to reduce the number of variables to a few which capture the properties of the data. This is especially advantageous when thousands of variables are common. Thus, we begin with the matrix of terms A, wherein each row contains the count of instances of a particular word in the document. Main component analysis is a very familiar approach in multivariate statistical analysis [HAS 01]. It begins with the correlation matrix $A'A$ of all the variables and uses singular value analysis to determine the most important singular vectors based on the correlation matrix. Finally, LSA is a technique which is popular in text mining, but which yields the same results are main component analysis [THI 88]. A variety of comparable techniques have been described under the denomination of factorial analysis. The factors are considered linear combinations of descriptive variables, which account for a maximum proportion of the variation in the dataset. In subsequent analyses, such as a classification, the factors may be used instead of the original variables without too great a loss in terms of expressive power. The similarity of documents in terms of main components can be interpreted as topical similarity and can be used to look for similar documents, or for documents which correspond to a specific request. Using this approach, we can estimate a degree of similarity between documents, even if they do not have any words in common [LAN 97]. If different words have a strong correlation to the same factor, this often indicates similarity of meaning: synonymy. On the other hand, the same word may have substantial correlations with two or more factors, which indicates the existence of different meanings for the same word: this is polysemy. One objection that may be leveled at LSA is that it is based on a correlation matrix, and implicitly minimizes the squared distances. For enumeration in text mining, probabilistic LSA, or PLSA, appears more appropriate [HOF 01]. This technique assumes the existence of a non-observable discrete variable z, a latent factor, which can assume values between 1 and m. The model works on the assumption that for each word w_{ij} in a document d_i, a value for the latent factor is generated in accordance with a specific distribution of the document $p(z|d_i)$. Depending on the value of the latent factor, the word w_{ij} is then generated in accordance with the specific distribution of the factor. The probabilities are estimated iteratively using the Expectation Maximization (EM) algorithm which was introduced by Dempster *et al.* [DEM 77]. PLSA yields better linguistic intelligibility and compatibility with well-corroborated linguistic models [CHI 93] concerning the distributions of word frequencies. This makes it possible to perform a conceptual search where synonyms also indicate a relevant target for a request, and documents in which a word appears with different meanings are excluded.

14.5. Iterative construction of sub-corpora

Very early on, information access systems – particularly in document retrieval – began to integrate functionalities associated with the users' behavior, because of the sometimes-ambiguous intentions of a user and also the complexity of the language. This resulted in query reformulation techniques. If we imagine that a query is generalized to an approach, we can instantly see that the user will chop and change, to-ing and fro-ing between modalities offered by a graphical interface and iterative accesses to a corpus, either to verify a piece of information "*in situ*", in the context of access to a document by an exploratory approach, or to gradually refine a query which was initially wrongly formulated. Here, we find ourselves in a circuit of serendipity far more than data-based verification. Involving a user in the loop of the process ensures validation based on utility – an extrinsic utility, i.e. originating beyond the bounds of the algorithm's properties. The advantage of involving a user in the approach is illustrated by the fact that the designer of an information-extraction algorithm invites users to integrate his/her means of computation into a knowledge-extraction approach; remember that knowledge results from interpreted information, and is therefore linked to a situation and to actors in a social environment. A document which is useful for one approach will not be useful for another; the user gives his/her judgment by adjustment of the parameters during the process.

14.6. Ordering approaches or ranking method

Frequentist approaches may be qualified as "chopper" methods. The capture a strong signal expressed by a minority of elements which occur most commonly. The reputed laws of textual statistics have told us this since the very advent of modern linguistics. Nevertheless, the information channeled by simple and frequent elements enjoys a certain consensus or appropriation of a concept on a certain scale. To begin with, and with no knowledge of a subject, ranking of frequent terms provides an interesting reading. On the other hand, the extraction of frequent elements can have a part to play in the search for key concepts and contribute to the acquisition of a taxinomy for a domain. The frequency may be normalized by the number of documents, and by ranking, different corpora or parts of corpora (sub-corpora) can be compared by classic inferential tests (e.g. Kolmogorov, χ^2). The overall frequency is a numerical factor which facilitates preliminary ranking. More sophisticated indicators are based on the computation of a relative weight. For instance, TF–IDF or the marginal (sum of frequencies) on a set of sub-corpora may be coupled with a simple global enumeration. Language is a standardized representation of exchanges between social actors dependent on elements acquired and in the process of acquisition, on the evolution of culture and on contingent economic factors. Consequently, taking account of the diachrony can modulate the reading of global rankings. The computation and ranking of new, lost and invariant elements provides content information about the value of the ranked elements. The TreeRank method facilitates ordering in a binary tree structure.

14.7. Use of ontology

The notion of ontology was presented in Chapter 8. We must recontextualize it as a technique connected to text mining, which can guide the mining approach, i.e. the acquisition of an ontology, or support the mining process as a intermediary means of structuring. It is not a method typically used in text mining, because we can conceive of ontologies founded on any structured database. However, there is a strong connection with the textual nature of the information, in that the vocabulary and concepts, the relations and the instances of them are in the form of an agreed vocabulary, specialized and/or general. The OWL language is universally used to format an ontology – examples are to be found in NASA's ontology at CalTech on climate change: SWEET 2.0 (Semantic Web for Earth and Environmental Terminology). This ontology covers astronomy, the atmosphere, biology, chemistry, the climate, physics, earth sciences, the cosmos, geography, space, time, oceanography, hydrology and geology; hence, it includes 6,000 concepts and 200 taxinomies. Another example is GO (Gene Ontology), which is intended to describe all biomolecular mechanisms of the living world. It covers the names of 60,000 species with 16,000 additional technical terms. In a neighboring domain, the Unified Medical Language System (UMLS) has 100 taxinomies, 5 million terms and 16 million relations, 135 semantic types and 54 types of relations, with the goal of describing the biomedical sciences. While there appears to be consensus as to the definition of the term "ontology" [MUS 92; CHA 00; IKS 02], its use in the real world is far less clear-cut. From a general point of view, an ontology serves to uniformize (standardize) the use of a language, or at least disambiguate a vocabulary, and therefore must favor communication between the actors of a project. In fact, although this point often falls by the wayside in discussions of the topic, above all an ontology is a formidable tool to force the actors on a project to structure their information, even if that is the extent of its role. In the semantic Web and Artificial Intelligence community, it is also frequently used to index documents in that it is directly inspired by the thesauruses of which documentalists make abundant use in their classification. Figure 14.1 illustrates the uses of GO.

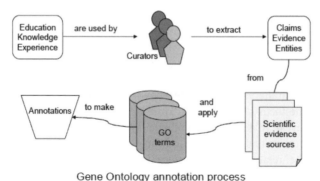

Gene Ontology annotation process

GO *Bibliography* 'use' categories and article quantities

Category	Articles
Use of GO in gene expression studies	857
Use of GO in clinical applications	485
Use of GO in biological databases	164
Use of GO in proteomics studies	125
Use of GO in network modeling and analysis	122
Use of GO in comparative genomics and evolutionary analysis	109
Use of GO in data or text mining	98
Use of GO to support predictions	59

Figure 14.1. *Uses of Gene Ontology (GO). Left: cycle of enrichment of GO; Right: quantity of articles per use category [MAC 08]*

14.8. Interdisciplinary techniques

Generic data-mining techniques find their natural place in text mining. In particular, this is due to the fact that – on the one hand – textual data can be transformed into more universal representations, such as a vector space in which algebraic and analytical tools are applicable, and – on the other hand – a great many research projects have shown that the adoption of such universal representations yields a good performance in terms of certain evaluation criteria.

14.9. Information visualization techniques

Visualization techniques are typically exploratory approaches to data [BER 67; BOR 97; BÖR 03; FRI 07]; they are related to knowledge extraction techniques.

They cannot explicitly be qualified as knowledge extraction methods, in that the visualization algorithm performs a layout on a two-dimensional space for an interactive navigation. It is a change in the means of representation. Thus, visualization contributes to the representation of knowledge which is available prior to the acquisition or extraction of knowledge from the documents. An entire chapter could be devoted to the visualization of knowledge, but to do so would fall outside of our remit – the focus of which is on knowledge extraction. A new representation may help to reveal relations (in synthetic form) which were hitherto rendered invisible by the mass and mixture of information. "Information organization" will help valorize the relations and therefore facilitate exploration-based knowledge extraction. In that sense, it is important to mention knowledge visualization as an effective means of navigating through the information, when used in conjunction with a specific knowledge extraction process. Thereby, we are able to link analysis of the structures of the data and visual metaphors. Tufte [TUF 01] holds that visualization of data requires that we choose a dataset with a genuine value for a researcher or an artist analyzing that dataset to find significant means of representing it, creating a structure for those data, exploring them, analyzing regularities, expressing the analysis by way of an aesthetic representation, refining that representation in order to better communicate, and creating a means of manipulating the data. In Tufte's view, the data express their own structures. Information visualization techniques are highly varied and aspire to encapsulate datasets by way of an interpretation which affords them the status of pieces of knowledge. The current challenge for visualization is the visualization of knowledge on subjects for which a certain boundary can be drawn (see Chapter 15).

14.10. The k-means technique

The technique of k-means clustering is an unsupervised method which aims to produce classes or clusters in the form of a partition of n observations in k clusters in which each observation belongs to the cluster with the closest mean (average). Given a set of observations (x_1, x_2, ..., x_n), where each observation is a real vector of dimension d, the k-means clustering technique aims to create a distribution of n observations into k sets ($k \leq n$) $S = \{S_1, S_2, ..., S_k\}$, such that it minimizes the sum of the intra-cluster squares:

$$\arg min \sum_{i=1}^{k} \sum_{x_j \in S_i} \left\| x_j - m_i \right\|^2 \qquad [14.1]$$

The most common algorithm uses an iterative refinement technique. Given an initial set of k-means $m_1^{(1)}, ..., m_k^{(t)}$, the algorithm performs two steps alternately.

The k-means clustering algorithm:

1: Assignment step: Assign each observation to the cluster with the closest mean (i.e. partition the observations according to the Voronoi diagram generated by the means).

$$S_i^{(t)} = \{x_p : \|x_p - m_i^{(t)}\| \le \|x_p - m_j^{(t)}\| \forall 1 \le j \le k\}$$

where each x_p goes into exactly one $S_i^{(t)}$, even if it could go in two of them.

2: Update step: Calculate the new means to be the centroid of the observations in the cluster.

$$m_i^{(t+1)} = \frac{1}{|S_i^{(t)}|} \sum_{x_j \in S_i^{(t)}} x_j$$

The algorithm is supposed to converge when the assignments no longer change.

14.11. Naive Bayes classifier technique

Bayesian probabilistic classifiers are supervised classifiers. They are based on the firm hypothesis that the words in a document d_i have been generated by a probabilistic mechanism. For instance, for classification, only the influence of the underlying class such as sport or politics is worthy of interest. Thus, we suppose that the class $c(d_i)$ of a document determines the probability $p(w_1, ..., w_N| c(d_i))$ of its lexical constituents. Now we can use Bayes' formula which determines the probability of considering a class if the words $w_1, ..., w_N$ in a document are known:

$$p(c_m|w_1, ..., w_N) = \frac{p(w_1, ..., w_N|c_m)p(c_m)}{\sum_{i=1}^k p(w_1, ..., w_N|c_i)p(c_i)} \qquad [14.2]$$

It should be noted that documents can belong to several different k classes. The *a priori* probability $p(c_m)$ denotes the probability that a given document will belong to a certain class c_m before its words are known. It frequently occurs that the *a priori* probability distribution across all the classes is uniform. The probability on the left-hand side of equation [14.2] is the desired *a posteriori* probability that the document with the words $w_1, ..., w_N$ will belong to the class c_m. The goal is to assign the class with the highest probability score to a given document. For document classification, it transpires that the specific order of the words in a document is not important. Furthermore, we may imagine that for the documents in a given class, a word appears in the document independently of the other words. This gives us a simplified formula for the probability of a word's presence:

$$p(w_1, \ldots, w_N | c_m) = \prod_{i=1}^{N} p(w_i | c_m)$$ [14.3]

Together, equations [14.2] and [14.3] define a naive Bayes classifier. Simplifications of this sort are necessary because thousands of words appear in a corpus. The naive Bayesian classifier involves training, which simply requires estimating the probabilities of the words $p(w_n | c_m)$ in each class based on their relative frequency in the training classes. In the classification step, the estimated probabilities are used to classify a new instance, i.e. a new document, in accordance with Bayes' rule. Although this model is not very realistic, it yields excellent results for classification [DUM 98; JOA 98; TUR 02], and the model can be extended to other processing operations [LEW 98; SEB 02].

14.12. The k-nearest neighbors (KNN) technique

The nearest neighbors algorithm is used both as a supervised and unsupervised technique, by case matching between them or with an example specified by an expert in the domain. A simple example of the nearest neighbors method can be formulated thus: given a set $X = \{x_1, x_2, x_3, \ldots x_m\}$ of vectors composed of n attributes with binary values, for each pair (x_i, x_j), we create a vector v_{ij} of length n by comparing the values of each corresponding attribute a_k of the n pairs (x_{ik}, x_{jk}), assigning a value of 1 for each a_k which corresponds and of 0 if it does not. Thus, the sum of the values v_{ij} calculates the score of the degree of correspondence. The pairs (x_i, x_j) with the highest score are the nearest neighbors. In more complex nearest neighbor methods, the attributes may be weighted to reflect the degree of importance. Expertise in the domain is needed to select the salient attributes, calculate the weights for these attributes and select a distance or a measure of similarity. Nearest-neighbor approaches have been used for text classification [COS 93). The KNN method gets around approaches intended to construct an explicit model for different classes: we can select training documents which are similar to a test document. Consequently the class of the test document is deduced from the class labels of the "similar" training documents. The approach gets its name from the number k of documents which are considered similar. As mentioned above, there are many similarity measurements used for knowledge extraction. One very widely used measurement is the cosine measure. If w_{in} is the number of occurrences of the nth word in a document d_i, the measure of similarity of the cosine between the documents d_i and d_j is defined by:

$$S(d_i, d_j) = \left. \sum_{n=1}^{N} w_{in} w_{jn} \middle/ \sqrt{\sum_{n=1}^{N} w_{in}^2 \sum_{n=1}^{N} w_{jn}^2} \right.$$ [14.4]

Other measurements are discussed in [BAE 99]. In order to decide whether a document d_i belongs to the class c_m, the similarity $S(d_i, d_j)$ of all the documents d_j in the learning set is calculated. The k most similar training documents (nearest neighbors) are selected. The proportion of neighbors with the same class can be taken as an estimator of the probability of a document belonging to that class. If the highest proportion is above a certain threshold then the corresponding class is assigned to document d_i. The threshold, just like the optimal number k of neighbors, can be estimated from additional training data by cross validation. Nearest neighbor classification is a non-parametric method, and it has been demonstrate that for large sets, the rate of error of a 1-NN classifier is no greater than twice the optimal error rate [HAS 01]. Many research projects have shown that nearest neighbor methods have very good performances in practice [JOA 98b; YAN 99]. The drawback to them is the computational effort required during classification, for which the similarity of a document in relation to all the others in a training set has to be determined [SEB 91].

14.13. Hierarchical clustering technique

Hierarchical classification is an unsupervised technique [SOK 63]. It does not specify the number of clusters to be identified and classes the elements defined by a vector space, the dimensions of which are the attributes (e.g. the elements of a language model). The technique creates clusters in an iterative fashion by fusing (agglomerative clustering) or separating (divisive clustering) clusters computed in the previous phase. The process of hierarchical clustering leads to the creation of a dendrogram, which is the tree of clusters, so as to visualize the interrelations between partitions (see Figure 14.2). It enables us to adjust the granularity of the clustering in accordance with the requirements. The process begins by placing each variable in its proper cluster and calculating similarity values for all possible pairs of clusters. One very common distance between two points in space (one point being an observation of the vector representing a cluster) is the Euclidean distance:

$$d(x_1, x_2) = \sqrt{\sum_{i=1}^{N} (x_{1i} - x_{2i})^2} \qquad [14.5]$$

The two most similar clusters will then be combined and the process will be repeated until a finite number of clusters is formed or the similarity between two clusters does not exceed a certain threshold. The similarity between two elements is not the same as the similarity between two clusters of elements. In fact, there are a number of ways to calculate the similarity between two clusters.

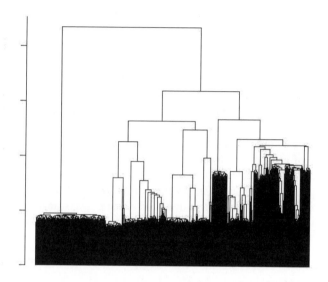

Figure 14.2. *Clustering of 2,000 terms using the software package hclusterpar with a Euclidean distance (amap library in R)*

We can measure the distance between the elements of each cluster which are nearest (simple link) or also the most distant (complete link) from the outside, and finally we can calculate the average similarity of the group (average link) between all the pairs of elements of the two clusters; most works highlight this last link as being the most precise approach [ASS 97].

14.14. Density-based clustering techniques

Model-based clustering assumes that the classes are generated according to a statistical model. For instance, for discrete distributions of textual documents, multinomial distributions are fairly appropriate. This enables us, using these statistical techniques, to estimate the most probable clustering and the appropriacy of classes [NIG 99]. The measure of similarity is implicitly defined by the distributional model. If there is no statistical model, it is difficult to determine the optimal number and the validity of the classes. In this register, we often find mixed models.

$$P(x) = \sum_{\alpha} P(\alpha)P(x|\alpha) \qquad\qquad [14.6]$$

This enables us to approximate any continuous distribution and explain an observation as emanating from several sources and from several points of view. If x_i is the number of occurrences of the word i, x_i^d the number of occurrences of the word i in the document d whose length is l_d and M is the size of the vocabulary, we can define the *burstiness*, which is a behavior of words which tend to appear in packets or bursts. Once these words have been found, there is a greater chance of finding them again. Church and Gale [CHU 95] propose the following definition for burstiness:

$$B_P(x) = \frac{E_P[x_i]}{P(x_i \geq 1)}$$

[14.7]

Elkan [ELK 06] proposes a measure of burstiness based on a Dirichlet Compound Multinomial (DCM) model and an exponential DCM (EDCM) model:

$$P(x_i^d|\beta) \approx \frac{\Gamma(s - \beta_i + l_d - x_i^d)}{\Gamma(s - \beta_i)} \frac{\beta_i}{x_i^d}$$

[14.8]

The coefficients $\beta_i(1 \leq i \leq M)$ are the parameters of the model with $s = \sum_{i:x_i^d \geq 1} \beta_i$. Density-based models evolve toward simple models, whose estimation of parameters is direct and in accordance with empirical properties such as burstiness. The EM (Expectation Maximization) algorithm put forward by [DEM 77] is able to estimate parameters based on data. We recall the following highly advantageous algorithm.

We observe n variables $X = (X_1, \cdots, X_n)$, independent and identically distributed in accordance with $f(x|\theta)$. Maximization of the likelihood $L(\theta|x)$ enables us to estimate the parameter θ:

$$\theta^* = \arg\max_\theta L(\theta|x) = \prod_{i=1}^{n} f(X_i|\theta)$$

[14.9]

We note the expectation of the log-likelihood, stressing the dependency in θ_0 and at the sample x:

$$Q(\theta|\theta_0, x) = \mathbf{E}[\log L(\theta|x) \mid \theta_0, x]$$

[14.10]

When using the EM principle, we construct a series of estimators $\hat{\theta}_{(j)} = 1, 2, \cdots$, by iteration of the expectation and maximization stages:

$$Q(\hat{\theta}_{(j)}|\hat{\theta}_{(j-1)}, x) = \max_\theta Q(\theta|\hat{\theta}_{(j-1)}, x)$$

[14.11]

EM algorithm

1: Iterate in m

2: Stage E calculate $Q\left(\theta|\hat{\theta}_{(m)},x\right) = E\left[\log\ L(\theta|x)\ |\ \hat{\theta}_{(m)},x\right]$

3: Stage M maximize $Q\left(\theta|\hat{\theta}_{(m)},x\right)$ *in* θ and take

4: $\hat{\theta}_{(m+1)} = arg\ max_{\theta}\ Q\left(\theta|\hat{\theta}_{(m)},x\right)$

5: such that a fixed point of Q is not obtained

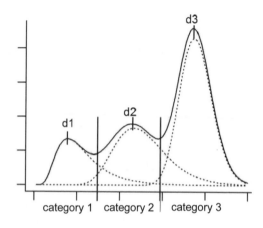

Figure 14.3. *Hypothetical case of a mixture of three densities*

If we suppose that the overall density stems from a mixture of Gaussians (MoG) as Figure 14.3 shows, this means that:

$$f(x) = \sum_{i=1}^{K} p_i\ \varphi(x, m_i, S_i) = max_{\theta}\ Q(\theta|\hat{\theta}_{(j-1)}, x) \qquad [14.12]$$

We shall then estimate the parameters (p_i, m_i, S_i), by maximizing the likelihood at random. In order to do so, we begin with a number of Gaussians K decided upon *a priori*, and then look for a local maximum using first-order null gradient conditions:

$$\begin{cases} p_i = \dfrac{1}{N}\displaystyle\sum_{k=1}^{N} P(C_i|x_k) \\ m_i = E(x|C_i) \\ S_i = V(x|C_i) \end{cases} where \begin{cases} P(C_i|x_k) & probability\ of\ being\ in\ the\ Gaussian\ i,\ knowing\ x_k \\ E(x|C_i) & conditional\ expectation\ of\ x,\ knowing\ the\ Gaussian\ i \\ S_i=V(x|C_i) & conditional\ variance\ of\ x,\ knowing\ the\ Gaussian\ i \end{cases}$$

$$[14.13]$$

We proceed iteratively by performing:

$$\begin{cases} p_i(t+1) = \dfrac{1}{N}\sum_{k=1}^{N} P(C_i|x_k)(t) \\ m_i(t+1) = E(x|C_i)(t) \\ S_i(t+1) = V(x|C_i)(t) \end{cases}$$

[14.14]

Thus, we get relatively "smooth" functions, and in particular, we know what we will obtain at most K modes for the estimated density. It is tricky to choose an optimal number of Gaussians; we can consider K to be the maximal number of classes to be observed.

14.15. Conditional fields

Conditional fields are probabilistic formal frameworks to annotate and segment sequential data, based on a conditional approach. We find the formalism of the conditional random field (CRF) [LAF 01]. Let $G = (V, E)$ be a graph such that $Y = (Y_v)_{v \in V}$; thus Y is indexed by the vertices of G. Thus, (X, Y) is a conditional random field if, when it is conditioned on X, the random variables Y_v obey the Markov property in relation to the graph:

$$p(Y_v|X, Y_w, w \neq v) = p(Y_v|X, Y_w, w \sim v)$$

[14.15]

where $w \sim v$ means that w and v are neighbors in G. This means that a CRF is an undirected graphical model whose nodes can be divided exactly into two disjoint sets, X and Y – respectively the observed variables and the output variables; the conditional distribution $P(Y|X)$ is thus modeled. For general graphs, the problem of exact inference in the CRFs is intractable. However, by approximation, we can use algebraic matrix calculus. For a CRF structured chain in which a sequence of labels is augmented by start and end states, y_0 and y_{n+1} respectively, with the appropriate labels, the probability $p(y|x, \lambda)$ of having a sequence of labels y given an observation sequence x can be efficiently calculated using matrices. Let U be the alphabet from which the labels are drawn, and y and y' labels defined from that alphabet, we define a set of $n+1$ matrices $\{M_i(x)|i=1,\ldots,n+1\}$, where each $M_i(x)$ is a $|U \times U|$ matrix with elements of the form:

$$M_i(y', y|x) = \exp\left(\sum_j \lambda_j f_j(y', y, x, i)\right)$$

[14.16]

The non-normalized probability of the sequence of labels y, in view of the observation sequence x, can be written as the product of the appropriate elements of the $n+1$ matrices for each sequence pair:

$$p(y|x, \lambda) = \frac{1}{Z(x)} \prod_{i=1}^{n+1} M_i(y_{i-1}, y_i | x) \qquad [14.17]$$

Similarly, the normalization factor $Z(x)$ for the observation sequence x can be calculated from the set of matrices $M_i(x)$ using closed semirings, a algebraic structure which gives us a general framework for solving path problems in graphs. $Z(x)$ is given by the input (start, end) of the product of all the $n+1$ matrices $M_i(x)$:

$$Z(x) = \left[\prod_{i=1}^{n+1} M_i(x) \right]_{start,\ end} \qquad [14.18]$$

We can compare CRF to a Markovian random field and a conditional belief field [SHA 76].

A family of probabilistic or stochastic models is commonly used to characterize near-neighborhood dependencies. These are hidden Markov models (HMMs). A HMM is able to find sequence correspondences in data in the form of a Markov chain wherein the transitions between the states depend on the previous two states (2nd-order model). One advantage of this method is the existence of an unsupervised learning algorithm (the EM algorithm), which enables us to estimate the parameters of the Markov model from a corpus and an initial model. The resulting Markov model is able to segment each sequence of data into stationary or transient parts. Markov models have been widely used to implement automatons to perform syntactic labeling: in this case, finite state automatons – 1st-order HMMs – functioning in accordance with a supervised mode on an annotated database.

14.16. Nonlinear regression and artificial neural networks

Nonlinear regression algorithms, just like feed-forward artificial neural networks, adaptive spline methods and continued projection methods are used to carry out classifications and clustering. Neural networks implicitly determine rules for which the classes are not defined conventionally – i.e. they do not conform to the principle of the excluded third (or excluded middle), or are poorly defined and therefore cannot be reduced into linear classification [MAC 43; ROS 58; AND 94; TWE 96; CAR 97; TOW 98].

A neural network is designed based on layers of neural units in accordance with varied network typologies (number of units, layers, connections, intensity of the connections and methods of information propagation). One objection to the use of neural networks is that the results often depend on the designers who built the model. This is due to the fact that the model, the topology and the weights can change from one implementation to another for the same data.

There is also a "black box" syndrome apparent in neural networks because there is little semantic gain of introspection of the final network. Unsupervised neural networks require little in terms of *a priori* investment by an expert in the field; however, the network is used to uncover categories based on correlations in the data. Unsupervised learning, using a variant of the k-means clustering algorithm, has been performed with textual data by way of the self-organizing map (SOM) method [MER 94].

14.17. Models of multi-agent systems (MASs)

Chapter 9 showed us the capacity of computational models to deal with the notion of belief and motivation – multi-agent systems belong to this category. There are many forms for managing interaction between agents. The best-known is the "blackboard" approach, where the configuration of the agents is limited and the transactions between the agents are centralized. Another family is that of stochastic systems [SCH 02], which take account of a large number of agents without holistic regulation. An unpublished work shows that the clustering around a target object in a set of associations of objects can determine certain similarities in specific data. This is particularly so in two cases: gene-gene relations and term-term relations, which gives us a common principle of organization for cognition, defined by random and deterministic effects. A Brownian agent model provides a solid theoretical framework, combining determinism and stochasticity of self-organization converging over time. The time, order and stochasticity are important parameters of the natural systems of the real world, in which the complexity stems from the fact that the system is composed of a large number of components, and cannot be accounted for by traditional functional modeling. This theoretical framework is also, implicitly, the nucleus of a pragmatic implementation as a large-scale multi-agent system, ensuring the required observation of the dynamic and the convergence of a relational model. The model is, itself, defined by a set of rules and populations of agents.

This framework has been adopted to develop an aggregative model of the dynamics of a set of genes (genetic network) and that of a set of terms (semantic network). The set of rules is defined by a set of features of interaction and a matrix of relations between the populations of agents (an agent is a term or a gene).

Knowledge about the relations is gained by extracting knowledge from an extensive body of literature. It can be shown that by choosing a target population, its neighborhood is not random but is consistent with reality, both in the vicinity of a gene and in the vicinity of a term, with the same style of self-organization (i.e. contextual aggregation). By analogy, we can assume that the way in which the terms are aggregated could be inspired by the way in which genes self-organize. Thus, the semantic nature of language is not purely deterministic but also has a stochastic origin which is not guided by intrinsic organization. Such a principle may not be surprising, when we know that any and every speaker is, first and foremost, a biological entity.

14.18. Co-clustering models

Recently, co-clustering has become an attractive tool for data exploration, which is able to analyze dual data connecting two entities. Almost all methods create divisions, so the variables in the rows and columns of a matrix may belong to a single cluster. Many co-clustering methods [HAR 72], i.e. simultaneous clustering of the rows and columns of a data matrix, can offer a better performance in terms of uncovering a structure, in view of the relations between two entities. Dhillon *et al.* [DHI 03] applied probabilistic co-clustering to document exploration, and it has been applied in other fields such as bioinformatics and recommendation systems. The most widely-used techniques are the latent block model (LBM), the technique based on a Kullback-Leibler distance, generalized Bregman co-clustering and Bayesian co-clustering. The hypothesis of partition is often restrictive because the objects in real-world data typically belong to several clusters, sometimes to varying degrees.

The LBM approach was described by Govaert and Nadif [GOV 03]. LBM was developed as an intuitive extension of a finite mixture model used in model-based clustering [FRA 02] to perform clustering of the objects and attributes. The probabilistic model is considered in a general context, originally based on a CEM (classification-expectation-maximization) algorithm. Suppose we wish to "re-order" the rows of a joint distribution p such that all the rows which match cluster x_1 are displayed first, followed by all the rows which correspond to x_2, and so on. Similarly, we re-order the columns of the joint distribution p such that all the columns corresponding to cluster y_1 are displayed first, followed by all those corresponding to cluster y_2, and so on. This row/column reordering has the effect of dividing the distribution p in small two-dimensional blocks. Such a block is called a co-cluster (see Figure 14.4).

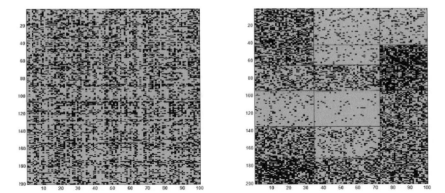

Figure 14.4. *Re-organization of the data matrix. Left: initial data; Right: data blocks*

14.19. Dependency models

Dependency models can be divided into two categories in accordance with the nature of the dependencies which are modeled. Sequential dependency modeling analyzes temporal information encoded in the data in order to detect regularities in the variation over time. Conversely, static dependency models explore relations between the data, independently of the temporal order. Dependency models can also be looked at from the point of view of the models which are considered. In structural dependency models, the objective is to discover unknown dependencies which exist in the data. These affinities can be expressed by qualitative rules such as "A causes B," or by quantitative summaries such as "80% of documents which contain A and B also contain item C". Quantitative dependency modeling, for its part, supposes that a specific model exists and seeks to estimate the parameters of that dependency relation. Regression is an example of a quantitative dependency modeling technique.

14.20. Decision tree technique

Decision trees are a case of linear regression, assuming univariate and multivariate variables with symbolic or numerical values [QUI 86]. Decision trees are supervised classifiers which rely on a set of rules (the branches of the tree), applied sequentially and leading to a decision. They are induced by observing a training process, initiated by an explicit training dataset. The algorithm is based on a "divide and conquer"-type strategy: for a set of training documents M with labeled documents, the word or term w_i is selected to predict the category of documents as best it can. Thus, M is divided into two subsets: the subset M_i+ with the documents where w_i is to be found, and the subset M_i- containing the documents without w_i. This procedure is recursively applied to $Mi+$ and $Mi-$. The procedure stops if all the documents in a subset belong to the same class c_j, generating a tree of rules with assignment to the real classes of the leaves of the tree. The decision tree is a traditional tool for knowledge extraction [MIT 97]. The number of leaves characterizes the complexity of the model. Using cross validation, we can establish a pruning procedure, whilst preserving the quality of the model. The technique is quick and applies to a large number of variables and an extensive training set. In text mining, however, this model has the disadvantage of producing a final decision which depends only on a relatively small number of terms. A significant improvement is to be gained by computing a boosted decision tree. This leads us to determine a set of complementary decision trees, constructed and combined in such a way that the overall error is minimized. The induction of a decision tree is fairly direct, but the results will only be useful if available variables provide a significant basis for categorization. In order to reduce the computational complexity, heuristics are often applied to ensure a linear selection of the properties which implicitly exclude a vast majority of potential rules. This approach may leave out interesting rules which have not been discovered because of decisions implemented earlier in the process, preventing other rules from being discovered at a later stage. The extraction of rules using decision trees may consolidate the validation of a hypothesis. Schapire and Singer [SCH 00] even used very simple decision trees containing only one rule, and obtained impressive results.

14.21. The Support Vector Machine (SVM) technique

The SVM technique is a supervised classification method which produces surprising results in terms of robustness and precision for a text classification task [JOA 98A; DUM 98; DRU 99; LEO 02]. As with other supervised learning methods, an SVM operates in two phases: training and classification, where an element is classified based on the decision boundaries of the previously-acquired model.

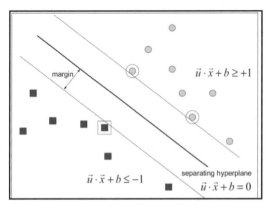

Figure 14.5. *Decision hyperplane separating two classes*
(squares: y = -1 and circles: y = +1)

The SVM algorithm attempts to maximize the margin around a hyperplane which separates a positive class from a negative class (see Figure 14.5). The computation of the margin is comparable to a linear regression such as the monolayer perceptron, for which the boundary of the margin is determined by particular points: the bounded points shown in Figure 14.5, called support vectors. These vectors enable us to find the parameters of the separators. A simple SVM can only separate two classes: a positive class c_1 (indicated by $y = +1$) and a negative class c_2 (indicated by $y = -1$). The SVM model is supposed to find a class separated by a hyperplane (a plane in three dimensions or a straight line in two dimensions) [VAP 98; JOA 02]. The result is the hyperplane defined by a normal vector $\vec{u}$ and the ordinate b. During the classification phase, a vector constituted by frequencies of terms in a document is estimated to belong to a class:

$$\hat{y} = \text{sgn}(\vec{u}.\vec{x_1} + b) \tag{14.19}$$

where $\vec{x_1}$ is the vector of frequencies of terms which represents the document d_i. The SVM model can be adjusted for different geometries in attributes space by replacing the scalar product with a kernel function $K(x_i, x_j)$. It has been observed that in the case of textual data, the choice of the kernel function has a fairly minimal impact on the precision of the classification. Kernels which can manage a large space show better results in terms of precision and recall, but they are subject to overlearning [LEO 02]. The most interesting property of SVMs is that the learning is independent of the dimensions of the input space. An SVM model looks for a hyperplane which is defined in terms of points of the data which touch the margin – the support vectors – rather than the coordinates of the input space. This offers a good generalization, even when dealing with a large number of attributes, and makes SVM a good model for classification of textual elements.

A fast and efficient unsupervised variant has been established: support vector clustering (SVC). This method creates clusters by making the entire dataset into a hypersphere which, when it is projected into two-dimensional space, is flattened into various clusters, much like a 3D orange peel which we attempt to flatten onto a 2D table, and which tears into small pieces.

Using a grid-based technique and a KNN approach, we can extract the clusters in quasi-linear time. The package *svcR* available for the software platform R offers an implementation of SVC with a geometric hashing approach, which can be applied to the discovery of lexical regularities. A Jaccard kernel is used. Jaccard's similarity index [JAC 01] is interesting to test the similarity between two objects when we only know their attributes rather than all the attributes (this global set of attributes is often extremely extensive). Its expression is as follows, if we posit that the string s_1

is composed of the forms $s_{10}, ..., s_{1m}$ and the string s_2 is composed of the forms $s_{20},..., s_{2k}$:

$$J_{12} = J(s_1, s_2) = \frac{|\{s_{10}, ..., s_{1m}\} \cap \{s_{20}, ..., s_{2k}\}|}{|\{s_{10}, ..., s_{1m}\} \cup \{s_{20}, ..., s_{2k}\}|} \qquad [14.20]$$

Thus, we define a Jaccard-Radial base kernel in accordance with a vector defined with the Jaccard index (the data matrix is symmetrical):

$$JRB(x_1, x_2) = e^{-q \cdot \left\| \Sigma_{i=1}^{N}(J_{1i}-J_{2i}) \right\|^2} \qquad [14.21]$$

Figure 14.6 shows an illustration of clustering on a dataset comprising 1893 terms (nominal groups) manually extracted from an annotation of 1471 documents (5730 sentences) in the PubMed database. The nominal groups describe seven stages of the biological development of bacterial sporulation.

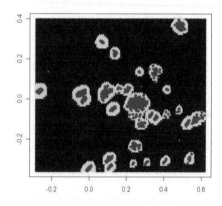

Figure 14.6. *Clustering with SVC geometric hashing*

14.22. Set of frequent items

Sequence mining is a subject which has been abundantly discussed in the field of knowledge extraction, aimed at identifying statistically pertinent regularities in examples of data whose values are provided by sequences. It is generally assumed that the values are discrete, and in a related point, temporal series mining is similar to that aspiration. Sequence mining is a particular case of structured data mining. We can cite many traditional computational problems closely related to the subject. This also involves the construction of effective databases and indices for sequential information, the extraction of frequently-occurring regularities, the comparison of sequences for similarity and the restoration of missing elements in the sequence. In principle, sequence mining problems can be classed as character string mining, the argument of which is founded on string processing algorithms, and mines the set of items which is based on learning of rules of association. Key algorithms for sequence mining include:

– Repetition-based problems. The methods here relate to operations on simple sequences, and are based on exact string matching or approximate matching to look for repetitions of maximum length or fixed length, look for unique sub-sequences and missing sub-sequences. The method of extraction of repeating segments to extract nominal groups is based on this type of algorithm.

– Alignment problems. These are concerned with comparisons between strings by aligning one or more sequences at first; well-known examples are the algorithms Blast [ALT 90] to compare single sequences with multiple sequences in a database, and Clustal [HIG 88] for multiple alignments. Alignment algorithms may be based on exact or approximate methods, and can be classed into global alignment, semi-global alignment and local alignment.

– Frequent pattern problems. Certain problems in sequence mining relate to the discovery of frequent sets of elements, taking account of the order in which they appear. For instance, we might search for rules of the form "if a {customer buys a car}, he (or she) is driven {to take out an insurance policy} within a week", or, in the context of share prices, "if {Nokia's shares go up and Ericsson's shares go up}, then it arises that {Motorola's shares go up and Samsung's shares go up} within two days". The mining of a series of items has been widely used in applications relating to market studies to reveal regularities between items that co-appear frequently in numerous transactions. For instance, by analyzing the transactions on a consumer's checkout receipts, we can produce rules which read that "if a consumer buys onions and potatoes at the same time, he will likely also buy hamburger meat". The two main techniques which are applied in sequence mining in databases are the Apriori algorithm [AGR 94] and more recently the FP-growth (frequent pattern growth) algorithm [PLA 09].

A significant problem in the extraction of rules of association, and therefore frequent patterns, is that the extraction process generates a very large number of rules [CAR 96]. Thus, it is a difficult task for an analyst to select an interesting rule which involves new units of knowledge. This leads to the process of extraction of rules and frequent patterns to integrate a phase of sorting and evaluation of the rules. The basis for this sorting is the number of documents in which the frequent pattern occurs. The confidence is the proportion of documents in which the items appear together over the overall number of their occurrences. These are the two main indicators which can help to reduce the computation time and the number of rules generated. Workflow and interpretation can draw upon other indicators such as interest, dependency and novelty. The rules, sorted by such indicators or combinations of these indicators, can be presented to an expert in the domain. Sometimes the rules extracted related to aspects which are already known – the rules simply reaffirm this knowledge. In order to claim a genuine discovery, it is important to compare the rules with a reference knowledge space. The use of metarules elaborated on the basis of prior knowledge is necessary and useful at this level of interpretation.

14.23. Genetic algorithms

Genetic algorithms can be used both for classification and discovery of rules. The method is metaphorically linked to the recombinations of DNA. A population of variables, each one representing the solution to a problem, is initially created randomly, or randomly created from a larger population. Variables combine in pairs to create a "progeny" for the next generation. Mutation processes are used to randomly modify the genetic structure of certain members of each generation. Genetic algorithms perform categorization by using supervised learning, training with a dataset and therefore using known correct responses to guide the evolution of the algorithm by way of techniques which mirror natural selection. Genetic methods offer certain advantages over neural networks, because they provide more perspicacity in the decision-making process. Sheth [SHE 94] described an example of the use of a genetic algorithm for document processing.

14.24. Link analysis with a theoretical graph model

A very large number of dependency methods use theoretical graph approaches which structure the data in a representation of causal links or influence diagrams in order to assist static or sequential dependency analyses [CRA 11]. The formalism adopted and the semantics of the links and nodes may vary with the domain, and thus domain-specific knowledge may be required in order to effectively design the graph. Theoretical graph models are generally and easily viewed as a visual representation of dependency between links and nodes. Bayesian networks are probabilistic graphs which represent causal events as nodes (a node is a variable) and factual dependencies as links. Belief in a leaf node is attributed in the system of links in accordance with an *a priori* distribution of root nodes. The most easily computable Bayesian networks are those which are instantiated in acyclical directed graphs. The vertices of the graph correspond to correlated or causal relations which are based on declarative facts instantiated between the nodes. With each node we associate a value corresponding to a belief or a probability in the interval [0,1]. A Bayesian network is evaluated by calculating the conditional values of the nodes of the network based on the inputs applied to the root nodes which do not have entering vertices. Formally, for each node n, we associate a fact e. $P(e)$ is either given by the probabilities (from the root) which are *a priori* independent, or it is derived using Bayes' theorem. Bayes' rule offers a calculable method to model the strength of the belief that an *x* will be a *y*, given the knowledge that we have that *x* may also be a *z*, but the conditions to estimate the *a priori* probabilities restrict the range of Bayesian networks in the context of text mining applications. Freeman *et al.* [FRE 98] describe an interesting case of knowledge discovery by visualizing a social network in the form of a 3D graph. By rotating the image of the network around its center using VRML (Virtual Reality Markup Language), a clustering result was able to be explored. After rotation, a dependency was discovered which could not have been discovered without rotating the network.

14.25. Link analysis without a graph model

With any graph, we can associate an incidence matrix where the intersections between rows and columns represent values of links. Based on that structure, we can analyze the links [BÉD 91; NAG 11]. In the context of the Web, socio-semantic networks (authors, usernames and terms associated with discussion threads or comments) are sources of data to apply link analysis to [AUG 70]. Graph mining and analsysis of social networks is a particularly thriving context in this respect [SCO 00; SCO 03]. For link analysis we can cite algorithms which have become famous and references on the subject. Albert and Barabási [ALB 99] conceived a preferential attachment algorithm which has been used to evaluate the diameter of the Web.

Preferential attachment algorithm

1: M_0 vertices (pages) at time 0

2: At every time step a new vertex (page) is generated with m($\leq M_0$) edges that link the new vertex to m random vertices

3: ...the probability of selecting a vertex for an edge is proportional to its degree

4: ...after t time steps, the network has M_0+t vertices (pages) and mt edges

5: ...the probability that a vertex will have connectivity k follows a power law

Two other approaches developed to exploit links are the HITS (Hyperlink-Induced Topic Search) method (also known as "hubs and authorities") advanced by Kleinberg [KLE 99], and PageRank, used by Google for document retrieval and conceived by Brin and Page [BRI 98]. These two approaches use a singular value decomposition method such as that drawn from main component analysis. This method is calculated on the basis of the link adjacency matrix. The intuition behind the HITS technique relies on the idea that the Web has two natures: having pages with attractive content (weight of authority) and having good concentrators (weight of concentrators). In view of this, the idea of the algorithm is recursiveness, assuming that good concentrator pages (hubs) point to good authoritative pages, and good authoritative pages point to good hubs. The basic idea behind the PageRank algorithm, for its part, is to calculate the unique vectors of the adjacency matrix. Each page is given a value which corresponds to the significance of the node in the network. The algorithm can be efficiently computed using an iterative procedure. Nodes with a similar set of links (the same set of inbound and outbound links) will be able to represent the same category. Blondel *et al.* [BLO 04] use this technique to identify synonyms in documents by constructing a graph of lexical tokens using a dictionary. Only the linked words are considered as potential candidates for synonymy: two words are considered to be synonyms when one appears in the definition of the other.

14.26. Quality of a model

The quality of a model relates to the utility factor which we find using the exploration approach. The question is how to rationalize the performance of such an approach. Is it conceivable, and if so, how? There are many criteria traditionally used to measure the quality of a model:

– rapidity in creating it;

– rapidity in using it;

– comprehensibility for a user;

– good performances;

– reliability of the model;

– degradation of the performances over time;

– easy evolution.

There are three relatively universal criteria to estimate the quality of the result of a model: its precision (similar to specificity), its recall (also known as sensitivity) and the F-score. For our purposes, we of course have to begin with a "gold standard". Based on the gold standard and the results, we evaluate a series of parameters to establish a confusion matrix (contingency table) which combines judgment and result. The parameters are as follows:

– TP (true positives): predicted positives which are indeed positive;

– FP (false positives): predicted positives which are in fact negative;

– TN (true negatives): predicted negatives which are indeed negative;

– FN (false negatives): predicted negatives which are in fact positive;

– P (positives): all the positives, regardless of the state of their prediction. $P = TP + FN$;

– N (negatives): all the negatives, regardless of the state of their prediction. $N = TN + FP$.

Table 14.1 shows the confusion matrix for a category c_i.

category c_i		expert's judgment	
		belongs to c_i	does not belong to c_i
choice of classifier	assigned to c_i by the classifier	TPi	FPi
	rejected from c_i by the classifier	FNi	TNi

Table 14.1. *Expert's judgment and choice of classifier*

The effectiveness of a model is measured for a given category by the precision P_i, the recall R_i and the specificity S_i in relation to the category c_i under observation:

$$P_i = \frac{TP_i}{TP_i + FP_i}$$, denoting the number of correct results over the total results

[14.22]

$$R_i = \frac{TP_i}{TP_i + FN_i}$$ denoting the number of correct results over the number sought

[14.23]

$$S_i = \frac{TN_i}{TN_i + FP_i}$$

[14.24]

S_i is the rate of true negatives in the results and $(1-S_i)$ is the rate of false positives, which can also be estimated from the measure of precision. We can perform linear integration on all the categories to obtain an average value:

$$P = \frac{\sum_{i=1}^{n} P_i}{n}$$

[14.25]

$$R = \frac{\sum\limits_{i=1}^{n} R_i}{n} \qquad\qquad [14.26]$$

The parameters P and R can be combined to form a global parameter which is the F-score, the expression of which in the sense of a harmonic mean is as follows:

$$F = 2\frac{P.R}{P+R} \qquad\qquad [14.27]$$

In terms of Google-style document retrieval, the recall expresses the ratio of correct documents displayed in relation to what was being sought; the precision the number of correct documents over the number of documents thrown up; and the F-score the average of the two. An F-score = 0 means that the results list contained no correct documents. An F-score = 1 means that only correct documents appear in the response, which includes all those that exist. In practice, a correct F-score is between 60 and 95%. It is rare for excellent scores to be obtained in terms of both recall and precision at the same time. By analogy, we recall the Heisen principle in physics, which holds that it is impossible to know both the velocity *and* position of a particle – which, in information extraction, is equivalent to obtaining *either* good precision *or* good recall. It is common to favor a good rate of recall, i.e. avoid the silence of good results, or else employ heuristics and a human user to clean up the results.

For the purpose of economy of obtention of annotated data, which are costly to obtain for evaluation, certain studies have shown that it is helpful to divide the sample dataset into three groups: a training set, a test set to adjust the parameters of the model acquired from the training set and a validation set, to obtain a final score for the quality of the model. In order to take advantage of the data as fully as possible, a technique known as "cross validation leave-one-out" was developed. This method of validation simulates a process which consists of separately developing a model on a dataset and making predictions about a previously-unseen dataset. The error estimation by this method is not specific to an adjusted classifier but applies to the process of adjustment using a classifier. The procedure is as follows:

– keep one point apart, train the classifier on the n-1 other points and then use it to predict the last one;

– perform a permutation with the n points, whilst keeping one back.

The error estimation is to total error over all the n test values.

We can conceive of V-fold validation. The procedure becomes:

– divide the data into V groups;

– keep one group back, train the classifier on the V-1 other groups, and then use it to predict the last one.

It should be pointed out that the setting up of a processing procedure is multi-agent or modular depending on the point of view. This causes errors in each sub-system of the set. The error is not necessarily passed on from one subsystem to another in a linear fashion. Certain singular elements can render the totality of the system completely unstable (e.g. a specific type of human voice in a speech recognition system). It is interesting to focus on the influence of certain noises on the rate of error and their impact on other systems.

The cost and the time required for a data mining study will depend on the objective of that study and the desired quality of the final product. We can hold up a number of influential factors, such as:

– the complexity of the request, the number of iterations of the requests and the level of analytical effort applied at each iteration;

– the number of domains dealt with;

– the number of computational techniques employed and the number of different applications for each technique;

– the number and degree of sophistication of the mining techniques used; and

– the complexity of the interpretation and presentation of the results.

A complete mining study can range from a single request in a given technical domain with a small amount of training, to a complex refinement of requests and a process of analysis needing to be accompanied by prototyping. The cost associated with such studies ranges from an expenditure of "zero pounds in your pocket" for a simple request to six-figure costs for complex requests. The time necessary ranges from a few minutes to several months.

14.27. Model selection

In certain use cases, it is helpful to choose between a certain number of available models. It is even possible to gauge the correctness of the models and act on the complementarity of the models. The method of boosting indeed supplements models. A new model is to be encouraged if it is capable of correctly classifying a point which is incorrectly classed by other classifiers. The intuitive idea is based on viewing the models as experts which complement one another. The theoretical result is an exponential decrease in error. Below is the best known algorithm for this purpose – Adaboost [FRE 96].

The Adaboost algorithm:

1- Assign an equal weight to each instance in the learning set;

2- Apply a learning algorithm to a weighted set and store the resulting model;

3- Calculate the error e of the model on the weighted set. If $e = 0$, or $e > 0.5$, terminate generation;

4- For each instance in the set;

5- If the instance is correctly classified by the model;

6- Multiply the weight of the instance by $e/(1-e)$;

7- Normalize the weight of all the instances.

Another solution consists, not of reducing the error by modifying the weight of the instances but by modifying the weight of the classifiers: this is known as "bagging". This technique uses the easiest method of combining predictions: vote/average. Each model is given an equal weight. The idealized version of bagging is presented as follows. We sample several learning sets of size n instead of using only one learning set of size n. We construct a classifier for each learning set and then combine the prediction of each classifier. This improves performance in almost all cases if the learning model is unstable. Bagging reduces the variance by vote/average and thus reduces the total expected error.

Chapter 15

Fields of Interest for Text Mining

In view of the definition of text mining which is heavily influenced by the opinion of users (be they experts in a domain or simply general public users), we have represented the practice of text mining in accordance with the technical uses and their context. We can distinguish two main axes for text mining. One, which is to be found fairly widely in the academic world but which, bit by bit, is seeping into the domains of research and development in large companies, is the *discovery* axis. This covers text-mining practices that are aimed not at accelerating access to information but rather to gathering information in order to uncover hitherto-unknown relations. The other axis is more mechanistic, as it aims to take advantage of the computational capacity of machines to deal with a vast quantity of data, so as to skim through the information quickly and summarize it. This axis is that of *organization*. We shall here enumerate sub-categories of the usage of these two axes, which benefit from the availability of large amounts of data, which may or may not arouse the interest of a large number of users.

15.1. The avenues in text mining

15.1.1. *Organization*

15.1.1.1. *Decision support*

15.1.1.1.1. Watchfulness

When a decision-maker wishes to take a decision, he must do so in full knowledge of the facts, and therefore must be well informed. The application of watchfulness or vigilance (also referred to as competitive intelligence) is intended to give an overview of the situation as it stands, and possibly an information flow. The aim here is to "map" an overall situation so as to "get an idea" of the content, and position the pieces accordingly. The uses are: alarm-raising, information filtering, detection of e-reputation (reputation on the Internet) and mapping of the lay of the land and the arrangement of the actors. The objective of competitive intelligence is user-centered.

15.1.1.1.2. *Strategy*

A decision-maker is led to take a stance towards other players on the field. To this end, he has to take account of "hot" short-term information, and grasp what is at stake in order to know how best to invest time and money on an active front. Again we see the basic idea of mapping the arrangement of the players, but here the analysis is profile-centered. The uses are: analysis of the state of the art, trend analysis, bibliometrics and marketing.

15.1.1.2. *Archiving*

15.1.1.2.1. Digital library

The extremely widespread emergence of the Internet in societies is transforming the means of access to information: particularly "paper" information. Documentation centers and libraries, information bulletins and other traditional information carriers are accepting the transition, and offer windows to information consumers by way of digital technology. This is conditioning for means of navigation peculiar to Internet portals.

15.1.1.2.2. Learning

Education – which is heavily involved in processes of exchange and communication – is also a consumer of written supports. Traditionally, schoolbooks facilitate the transmission of knowledge, along with a teacher who guides that transmission. Today, Internet-based means and other media (particularly e-books) are opening up new windows on knowledge transmission, the uses for which are: reading aids, distance learning, foreign language learning or learning of jurisprudence.

15.1.1.2.3. Feedback from past experience

The accumulation of digital data means that research no longer generates stores of information in material form (e.g. magnetic reels or paper files) but rather digital archives. These archives may be very diverse in nature, but are generally documents with heterogeneous content, including images and texts. Hence, with a view to exploitation of such archives, one is led to consider means of storage and possibly avoid memory loss (memories of informal practices, company memories, etc.). The uses are, notably: incident or nuisance analysis and analysis of flows such as e-mails.

15.1.2. *Discovery*

15.1.2.1. *Biomedical sciences*

15.1.2.1.1. Pharmacology

Pharmacology is an industry which requires highly-costly protocol efforts in order to select a molecule that acts on a particular protein or tissue. The exploration of bases of technical documents is one way of isolating genes which are likely candidates in view of certain sought properties. Text mining is particularly advantageous because of the staggering complexity of the task, and the vast range of possible targets (over 100,000 proteins in the human body). The public database PubMed, which hosts 22 million publications, is a reservoir of information that is hugely valuable for consulting.

15.1.2.1.2. Molecular biology

In the same vein, because it is linked to PubMed and focuses on the functional properties of genes, molecular biology aims to comprehend the deep mechanisms which enable a cell to "work". Studies in this field focus on tissues and species, thereby leading to models which associate networks of genes and dynamic models of the contribution of each of the genes depending on their concentration. These models are complex in parametric terms, and text mining is useful in order to isolate the meaningful components.

15.1.2.1.3. Medicine

The field of medicine is becoming more and more closely linked with that of genetics, but it remains heavily influenced by a non-scientific mode of reasoning. Indeed, this reasoning is closely linked with experimentation on a statistically-representative spread of patients. In this mode of practice, the patient and empiricism play a more important role than the model. In this context, there is a clear interest in mining of diagnostics reports. Historically, this was the object of the earliest studies of corpora in the 1970s.

15.1.2.2. *Humanities and Social Sciences (HSS)*

15.1.2.2.1. Sociology and law

Sociology is a vector of analysis of society in order to comprehend the way in which it works and is mutating. Gesture and representation are important parameters, and communication is no less important, in a world where digital technology is growing and the participation of both civilians and experts in opinion is increasing. Text mining has a naturally apparent place in this world, to analyze: interactions and their weight in political and techno-scientific world history, but also the impact of new virtual interactions on culture.

15.1.2.2.2. Linguistics

Language is the fundamental material in text mining. The methodical analysis of language – linguistics – has taken on a computerized form. Certain mechanisms are difficult to deal with from the computational point of view, such as anaphora or the creolization of a language (e.g. SMS language or "text-speak"). Other mechanisms are also very complicated to implement properly, such as automated translation. Cultures remain firmly attached to their natural languages, and as yet, no effort has produced a consensus as to an artificial lingua franca that can be easily translated into any natural language. Machine translation remains an immovable barrier, but text mining can help progress in this area by helping to construct ontologies and dictionaries.

15.2. About decision support

The key issue is the ability to provide each and every recognized user with information that is useful in his particular working situation. Contemporary decision support methods are based on the principles enumerated in the 18th Century by Daniel Bernoulli. These methods require a great deal of feedback, particularly in order to determine the reliability and the predominant factor in the decision. Knowledge extraction methods may come into this framework if it is a question of exploring situations to find a solution that is optimal in relation to a given criterion. Knowledge extraction may be viewed as a technique which explores the solution space. Decision support methods are divided into two main families: primarily formal methods and more cognitive methods. Mathematical methods will include knowledge extraction from databases, but also operational searching, one of the cornerstones of which is the exploration of graphs and networks, but also linear programming; random choices; strategies for competitive situations using game theory; and finally, multicriterion aggregation methods. Cognitive approaches will include the design of information systems coupled with knowledge management, the creation of graphic models and probabilistic belief modeling, models which deal with the pitfalls of reason, such as logic errors or decision-making in emergency situations, and the relation between rationality and information transmission.

We cannot emphasize strongly enough the informational structures which are the text and image: documentary elements that are omnipresent in data and are therefore available in any data-mining approach. The questions that one might ask are numerous, such as "What are the 'hot topics' at the moment?" or "What are the relations between these hot topics?" "Which avenues seem promising in order to initiate a new field of research?"

The analysis of one's reputation, also called "e-reputation" for electronic reputation or digital reputation is one topic of analysis. This can sometimes be boiled down to the study of the use of a product. The way in which a document is used can provide relevant indicators about the document itself. For instance, if the vast majority of the links that point to a document on the Web are pages which mention known chemical compounds, this means that the document will likely be of interest for chemists. Oard and Kim [OAR 98] identified four categories of possibly observable user behavior which can provide usage support: examination, retention, reference and evaluation.

The analysis of responses to open-ended questions, such as those posed in marketing, often includes themes under the auspice of investigations. The idea is to enable participants to express their "points of view" or opinions with no constraints framing the dimensions of the response in accordance with a certain format. This may offer an insight into the points of view and opinions of consumers which would not be observable were we to focus only on questionnaires with closed questions defined by "experts".

15.3. Competitive intelligence (vigilance)

The notion of competitive intelligence is akin to that of strategy, because it accentuates the process of computerization: for instance, it enables us to automatically create satisfaction barometers and reports on the image of a company or the state of the competition. However, we find numerous examples of applied research in the United States where, since the 1980s, research has been used to respond to many different demands, such as security, analysis of question-and-answer [CHE 02], bioinformatics and information searching within terabytes of data. In the domain of civil security, the MUC campaigns (Message Understanding Conferences) serve as a reference. These conferences were launched in the late 1980s by the US Department of Defense (DARPA – Defense Advanced Research Projects Agency), which wished to automatically analyze dispatches appearing in newspapers so as to detect and track terrorist activities by computerized means. In the same vein, one could also cite the wireless network Echelon created by the NSA (National Security Agency) in order to monitor wireless communications using a network of parabolic antennae. The encryption of data on telecoms networks – particularly VPN (virtual private networks) of IPv6 (Internet Protocol Version 6) – renders this type of espionage more difficult; however, free data access, in the wake of the MUC challenges, can take up the baton for this type of action. Technological competitive intelligence is the democratic side of Echelon-type espionage, whereby the listening is underground and is expressed in a form of economic activism or economic warfare. It has a variety of appellations, such as "economic intelligence" or "scientific and technical vigilance" [LEI 10]. While essentially, vigilance projects are based on data from news networks and scientific publications for reasons of availability, they penetrate the entire spectrum of data on the Web; we can see economic applications for vigilance projects as meta-search engines which aggregate information from different sources and make that information available to consumers. Applications are at work in all the services of a firm, including human resources. The company Koltech, using Temis technology, created an efficient tool (CV Distiller) for automatic processing of electronic applications, CVs, covering letters etc. to absorb the flows of applications coming in from various sources. This enables the user to create a CV library, and eliminate manual and mechanical processing tasks.

The now-popular example of price comparison Websites regarding car insurance, travel packages or any number of other products is also a good illustration of means of electronic monitoring. Such Websites are very powerful meta-search engines on a very large scale. For the moment, these tools act on a numerical parameter. The monitoring is multi-criterion (e.g. date, brand, size, location) but the display is sorted in a list according to a single criterion (e.g. the price or date), reduced to a tabular format, although a large proportion of the data is textual (name of the product, destination, etc.).

Again on the Internet, we find automated processes for tracking discourse in messages between different actors. Indeed, the Web is not simply an online shopping mall, a digital library or an electronic messaging service, but also a collaborative tool which allows users to interact and communicate by way of an interposed medium. Memetics, which comes from the epidemiological metaphor, looks at the diffusion of information. A *meme* on the Internet might be, e.g. a character string which can undergo transformations. The term "meme" was first put forward by Dawkins [DAW 76] and stems from an association between "gene" and "*mimesis*" (from the Greek for "imitation"). Dawkins also highlights the roots of his term in the French word "*meme*", meaning "same". Dawkins presents memes as replicators, which in this respect are comparable to genes, but which are responsible for the evolution of certain animal behaviors and cultures. Leskovec *et al.* [LES 09] designed a "meme-tracker" to study the dynamics of Internet news on the scale of the information cycle. The tool was famously applied to the analysis of the most frequently-repeated phrases during the American electoral campaign in 2008. This tool only works on citations – i.e. expressions contained between quotes – and on variations of these citations, but not on their negation.

Another means of information tracking consists of taking account of user interactions, as does the platform "xPatterns", offered by Atigeo. This tool takes account of users' actions to facilitate a better computerized and decisional response on disparate and evolving data.

15.4. About strategy

Strategy consists of being aware of our strengths in relation to the other players around us, and envisaging alliances. The sociology of sciences has come up with a vision of the function of laboratory life, where information processing has come to represent an affirmation of the models [KUH 62; LAT 86; DUB 01]. Since the dawn of the Information Age, there has been a genuine taste for analysis of scientific literature and patents in instances of advice in boards of directors. Bibliometric indicators relate to science and technology. Such indicators enable us to measure scientific activity by analyzing bibliographical notices relating to scientific articles indexed in scientific databases. They also enable us to detect trends and provide elements of information to nourish strategic reflections relating to sciences and techniques. Archives of publications have been available since the early 1960s, and at this time the interest of analyzing collaboration networks became apparent, with the notion of the invisible college [PRI 66; CRA 72].

More recent works continue the study of the properties of epistemic communities [KAT 94; NEW 01]. Swanson's investigations [SWA 86] uncovered hidden relations within scientific literature. Documents and authors can be grouped together in epistemic communities on the basis of the articles that they cite [KAN 07]. The works which are most representative of the co-citation approach are those of H. Small and E. Garfield [GAR 70], who founded the Institute for Scientific Information (ISI) in the 1960s. They developed the bibliographic database called the Science Citation Index (SCI) (which has now become the Web of Science), with the aim of implementing precise indicators to measure the "consumption" of scientific results. In their work, they propose to conduct an analysis of these articles, factoring in citations in order to calculate the impact factor (IF) of a publication. This indicator is still used today, and is calculated as follows. Suppose we wish to calculate the IF for the year n. Let A represent the number of times that articles published in n-1 and n-2 have been cited in publications indexed during the year n. Let B represent the total number of elements which the journal could have cited from years n-1 and n-2. We get the formula:

$$IF_n = \frac{A_{n-1,n-2}}{B_{n-1,n-2}} \hspace{3cm} [15.1]$$

According to Small and Garfield, the fundamental articles or those which are cited in clusters tend to share a common theme from a theoretical or methodological standpoint – or indeed both. More recent works have attempted to formulate new indicators of scientific activity, such as the indicator of "research front activity" advanced by Lucio-Arias and Leydersdorf [LUC 09].

The evaluation of research is not the only goal of bibliometrics. It can also serve as an auxiliary method to peer reviewing, in three directions:

– measurement of productivity (*pub[lishing] output*);

– co-authorship (collaborations);

– number of citations (impact factor).

The latter two directions give rise to indicators associated with the notion of a network. Other determining factors are:

– the researcher's age;

– his/her environment or social status;

– the subject;

– the type of document;

– the period covered by the analysis.

Barirani *et al.* [BAR 11] developed a methodology that enables us to set up a social network of inventors, segment these inventors on the basis of their social capital and find the social profiles which are most productive in terms of the number of patents produced.

On the other hand, an approach which automatically exploits the activity summaries provided by the laboratories to their host organization enables us to define anticipatory practices. Such activity summaries reflect the direction of the work undertaken year after year and, consequently, touch on their approach of anticipation. This information source represents a large quantity of data, and computerized exploitation of these data helps to extract the main scientific trends underlying them. Researchers pursue their work in accordance with their own passion, curiosity and intuition, whilst adapting more particularly to the rhythm at which their intellectual environment and their experiences are evolving because of the evolution of technologies and the advancement of scientific knowledge. Tacitly, this notion of "anticipation", which is inherent to time-specific research, is an advance toward multiple orientations, owing to the initiatives of the different actors at a research institution. It results from a comparison between the timeslot in which an event is likely to occur and the time needed for the organization to respond to that event. Two concepts are recurrent:

– The knowledge base, constructed on the basis of the terminology used in clusters of cited articles.

– The research fronts, based on clusters of bibliographically coupled articles.

Similar content is spotted in lexical terms by co-occurrences or associated words [CAL 93a; CAL 93b], keywords [NOY 99], frequent terms used as a weight such as TF-IDF and LSA (latent semantic analysis). Specifically bibliometric databases are not enough. Other bases also form part of the reference databases, including thesauruses, standards, documents in OAI (Open Archive Initiative) format and geographical information. Van Looy *et al.* [VAN 10] combine bibliometrics, patents and R&D (research and development) to account for the performance of transfer of technology created in universities. Another example of a study of a socio-technical system to extract empirical knowledge from bases of economic literature, patents and R&D is presented in [GUO 12]. Its authors set out a ten-stage analytical methodology to gauge the state of development of a piece of technology and describe the socio-technical system of the actors and the institutions, for the specific case of dye-sensitized solar cells (DSSCs).

Rafols and Meyer [RAF 10] present the notion of variety and cross flow about knowledge dynamics. We must highlight the importance of "sleeping beauties", which correspond to articles being cited over 10 years after their publication, and of "pearls" or "hidden jewels". The objective of the citations score, of the Leiden Ranking classification method, is to compare the team, the journal and the field of research. The score applies to a team, and is calculated in view of the journals and reviews in which that team's work is published. Such a measurement shows that a narrow window of two years limits the opportunity for the work to have been digested and cited, and therefore introduces a certain degree of falsehood into the calculations. The ranking scheme enables us to combine a conceptual map and a measure of the local density of citation. Finally, it helps evaluate the performance of a team on the basis of the uptake of its citations within a domain, rather than in a cluster of journals covering a wider discipline (i.e. which is not specifically defined in disciplinary terms).

The most widely used technique in bibliometric text mining is co-word analysis, which involves a chain of processing beginning with an extraction of co-occurrences of words (lexical associations), clustering of the associations and visual rendering (visualization of the information). This technique is one of the processes involved in a rather widespread approach of content analysis or lexical method, in conjunction with techniques for knowledge extraction from databases. Co-word analysis was first proposed by Small [SMA 73] and later corrected by Small and Griffith [SMA 74]. In the body of literature, we find works by other authors [CAL 83; LEY 97; LEY 98] which have more recently made improvements to the co-word analysis method. Co-word analysis encompasses a fairly varied range of methods for knowledge extraction from the distribution of keywords in plain-text scientific articles, where we can cite Braam *et al.* [BRA 91] on the subject of combining co-citation and co-word analysis. The dynamic aspects in scientometrics, and long-term observation of scientific and technical literature, have of course been discussed

[LAT 92; GIB 94]. Today, the various traditional models of infometrics and citation analysis are still under study, in order to be able to take account of the heterogeneity of sources of information production and transfer between different arenas of communication. The debate about an impact factor beyond the domain of scientometrics is still a current topic for public policy makers. Classification following a ranking order for publications or institutions is also a useful tool for public decision-making.

Evaluation tools, including topics, actors and intellectual property, are key to strategic decision-making. It is because we have decisional legitimacy that we can make our strategic standpoints count and gain enough room for maneuver to enable us to enforce our policies. Industrial groups have computerized technology watch structures from which we could draw inspiration. They include "text mining" tools, information cross-referencing and search for local resources by way of internal social networks. A number of risks depend on the evaluation. The evaluation of research projects and their results does not obey the general spirit of a respectful evaluation of the researchers. An evaluation solely of the publications could lead to a total sterilization of research, with everyone performing research at the same time into fashionable topics using similar techniques and similar intuitions, with the researchers having all been given identical training. Without a certain degree of risk-taking, the tightening of financial means could lead to the undue sidelining of a team in category A, or prevent a team in category B from qualifying, or even give rise to an atmosphere which is not conducive to the emergence of differentiated characters, but rather ones which are competitive.

15.5. About archive management

Medical questionnaires and guarantee demands are usually written in natural language – these are examples of plain-text narrative documents, sometimes with metadata characterizing the context. Nuisance report bulletins contingent on the month or the week (police reports, agricultural reports, etc.) may also constitute archives of numerical information. Nor must we forget libraries of textbooks and school manuals. The State is also a major producer of official data; the official journal is a brilliant example of this in France. The Government Printing Office or GPO in the United States is another example; the Senate regularly produces numerous studies, which are made available on its Website, making this site one of the largest Websites containing numerical documentation. These documents are either picked up or broadcast electronically, which offers a potential source for exploitation by text-mining algorithms.

Electronic messaging is a flagship application of the Internet and a good target area for text mining – e.g. detection of undesirable messages (automatic filtering of spam or junk mail) or automatic classification of messages (categorization of a message to choose a response or store it; automatic routing to an advisor or a service) [COH 95; HUL 98; TUR 03]. These elements of automated processing, when dealing with very short messages, are based on morphological analysis and e-mail addresses, with a number of rules regarding the use of a word or term as an identifying criterion about the content of the message in order to deal with it automatically.

A flagship application of text mining, which therefore has appropriated a well-established methodology in document processing, is to automatically run a search for a certain number of documents based on keywords or key terms. As an excellent example, this is the approach used by Web-based search engines, which have developed techniques that are efficient in terms of storage, speed and regularity of response time, to handle hundreds of millions of documents in view of millions of simultaneous requests. Typically this is a significant approach which requires robust, multi-user, multi-criterion, precise and fast access to the content of enormous documentary spaces. Similarly to other large competitive markets (telephone operators, purchasing centers in distribution), we find a concentration of actors with phenomenal investing power in the world of digital publishing. The modern model of complex and integrated online publishing services is primarily observed around four major publishers: Thomson Reuters, Reed Elsevier, Wolters Kluwer and Springer. In France, a national excellence initiative (IDEX) project received substantial funding (€60 million for 10 years) for work on the topic of scientific and technical information (IDEX ISTEX), which brought together the CNRS (French National Research Center) and the research hub at the University of Nancy. Key aspects make digital publishing an active domain:

– the capacity to process electronic information using algorithms (which is impossible with paper-based documents). Springer uses the Biomed Central suite of tools and UMLS to consult biomedical literature. Reuters developed Thomson Analytics, and Elsevier the Illumina 8 system;

– the emergence of the topic of e-books from 2009 onwards;

– the development of new formats as an information carrier such as podcasts and Webcasts;

– the enrichment of content with ever-more-complex sets of metadata;

– the growing digitization of old documentary collections.

Publishers are tending to develop services for information discovery – i.e. a set of computerized tools which are able to find the proverbial needle (the relevant document) in a haystack (a documentary collection comprising multiple documents). These services stem more from simple documentary searching, but are able to pick up new knowledge, e.g. the manifestation *in abstracto* of the co-occurrence of two phenomena within a body of scientific literature which does not identify that relation *a priori*.

The notion of interoperability has long been a concern for document management tools. Indeed, this notion was at the very root of the Internet, with the conception of HTML (HyperText Markup Language), implemented by Tim Berners-Lee at the CERN (European Organization for Nuclear Research) in 1990, preceded by the documentary system SGML (Standard Generalized Markup Language). From which the loins of these two formats was born XML (eXtensible Markup Language) which is more adaptable in semantic terms. Encoding systems have seen the light of day, including TEI (Text Encoding Initiative) and OAI (Open Archives Initiative). OAI, based on XML, is an initiative aimed at facilitating the exchange of metadata between data providers and service providers. The TEI, for its part, acts like a consortium, in the same vein as the W3C, and aspires to implement a framework for the adoption of standard schemes based on XML for document exchange. Communication is developing widely on the Web, taking many forms that have hitherto been reserved for patented publishes: online publication of research results, free access journals, academic blogs, information portals and reports, and "open peer review". This muddies the notion of intellectual property and means of broadcast, not to mention the emergence of "free" publishing. Text mining is used by large journalistic companies to disambiguate information and offer their readers greater potential for finding information, the result of which will be to attract more readers and therefore increase revenues. There are consortium-type projects, aimed at designing new types of large-scale digital libraries. The MONK (Metadata Offer New Knowledge) project brings together thirty-odd partners in the United States, with a multi-million-dollar budget. It encompasses the project SEASR (Software Environment for the Advancement of Scholarly Research), the goal of which is to create a working environment for analysis of (primarily English-language) literary archives, facilitating access to those texts. MONK includes at least 525 works of American literature from the 18th and 19th Centuries and 37 plays and 5 works of poetry by William Shakespeare. Each text is standardized using Abbot, a complex XSL stylesheet, to a TEI schema designed for analytic purposes (TEI-A), and each text has been annotated, using Morphadorner, with: a process of tokenization, sentences boundaries, standard spellings, parts of speech and lemmata. Then a text is injected, using the tool Prior, into a database that provides Java access methods for extracting data for many purposes, including searching for objects, direct presentation to end-users in the form of tables, lists, concordances or visualizations. The project is also intended for getting feature counts and frequencies for analysis by data mining; the platform also enables users to get tokenized streams of text for working with n-gram methods, collocation analysis methods, repetition analyses and corpus query-language pattern-matching operations. MONK's quantitative analytics are run through the SEASR environment, with data extraction programs such as

NoraVis and Featurelens which transform unstructured (or semi-structured) data into structured data. Thus, these tools are considered increasingly important in the development of text study infrastructures, in view of the coexistence of highly differing protocols for archive structuring and management [BAT 02]. In Europe, we can cite the TextGrid consortium, including 10 partners, attached to the European program CLARIN (*Common LAnguage Resources and technology INfrastructure*), the aim of which revolves around ten commandments: interoperability, an all-in-one (user) environment, storage and computational resources, collaboration, security and stability, flexibility, extensibility, open standards, free programming and long-term sustainability.

15.6. About sociology and the legal field

An HSS text-mining tool must be co-constructed and interactive. It must be interactive at the level of analysis, in the sense that it enables users to articulate a corpus of texts and research hypotheses. Its interactivity can also be expressed between users to enable different analysts to contrast and compare alternative interpretations of texts or text segments.

Sociology and law are part of the social sciences. These are disciplines which share the same object of study: the norms in a society. They also share the same tendencies, borne by the "digital humanities", owing to the fact that the data used both in sociology and in law are generally in textual form. Lawmakers formulate their results (laws, decrees, conventions, etc.) in text format. Thus, it is possible to construct well-defined corpora of legislation even though the essential interest of such corpora lies in jurisprudence. Stavrianou [STA 07] and Pisetta [PIS 07] studied and positioned labor legislation from different countries. In the wake of this project, the International Labor Office then wished to draw up maps which would enable representatives from different countries to position themselves in relation to one another.

According to Gieryn [GIE 83], from the very dawn of sociological theories grounded in constructivist sciences, the institutional boundary between science and non-science is contingent. Rather than seeking to define what exactly the essence of science is *a priori* (Karl Popper's falsifiability, the discovery of the laws of Nature, etc.), Gieryn invites his readers to closely examine, from an anti-essentialist standpoint, the way in which it is defined by social groups driven by interests and ideologies. Social Construction of Technology (SCOT) is a theory of the domain of studies of science and technology. Social constructivists, defenders of SCOT, hold that technology does not determine human action, but that rather, human action defines the aspect of technology. The central argument rests on the idea that the ways in which a technology is used cannot be understood without first understanding how that technology fits into its social context. SCOT is an answer to technological determinism, and is sometimes known as technological constructivism. The principle of symmetry relates to the fact that historians and sociologists, explaining the origin of scientific belief – or in other words, evaluating the success and failure of various models, theories or experiments – could use the same explicative concept whether in the case of success or failure. Observing the beliefs, researchers could be impartial to the veracity or falsehood attributed to these beliefs *a posteriori*, and the explanations can be unbiased. The strong program adopts a relativist or neutral stance, observing the arguments that the social actors put forward for the acceptance or rejection of a technology. All the social, cultural, political, economic and indeed technical arguments must be dealt with equally. Ren [REN 03] describes interdynamic relations between the innovation of a regime (governance of a system) and the scientific development of a scientific community, analyzing the structure of the regime of that scientific community and a regime's general process of innovation. Today, the development of science is not merely an enrichment of the accumulation and expansion of scientific knowledge, but rather a reasoned guiding and distribution of the scientific resources. This depends on the state of perfection of the regime of the scientific community and whether the regime is consistent with the demand for scientific development. Carayol [CAR 03] described the importance of ecosystems favorable to innovation as the notion of a knowledge network or knowledge community, whose questions in sociology of scientific knowledge raise the issue of the interface between politics, organization and scientific production with the notion of an architecture necessary for creativity [GAR 82; AMI 04]. Sociology of scientific knowledge (SSK) is a sub-discipline of sociology which quickly adopted text-mining techniques – particularly from data in available publications contained in databases such as PubMed and Web of Science, but others as well such as PatStart or CAB Abstract. SSK focuses on epistemological issues such as truth and knowledge, with views which are often critical of positivism in favor of social constructivism. SSK has been transformed over the past thirty years, because of relativism. A number of different sub-disciplines touch on the sociological question of knowledge production, analyzing scientific activity: history of science, philosophy of science, epistemology, "science studies", etc. In many cases, the boundaries between disciplines are somewhat fluid. The SSK train of thought (which one will also hear referred to as Science and Technology Studies or Social Studies of Science) brings together two fairly similar points of view, which share the hypothesis that scientific content is entirely determined by society and culture [PRI 65; MER 79; LAT 79; WHI 81; CAL 83; JAS 85; LEI 89; VIN 07]. The dominant point of view holds that *social* rather than *natural* causes should be able to account for both successes and failures, and true beliefs and false ones alike. The empirical or micro-sociological view of relativism holds that social mechanisms impose a unique interpretation, with negotiation taking place within a small group of specialists called a *core set*, whose conclusions are accepted by other scientists. Historically speaking, the foundation of this discipline is attributed to Robert Merton [MER 42], followed by the famous works of Thomas Kuhn [KUH 62] about the social factors of dynamics of sciences. Obviously there were precursors to the discipline in philosophy of science and technology, spanning the centuries from Descartes in 1637 to Wittgenstein [WIT 53], including Hobbes [HOB 51], Locke [LOC 90], Hume [HUM 48], Leibniz [LEI 05], Kant [KAN 81], Hegel [HEG 16], Schopenhauer [SCH 19], Comte [COM 30], Bergson [BER 89], Popper [POP 34] and Bachelard [BAC 38]. Similarly to other disciplines in social sciences, SSK integrates a number of trains of thought, which are distinguishable by their goals, their methods and their conceptions of what SSK is and should be. One of the most influential approaches of the past half-century is the Actor–Network Theory (ANT). Developed in France by Michel Callon [CAL 83] and Bruno Latour [LAT 79], this school of thought had a profound impact on later forms of sociology, and is one of the approaches most cited in international works about science. Researchers integrated notions of documentary organization, as it is understood in scientometrics, and discovery of knowledge by knowledge extraction from texts. Such is the case with Yao *et al.* [YAO 09], who conceived of a combined approach involving the mining of texts from the perspective of sociology and that of biology. They linked information about the inventors and authors with data drawn from text mining in biology, facilitating the construction of a predictive model to guide researchers and organizations in assembling brilliant teams to discover new medicines. The notion of a network is a relatively old one. We can trace its serious scientific origin back to the 1930s in various disciplines in HSS (Human and Social Sciences). In psychology, Jacob Moreno [MOR 34] initiated a systematic program of recording and analysis of social interactions in small groups, primarily in school classes and working groups. In anthropology, the foundations for a social network theory were lain by the ethnographic work of Bronislaw Malinovski [MAL 19; MAL 29], Alfred Radcliffe-Brown [RAD 30; RAD 33], Claude Lévi-Strauss [LÉV 49] and Elizabeth Bott [BOT 57]. In sociology, the works of Talcott Parsons [PAR 37; PAR 51] elaborated a relational approach that helped better understand social structure. Later, using Parsons' model as a basis, the sociologist Peter Blau [BLA 55] made a significant contribution to the analysis of relational links of social units, with his work on social exchange theory.

Later on, we shall come back to the history of the notion of a network in physics and mathematics, which is a particularly long and interesting story. In brief, social network analysis [ERN 10] emerged in the 1970s from studies on social structure, graph theory, mathematical topology and statistics, as an analytical method in its own right, used by sociologists such as Harrison White [LOR 71], Scott Boorman [BOO 75], Linton Freeman [FRE 77], James Mitchell [MIT 85], Mark Granovetter [GRA 85] and Barry Wellman [WEL 83]. The diffusion of new information and communication technologies (ICT) crystallized efforts toward social networks and multi-level analyses which were then extended to large and complex datasets [HED 00]. The latest wave of computerization in the 1990s used more simulations and advanced statistical techniques to study extensive databases of electronic behaviors [VAL 09]. Electronic recordings such as e-mails, instant messaging communications (MSN, Twitter, Skype, ICQ, to cite only the best-known services), Web hyperlinks, uses of mobile telephony (SMS) and discussions on forums and blogs, enable sociologists to directly observe social behaviors at different times and different levels of analysis without the constraints of traditional empirical methods such as interviews, observation of participants or surveillance instruments. The constant improvements in automatic learning algorithms have also enabled sociologists to uncover significant forms of interaction and social evolution in extensive electronic databases.

E-infrastructure tools offer the possibility to combine text mining with social network analysis in order to extract knowledge from large datasets, or "datamasses", such as the Web. The techniques associated with data mining are once again used in major instruments for academic research in social sciences, partly because this requires computer resources. E-infrastructures offer the possibility to overcome this obstacle [WAS 94; SHA 11; LIN 12].

The adoption of computational simulation methods, artificial intelligence, text mining, complex statistical methods and new approaches such as social network analysis [WHI 73; WHI 76; WEL 88; FRE 95; WEL 08; FRE 04; CRO 10] has seen the development and testing of theories of complex social processes by bottom-up modeling of social interactions. The exploitation of socio-semantic networks has been dominated by bibliometrics for the purposes of strategic analysis of a specialist domain. However, other issues, focused on sociological hypotheses and co-constructed with data mining to refine them, can draw on the advances in digital sociology and text mining algorithms.

However, SSK is not the only form of sociology, and the electronic advances relate to all sub-domains of sociology. One would often speak of *e-social sciences*. Jeoffrion [JEO 09] highlights the advantage to using text-mining approaches to perform comparative studies of representational systems in order to improve communications and thereby fight more effectively against disease. The community of psycho-sociologists is expressing a growing interest in text-mining methods in the study of social representations [LAH 96; KAL 05]. That said, the compatibility between social representation theory and text mining has still to be demonstrated, and the applicative possibilities have as yet not been extensively exploited. This represents a significant methodological challenge, because a researcher in social sciences has to arm himself with text analysis methods, which will enable him to attain the three levels of social representation analysis: identifying indicators in those texts which are the expression of cognitive elements specific to the social representation that he wishes to study; identifying the structures which organize the social representation under study; and identifying the centrality of the cognitive elements which make up the representation.

Here are two concrete examples of studies which combine text-mining with sociology. Archaeology is a domain of social sciences. In the field of archaeology we can cite the project *Open Boek*, part of the Dutch program *Continuous Access to Cultural Heritage* (CATCH), the aim of which is to apply a digital information extraction system to archaeological reports. Paijmans and Wubben [PAI 08] describe this system, which functions in accordance with an automatic learning procedure, centered on the recognition of phrases containing chronological and geographic data such as dates, dimensions, coordinates and key elements in archaeology. Franzosi [FRA 10] studied the acts of violence in Italy between 1919 and 1922 between different social categories. Using texts and text mining, he was able to construct artificial diachronic visualizations that showed the evolution and the intensity of such acts (see Figure 15.1).

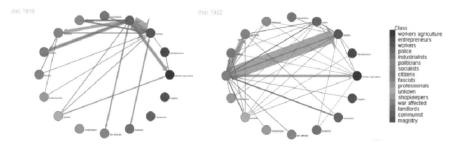

Figure 15.1. *Visualization of acts of violence, distributed across social categories [FRA 10]*

The avenues for research in e-social sciences are many and varied. For instance:

– The use of logs in computerized projects offer sources for social interaction data.

– The use of keyword filters opens up the possibility of tracking salience and judgment in texts. Determination of a special language in texts can express a value associated with significant learning, taking advantage of the gain from collaborative work [AHM 05]. This is based on comparison with a general dictionary.

We must have a schema in order to collect data. For instance, such a schema must enable us to distinguish the individual sources which have created a collective skill. These schemas group together the capital of individual skills, on the basis of opportunities for creation and development of collective skills, the affective interactions which condition that creation and development, the informal relations constructed by the actors who contribute to their stabilization, cooperation based on the will of the actors, compared to simple coordination which facilitates the development of collective skills. This schema begins with the hypothesis that analysis of the referential frameworks constructed should reveal the traces of the collective skill. Three main techniques can be used for data collection: interviews (e.g. interviews with employees), observation (e.g. observation of governing committee meetings) and document analysis (e.g. automatic analysis of the minutes of meetings and construction of an ontology on the skills, roles, activities and functions to create a common referential framework). Once these basic principles have been set out, we can lay out the elements that a text-analysis program has found in any given corpus.

Another context for data, life progression analysis, is an important topic in labor sociology, for which we can show significant connections:

1. scholarly progression and the process of orientation refer to the same period and the same sphere.

2. the context of childhood and scholarly progression relate to the same period or close periods such as childhood and adolescence.

3. professional progression and personal development demonstrate the reciprocal influence of the personal and social area on a person's professional life.

A textual analysis can pick up on certain external factors which influence a person's trajectory, such as:

– their age, e.g. "At 45, I want to move on in my career",

– their sex, e.g. "Since I am a woman, I have to organize my professional life around my private life",

– their social origin, e.g. "I am from a poor background, so my parents did not have the means to fund my education",

– their cultural origin, e.g. "I am of African origin. My family came to France in [date]",

– their current context, e.g. "I am unemployed and I need to find work to feed my family" or "I am the CEO of a major company and I have responsibilities",

– their life context, e.g. geographic location and living conditions, social status, etc.

– their childhood context, e.g. "I came from a modest background where people thought education was important in order to succeed in life".

Researchers in human and social sciences depend quite heavily on archives and dossiers (texts/images/videos) such as news, sound recordings (interviews), photographs, letters, diaries, tables, books, publications, birth, marriage and death registers, records in churches, schools and colleges, or maps. Any trace of human experience can be treated as data for a researcher in HSS. Laboratory logs can be analyzed to reveal patterns of activity problem areas and the way in which the participants in studies of social practices make the transition between reading from hard copy and reading from digital documents [OHA 98]. Participants who are used to specific models (e.g. biologists studying human stem cells) may find it difficult to apply these models in the digital world [MAK 07]. Semi-structured interviews help explicitize the use of physical and digital information supports, and thereby determine requirements, preferences and any prior experience of such supports [SIE 09].

Semiometry is, specifically, an empirical approach developed by Lebart *et al.* [LEB 03] which was used to determined personality types. A carefully-selected list of 210 words was presented to the individuals, who were asked to note their own emotional response to these words, ranking them on a scale from strongly negative to strongly positive. The results are examined and the personality type of an individual, a group or a nation is thus determined. Camillo *et al.* [CAM 05] noted that this approach is based on the principle that words do not simply mean *things* but also refer to values and affections to which an individual or a group of individuals is attached.

Sociology is interested in interactions, which leads to groups of interactions that are analyzed in the form of a network [BOR 09]. By extension, having analyzed the concepts in the corpora, we would speak of socio-semantic network analysis when the groups of actors are linked to associated groups of terms. This is the origin of the well-known concept of a network which has become popular – first in SSK, and more recently as regards Web-related topics. A network is a set of nodes with which we associated vertices; it is a mathematical structure born out of graph theory and therefore discrete mathematics. This domain of mathematics already has its own history. The pioneering work was done in the 18th and 19th Centuries. One might cite the famous work of Euler [EUL 36]. Leonhard Euler discussed the problem of the seven bridges of Königsberg, giving rise to the search for a path from one node to another which passes only once through each of the edges. This has also been nicknamed the problem of the commercial traveler. The term "graph" was introduced by Sylvester [SYL 78]. Cayley [CAY 57] had been led to study a particular analytical form of differential calculus of the trees corresponding to a category of graphs. One of the well-known and productive problems of graph theory is the four-color theorem, raising the question of whether it is possible to draw a map of regions on a four-color plane such that no two contiguous regions have the same color. The problem was posed by to geographer Francis Guthrie in 1852 [GUT 52], having noticed that four colors were sufficient to set apart the counties on a map of England. The conjecture went from mathematician to mathematician until it was published and partially proven by Cayley [CAY 79]. The autonomous development of topology between 1860 and 1930 contributed to the development of graph theory through the works of Jordan [JOR 70], Kuratowski [KUR 30] and Whitney [WHI 32]. Another factor shared between the development of topology and graph theory is the contribution of modern algebra. The groundbreaking work at this level was demonstrated by Kirchoff's laws of electrical circuits [KIR 45] to calculate the voltage and intensity of electric current. The introduction of probabilistic methods into graph theory by Erdös and Rényi [ERD 59] gave rise to a new branch, called Random Graph Theory, which is prolific in theoretical terms. König [KÖN 36] wrote the first textbook in graph theory, but it was the work authored by Harary [HAR 65; HAR 69] which became most popular amongst chemists, mathematicians, electrical engineers but also researchers in social sciences. The notion of connexity of a network was largely popularized in work on complex systems by so-called "small world" statistical distribution, illustrated in computer–server networks on the Internet [BAR 99; BAR 03], in online social networks [MOR 06), but also in genetics to describe the associations between genes. The founding work on social networks in sociology was certainly done in the 1950s by Barnes [BAR 54] and Bott [BOT 57], whose examination of the relations of urban families with society set out to look at the families' relationships with their neighbors, friends and relatives with a small sample of around twenty. The study showed that the local relations take the shape of a network which has no boundary, unlike a group. The other conclusion is the influence of the characteristics of the network on husband–wife relationships [SAV 08].

It is not to graph theory and topology that we owe the concept of a small-world distribution, but rather to an empirical study in social psychology about chains of social relations. Milgram [MIL 67] took up an idea developed in 1929 by the Hungarian philosopher Frigyes Karinthy, proposing the theory of six degrees of separation. This was the small-world experiment. [MIL 67], followed by Travers and Milgram [TRA 69] showed that the typical distances between pairs of nodes in a friendship network are surprisingly small. This would later be taken up in the graph theory advanced by De Sola Pool and Kochen [DES 78; WAT 98]. The study of friendship networks is still a current topic nowadays, e.g. with Milardo [MIL 82] or Brueckner [BRU 06], who developed friendship networks in which the links are formed stochastically; and even more so since the dawn of Internet social networks: political network (e.g. Twitter), generalist networks (e.g. Friends Reunited), sentimental networks (e.g. Meetic), professional networks (e.g. Viadeo or LinkedIn), cultural networks (e.g. Meetup) or solidarity networks (e.g. carpooling.com). In general, on certain topics such as auctions, many networks may spring up – we observe that the capacity to create a user-friendly Website, coupled with the confidence provided by investors, who will be agents for the large-scale promotion of the site and therefore for its popularity, will see a site buy out its competitors and emerge as the dominant social network on the Web. Such is the case of the

American Facebook, created in 2005, in comparison to the French site Copainsdavant created in 2001, or the French site Onvasortir.com (2007) in relation to the Parisian site Peuplade.fr (2003). Web-crawling in this context is used for large-scale knowledge extraction, for which analysis is performed on Web pages, or to analyze statistical properties [THE 01]. Other studies are envisaged to identify and analyze "Web spheres" or "controversy networks". Lusher and Ackland [LUS 09] used a crawler to analyze 211 target sites, highlighting the importance of the investigation tools for research in social sciences for the Web – among other things for link analysis. While social networks are sources for interactional data at one's fingertips, they are also sources of semantic data, in that the sites use Web 2.0 which enables users to interact and therefore post opinions, experiences or messages for the attention of other users. These comments supplement the data on inter-user relations or network access data. Web 2.0 drives forward the notion of an interactive network in the form of a collaborative network, and the network reality from which it arose. Let us recall the few general principles of Web 2.0. Tim O'Reilly [ORE 04] is usually credited with having coined the term. In a conference on the Internet, he stated that one of the crucial differences between the age of PCs and the age of Web 2.0 was the fact that the Internet was becoming a platform [TUR 11b]. While double-clicking to obtain the desired information was undoubtedly the preserve of Web 1.0, today, we no longer merely let ourselves be carried along by hypertext links on a journey of reading, but rather we add "meaning", seeking to supplement a search with other related content. The fairly stable hypertext architecture which had characterized the Web of human and social sciences up to that point, i.e. the Web as a passive archive of texts and documents, was transformed and yielded to new architectures which favor interaction and knowledge exchange in a mutation and often deliberate role reversal between those who had thitherto written the content and those who read it passively. These new Web architectures cater for the general public's needs for participation in networked activities in platforms. These platforms offer access to multimedia information but also the possibility to share that information and interact by creating fruitful collective content, in view of this constant fusion of roles between authors and readers. The fact of using technology to delegate content to individuals or collectives and of hoping they will thereby advance the activity and the Web content by responding, *en masse*, to the challenge posed, is now known as "crowdsourcing" (or open outsourcing) [EAS 10; HOL 10], a neologism related to the later developments of Web 2.0, which is being spoken about more and more since 2010. It should also be noted that the abundant communication of a single crowd has never produced intelligible discourse. The rise of interventions by means of crowdsourcing requires information processing that only knowledge-extraction techniques can offer in order to "tell the good from the bad". In the same vein, collections and social bookmarking services can be used to measure large-scale usage. Bookmarks reveal a perspective of use on content. A user profile can be established by classifying the actors depending on their means of access and usage of the tools on the software platforms, based on log information: duration of a session, frequency of login and type of activity.

Another major topic, which covers several domains in sociology, is sentiment analysis or opinion mining. The aim of this is to provide people – particularly politicians – with points of view that they can use to deal with questions of representativeness of the participants in debates. In particular, we can distinguish:

– institutional leaders, who are the officially recognized representatives but who have no real representativeness;

– and individuals who are true opinion-holders, although they have not been identified as such; classifications could be established in accordance with various pre-established points of view.

We find different styles of participation, e.g. those who express themselves in a register of opposition, rarely connect and do so only to "blow off steam". Linguistic material collected on the Web during a crawl for documents on the Web with a view to opinion mining stems from several types of statements: a judgment, an evaluation, an opinion, a feeling, a taste, an account of an experience, an account of a practice. There are many contemporary tools for opinion mining and consultation: registers in public spaces, records in public sessions, forms on the Internet, etc. A great many oral corpora form the material used by a sociologist looking for a "ground truth". For processing purposes, this material must be transcribed into written form. That transcription may be automatic or automatable. Unfortunately, this type of process entails a number of pitfalls due comprehension of spelling, which are also called disfluences (hesitations, silences, voice quality, regional aspects, aspirations, glottalizations, prolonged syllables, throat clearing, coughing, laughter and overlap), so that the cleansing required renders knowledge extraction impracticable. However, the noise caused by disfluences may not have an impact on statistical treatments, which means an oral corpus of hundreds of hours on an invaluable piece of material.

The studies envisaged for sentiment analysis aim to determine the polarity of sentiments and the degrees of positivity, to detect subjectivity and identify an opinion. One example of an application might be the analysis of perceptions of grades amongst university students. Hatzivassiloglou and McKeown [HAT 97] were among the first to have focused on opinion classification in an automatic text analysis context. They concentrated on adjectives and nominal groups in which the adjectives are connected with conjunctions such as "and" or "but". They constructed a loglinear regression model to clarify whether two adjectives had the same general meaning. The precision for this task was evaluated at 82%. Their technique is described as containing the following four steps:

– extracting from the text the conjoint adjectives which are connected by the word "and", "but" and others;

– applying a supervised algorithm which constructs a graph wherein the nodes are the adjectives and the links determine a similar or contrary orientation;

– applying a clustering algorithm to separate the graph into two classes;

– considering the cluster with the highest frequency to be the most probable orientation.

Another important piece of work in this field is that of Turney and Littman [TUR 03] who used pointwise mutual information (PMI) and latent semantic analysis to find a statistical relation between a specific word and a set of positive and negative words. Maurel *et al.* [MAU 08] analyzed forums in the domain of tourism, and extracted information relating to the users' feelings and the tourists destination. They applied semantic and syntactic processing techniques and adapted the grammatical rules or opinion words which they sought to identify in accordance with the domain.

Sentiment analysis may involve analyzing opinions about movies, for instance, to estimate whether an opinion is favorable for a particular movie. Such an analysis may require an annotated dataset or annotation of affective words. Word and concept resources about affectivity have been created for WordNet and ConceptNet respectively. The text is used to detect emotions in domains associated with affective computing. We can also process the text to detect emotions in corpora relating to student assessment, children's stories and brief news breakdowns [SAA 12]. We can also cite the iPinion project, piloted by the Parisian network Cap Digital, to analyze e-reputation. The aim of this project is to develop tools and services for semantic analysis and cartographic representation of data on the Web to measure the e-reputation of companies, organizations or brands. The project is divided into four intermediary missions. The first is the definition of conditions to define relevant corpora and establish a collection of data. The second aim is to develop tools which identify pertinent informational zones. The third is to develop linguistic and semantic tools to precisely categorize the opinions expressed on the Websites, including expressions of judgment. The final aim is to develop data analyses and cartography analyses to structure the opinion and its evolution on the Internet.

Content analysis is a classic approach in HSS [BAR 77]. Most of the time, the task of analysis and annotation of the texts is performed *manually*, after which the researcher classifies his textual documents into categories which he himself has defined. Sometimes this analysis is assisted by a computerized annotation and categorization support tool. That being so, once the research material has been collected, and especially when that dataset is particularly large, the annotator realizes that analysis of it risks becoming an incredibly laborious task, and that classic content analysis alone will be insufficient, despite its undeniable effectiveness. Knowledge acquisition from texts is a complex subject, because of the boundary between representation and interpretation. While the first annotated corpus was the Brown corpus [KUC 67], annotation as an in-text means of interpretation has been used since the late 1990s. This provided an impetus to involve experts in the acquisition loop [LEE 97; GUT 04; AFA 12]. The process is long and laborious with the annotations not often being re-used on a larger scale at the corpus level. Basing the work on a summary structure such as a graph could help reduce the task of annotation. In the context of this subject the originality lies in promising an informed user – a sociologist [LYN 85; WOO 90] – that the annotation will be taken into account profitably in the tasks of extraction and feedback to the text. The majority of works in the current state of the art include elements of annotation so as to explicitize relations within the texts. A user of the tool – a reader or a sociologist – must be able to immerse themselves in the community that they create or observe during debates. This creates peritext, an immersive space of annotation, much like an "author" or "keywords" field in a bibliographical notice generates peritext around a publication. Remember that a "keywords" field is a space for annotation generated by a documentalist who has the capacity to understand a domain, to enrich the documentary space. These annotation spaces will provide numerous subdivisions in accordance with the users' profiles: lobbyists, managers, experts or onlookers. Semantic analysis of the textual part of an annotation enables us to gain an initial idea of the relevance of the argument. It also enables us to detect unwanted annotations such as spam, or lobbying if we find too many redundancies between the arguments in the same debate. Analysis of the free text left in comments can reveal key terms or concepts other than those initially put forward. This enables us to work back from the hierarchy of concepts initially proposed, enriching it or refining it, revealing co-occurrences between terms and annotations. The ASSIST project is a specialized search engine to analyze the context of experiments [ANA 09]; it takes account of the natural language processing modules needed by a sociologist who wishes to annotate a document.

Conversation spaces or instant messaging services are rich in socio-semantic information. Instant messaging is relatively old. The first serious protocol was conceived in 1988 by Darren Red, called IRC or Internet Relay Chat – hence the name "chat" to denote tools for online conversation. Little by little, adaptations appeared in XML language and the IPv6 protocol, culminating in the XMPP (Extensible Messaging and Presence Protocol) standard, put forward in 2002 and accepted in 2004. Today, the major actors in social networking (e.g. Facebook), messaging (e.g. Google, Yahoo, ICQ) and videoconferencing (e.g. Skype) have all adopted this protocol. Donath et al. [DON 99] developed the tool Loom to visualize communications processing in Usenet groups. Visualization systems are often based on metaphors, which in this case are the "threads" of the conversation in the discussion group, and the ways in which the form and texture of the associated events are reflected in the form and texture of the digital fabric. The aim of the tool is to provide social schemas and the atmosphere of the group. *Conversation Map* [SAC 00; SAC 04] is a tool which indicates the potential of democratic discussion forums by visualizing how debates about political subjects on the Internet, forums or instant messaging services can cross national boundaries. Although the tool is not interactive as such, its users are able to choose the subjects which they wish to watch.

We can spot overall holes in current computerized approaches, which miss out a number of points:

– these approaches examine the social groups and interests which contribute to the construction of a debate, but ignore those groups which are silent in the process, but which are, nevertheless, connected to it. Similarly, when the choices and contingencies come to be documented, no mention is made of the different options;

– the studies are superficial in that they focus on the needs, interests, problems and immediate solutions of a particular social group which influences the choice, but disregards deeper cultural, economic or intellectual factors behind the social choices;

– there is a moral stance adopted or a judgment taken about the relative merits of alternative interpretations. This indifference weakens interpretation of debates or major controversies in human affairs.

15.7. About biology

The biomedical domain, which enjoys a great deal of interest from society and therefore massive investment, is replete with new concepts and new techniques. Consequently, there is a fast-growing body of literature in the field. The availability of large quantities of data incites scientists to ask new questions with new points of view [TUR 09b]. The researchers' environment can lead to longitudinal analyses and give rise to local comparisons between datasets compiled from various sources. Similarly, genomic data offer an analytical power of greater granularity and on a larger scale. The PubMed database, which houses over 20 million documents, attests to this. In fact, in biomedicine, we see needs for information searching but also for knowledge extraction. Natural language processing and the mining of scientific texts may be a useful tool to identify parts of knowledge and enrich the analysis of biological data [NAT 06; SIM 12]. Extraction and structuring of terms, terminology management, facilitates the identification of named entities. Various techniques have been implemented [ANA 05; ALT 08] in this field of biology, from genes to cells. This subject is evolving with the compilation and cataloging of knowledge in molecular biology as to the role of each of the thousands of genes making up the genome of a species (see the Websites GeneDistiller, UniProt, PubMed and Gene Ontology, for instance). Thus, this is a subject which is greatly influenced by the evolution of its ontology and the way in which that ontology can be managed and enriched by tools from the world of knowledge computing through universal encyclopedic viewers such as Gene Ontology (GO). Lexical ontological resources such as the UMLS biomedical ontology – particularly the modules *Specialist Lexicon*, *Metathesaurus* and *Semantic Network* – have been created to complement named entity recognition and information extraction (see section 14.8).

In molecular biology, text mining is a practice which has been firmly established for the past 15 years, used to identify genes and their possible interactants [HIR 05; HAH 07]. We can cite a broad range of works that mine texts in the biomedical domain, from the earliest papers in 1998 (see below) to 2006, published in [ZWE 07; STA 08). However, works in the field of medicine used the technique earlier [SAG 75]. Yet text mining is beginning to take its place amongst major practices in the "-omics" sphere (e.g. genomics, proteomics) – disciplines which are firmly anchored in *in-vitro* biology: electrophoresis, electron microscopy, immunoprecipitation, quantitative PCR and DNA microarrays. Data mining in biology is used to perform a variety of tasks: (1) classification of articles, (2) recognition of names of genes and proteins and (3) detection of protein–protein interaction pairs [KRA 08]. The best F-score (compromise between good precision and good recall) obtained for task 2 is 92% (weighting by a boosting approach of several contributions from different classifiers whose scores range between 82 and 87%, and the F-score is 29% for task 3, with pattern-based approaches [KRA 08]. Event extraction for biological entities has become a promising technique for information extraction [ANA 10]. Like in a jigsaw, each document is mined to extract a piece of knowledge relating to a gene identified in sentences, in order to reconstruct its context: the interactome and location of the products of the gene, and the biological processes involving that gene [AMA 06; TUR 06; IVA 07; SOM 10]. An illustration of the need for ontological enrichment in conjunction with text mining can be seen in the application GoPubMed. GoPubMed was the first semantic search engine in molecular biology on Web 2.0 [DEL 04]. Another example is PubGene, which combines text mining with network visualization as an Internet service. Since the publication of the pioneering works [PRO 98; SEK 98; FUK 98], we can cite over 50 tools that have emerged, intended to extract named biological entities in texts. These tools quickly integrated the detection of names of genes and then proteins. They are divided into other detectors, e.g. aimed at detecting metabolites or kinetic coefficients. These tools are regularly compared on the basis of shared corpora with specific tasks of extraction in evaluation campaigns organized by international conferences in the form of challenges (e.g. KDD – Knowledge and Database Discovery; COLING – Computational linguistics; BioCreative) in the tradition of the MUC (Message Understanding Conference) and

TREC (Text Retrieval Conference) programs. The work done between 2000-2010 in knowledge extraction from biological texts, as described in summary works, revealed a truth and a perceived idea. The truth relates to the complexity of computational systems that are both precise and robust – i.e. whose processing capacity goes beyond the data on which they have been tested and elaborated. The perceived idea held that a knowledge extraction system is exclusive and can function in "black box" mode, excluding the habitual working environment of a biologist or a doctor, excluding the existence of additional databases about the text of a protein, excluding interpolation from a model species to a target species. Ideally an archetype of a text-mining system should produce a form of proposal if it does not merely content itself with organizing the information by way of outputs, e.g. to uncover a new piece of knowledge. The solution of a problem in biology requires that we take account of scattered data, sometimes in numerical form, sometimes stored in databases in groups that must be sorted in accordance with the hypothesis of biology. Hence, we must stress the importance of ably combining text mining and data mining, as done in [TUR 12] and [NG 06]. Fruitful combinations of information from various sources can lend value to the contribution of text mining:

– sequential neighborhood – or display of the neighborhood of genes connected by a black line and which are immediate neighbors on the genome (300 base pairs);

– species fusion – or phylogenetic display of occurrence where a protein is conserved, defining a phylogenetic profile;

– co-expression in micro-arrays – or display of activation of genes in an RNA microarray, revealing experimental evidence of existence on a large scale;

– databases – or display of links between objects in different databases;

– a scan of the PubMed database by text mining – or establishment of the existence of proteins in a tissue and the relations between those proteins.

Of the numerous subjects for which knowledge extraction may be useful, we find the sub-domain of comparative genomics. Biologists frequently work on model species which facilitate experimentation and validation of the results. Comparison with the species under study becomes necessary, particularly in terms of molecular aspects and in relation with literary data. Genetic and molecular data obtained from model organisms are widely used in studies of biological processes. The problem is that the processes studied in the familiar model organisms often have specific characteristics which are different from those present in the non-model organisms. For this reason, a model organism alone cannot give us a complete picture of a process of interest. Hence, the development of bioinformatics approaches which facilitate the integration of information available about the function of a gene on the scale of several model organisms, with account taken of their specificity, is a ponderous task. This task is pertinent for nearly all domains in biology including biomedicine, veterinary sciences and agriculture. For instance, studies about the development of embryos in ruminants are important for i) understanding miscarriage/embryonic loss, particularly for very productive dairy cows, and ii) comparing the processes of development between species [HUE 12]. However, few molecular genetic data are available about the development of ruminant embryos, and blastocyst elongation is not observed in rodents and primates. Consequently, the number of properly-studied organisms to which we can refer on this topic is limited. A good way to describe the regulation of genes for embryo development in ruminants would be to consider the peculiarities of species similar to cows, such as sheep or pigs, and those of model organisms that have been abundantly studied, such as human beings and mice. Techniques to search for publications that describe the genetic and molecular mechanisms underlying complex biological processes have been developed. For instance, a service facilitating a search of the body of literature and sorting of the results on the basis of their biological relevance to a set of genes was presented by Soldatos *et al.* [SOL 12]. However, the approach adopted in [TUR 12] corresponds more closely to text-mining issues such as attribute selection or combination of literary information with biological databases [THO 12]. In animal sciences, mining is only just beginning to include *in-silico* methods [SAH 12], and the TF Encyclopedia proves the interest surrounding the factors of transcription in life sciences [YUS 12]. In addition to the question of text mining, here the issue relates to inter-species differences in the mechanisms of proliferation and differentiation, of which the molecular bases are relatively common between types of cells and between species [TUR 09a]. The body of scientific texts published on the organisms being studied is fairly voluminous; thus, computer-aided methods must be used, automating knowledge extraction. The general goal being to look for new transcription regulators involved in the development of bovine extra-embryonic tissues using a new text-mining approach (a transcription factor or TF is a protein which latches onto specific DNA sequences, activating or inhibiting the uptake of RNA polymerase to specific genes; see the TF encyclopedia [YUS 12]. Turenne *et al.* [TUR 12] created a workflow to identify genes of interest using: (1) cross-referenced information between several databases (tables of knowledge about proteins, and texts in free format); and (2) the offer of a sorted list to deal with the scarceness of molecular biology experiments. The end result is a list of similar genes that share identical properties, drawn from the databases Pfam and HomoloGene, containing between 15 and 20% of transcription regulators, as well as shorter sorted lists (cytokines, kinases, etc.) which could be the object of later, more specific data-mining projects.

In a domain more closely related to medicine, cohort study is enjoying an increasing amount of interest. A cohort is a group of individuals who share a certain characteristic or an experience over a given period of time: cohorts are generally defined by date of birth, length of exposure to a medicine or a vaccine or a pollutant, or by monitoring of a specific medical procedure. Thus, a group of individuals born on a particular date or in a particular year – e.g. 1948 – forms a birth cohort. It is then possible to use text analysis to study medical reports or other documentation in order to deduce typical properties in relation to a witness sample. The comparison group may be a general population on whom a cohort study is performed, or may be another cohort of people who have not been exposed to the substance being investigated or whose exposure to it has been slight, but who have been exposed to a similar substance. Alternatively, sub-groups within a cohort may be compared.

Given that an automatic system may have difficulty in deducing a hierarchy of categories from a corpus, manual annotation is sometimes required. On the other hand, named-entity marking systems can be used to add annotations which can be used to analyze the context. Winnenburg *et al.* [WIN 08] examined how automatic text analysis had already been used in previous annotation projects, and concluded with how these techniques could be properly integrated into a manual annotation process by new author-publishing systems to improve the quality of the manual cleansing. Leonelli [LEO 12] identified and discussed four key problems found by human contributors to the cleansing of databases when human and non-human data are integrated together in the same database: (1) choosing criteria for which counts are effective tests; (2) selecting metadata; (3) standardizing and describing the research materials; and (4) choosing a nomenclature to classify the data. As mentioned in the previous chapters, one of the pitfalls of natural language processing is ambiguity – be it semantic (polysemy) or syntactic (morphosyntactic variation). The handling of abbreviations is a subject which raises syntactic ambiguity and is clearly identified as a problem in the mining of biomedical texts. The issue here relates to the idea of linking an abbreviation with its full form – e.g. DNA and Deoxyribonucleic Acid. Chang *et al.* [CHA 02] developed the Stanford Biomedical Abbreviation Database. Various algorithms are capable of generating numerous types of abbreviations and can compare them against different databases.

15.8. About other domains

Human and social sciences (through sociology coupled with history, law and linguistics) and biomedical sciences (through medicine and molecular biology) find the greatest degree of success when it comes to issues of discovery and knowledge extraction from automatic corpus processing, encompassing the essential issues of financing and workforce in terms of personnel. However, other more marginal subjects occupy the applicational and finalized space of knowledge extraction tools designed to compile and exploit extensive databases. For the purposes of revealing certain attributes of a database, text mining proves advantageous.

Modern astronomy is no longer based on individual observation of a celestial body and the sky chart, but rather on the exploitation of satellite data for the entire electromagnetic spectrum (gamma, X-rays, ultraviolet, infrared and visible light). The recording of certain pieces of information about stars and galaxies may prove complementary to numerical data [EGR 98].

Physical geography (as opposed to human geography) is gaining popularity thanks to computer tools – particularly geographical information systems (GIS), which are now available to nearly anyone on their Smartphone. The advantage of corpus exploration, in this particular case, is to associate a location (latitude/longitude) with information about the content [TEZ 05].

Physics, in climate sciences and meteorology, creates predictive models relating to certain physical parameters such as temperature and pressure. Climate change is a major societal issue, which is causing questions to be asked about temperature-change. Climate-related taxonomies can be adapted and extended with concepts specific to other domains such as forest ecology, especially to describe the interface between scientific research and natural-resource management. In order to construct and maintain such collections of taxonomies, annotation and mining of archives on the state of the climate fifty or a hundred years ago is important. It ensures the collection and historicization of the information, which can then be turned into action and change, but also enables us to study boundary objects, like the term "watershed point", which may be an object both for a marine biologist and a hydrologist. Indeed, a model may be a boundary object if it is used differently in different communities [STA 00]. According to Bowker and Star, the boundary object is robust enough to maintain a common identity depending on local needs.

Conclusion

Over the past 100,000 years, the human brain has developed intellectual capacities thanks to natural languages which animals such as higher mammals do not have. This gives human beings the capacity to interact with their peers in a complex manner, but primarily – and this is too often forgotten – to talk to themselves.

Before this long period of cognitive development, human beings evolved in the same way as other species, serving natural needs, qualified as instinctive and still present even today, which regulate our daily and annual cycle of activity. Neurobiologists have isolated molecules which transmit a warning signal about the motivation to be attached to certain requirements which, if left unsatisfied, can have a damaging impact on our health. An individual needs air; he needs to breathe at least every three minutes; he can go at most three days without water; eight days without sleep; fifty days without protein; roughly six months without sexual gratification. Otherwise, his body suffers greatly – particularly when he is young.

The hypothesis and theory developed in this book hold that our linguistic capacities have given rise to a new, cognitive need, experienced at the level of the brain's motivational system by protein exchange, to serve an informational requirement. The timescale for degradation would not be three minutes as for breathing, but over the course of, say, three years, the mental state of an information-deprived individual will suffer terribly. An informational need does not, in this case, refer to immersing oneself in the news of the day every evening, but means having general orientations. Some would crudely call this "giving one's life direction" or "setting oneself goals"; it is preferable to qualify this need as "having principal activities". For instance, "worshipping a god" may be a principal activity, as may "betting on horseracing", "raising a child" or "advancing one's professional career". It is an activity outside of oneself and which results from an activity inside of oneself, an inner dialog, whereby one is able to wonder, to receive and exchange information and which is valuable in the long term. This does not mean that these activities are valid throughout one's entire life. A new activity may take up the baton from an old one – e.g. starting to chew gum after quitting smoking. It is in this respect that we give "an interpretation" to human and individual consciousness, which is also sensitive to a person's social environment because it depends on his language which gives him the aforementioned duality of reflexive and external communication. The subject of consciousness is far larger. It may refer to culture in the sense of a nationwide collective consciousness, or to animal psychology in the sense of a living being's consciousness. We can even associate consciousness with a bacterium, the oldest and smallest sentient organism on our planet.

This book is intended not to be mystical, but rather university-oriented. Thus, any theory must be able to be compared with experimental results and observations. Observation involves traces – in our case traces of an individual's behavior. A journalist, a detective, a physicist or a geneticist also seeks observable and analyzable traces. The geneticist and the physicist have the privilege of observing their objects of study in a laboratory environment, in a space devoted to this work (the word "laboratory" comes from the word "labor"). In terms of analyzing human behavior, and notably what is going on in an individual's head, it is a more delicate issue. There are of course media experiments about the link between authority and sanction, or hallucinogenic substances, and indeed the active areas in the brain. The problem becomes cyclical when we begin to characterize a process of dialog in natural language using categories of description which, themselves, stem from natural language. The problem also becomes an ethical one, if it is a question of isolating an individual from learning natural language to prove the role of inner dialog. The solution is to analyze the traces left in electronic media. We come across issues of knowledge-extraction, for which the range of techniques is relatively rich and often effective, although new applications are expected to emerge. While digital "footprints" are not enough, the possible alternative is to analyze non-dialoged traces and act as a detective, photographing an individual's every gesture and every action. If we were by his side 24/7, we would realize whether the individual "plays the horses" and how often. That said, all humanity has largely adopted modern means of telecommunication. Almost everyone has a mobile telephone, and often these telephones are Internet-connected, or may be a tablet or laptop computer. Analysis of digital footprints on the Internet and mobile telephones offers an opportunity which is closely related to language, relating to the cognitive and linguistic nature of thought. This analytical approach is similar to knowledge extraction from texts. For the past twenty-odd years, it has been an active scientific and technical domain drawing on various methodological, linguistic and statistical theories. These are sciences that were officially founded in the 19th Century, which have witnessed significant developments over the past thirty years. Either the extraction methods are transversal to the data (be they numeric or otherwise), or the methods are typical of the nature of linguistic data. Numerous domains such as human and social sciences (particularly sociology) and life sciences (particularly genetics) are domains where techniques of knowledge extraction from corpora have borne fruit, and will undoubtedly develop still further. These domains are appropriate to test the identification of traces of information relating to individual principal activities. Thus, a consciousness, inspired by informational need, and supposedly artificial in the same sense that we attach to informational need, could do the opposite of what detection does: artificially produce traces – e.g. on the Internet, simulating an artificial existence by means of pseudo-principal activities. On an anecdotal note, we can cite the still-famous article from 1948, by student Ralph Alpher working with his supervisor, the cosmologist George Gamow. The article was published under the name of a co-publishing group of authors "Alpher, Bethe, Gamow", in a nod to the Greek letters $\alpha\beta\gamma$ (Alpha, Beta, Gamma), giving a fictitious existence to a certain imaginary "Bethe" (credited to Alpher's friend Hans Bethe, who had no affiliation whatsoever with the article), but also – by way of the writing – simulating a certain artificial (individual and media-related) consciousness for this fictitious author.

In conclusion, to be conscious is to be self-motivated. Self-motivation is an internal cognitive informational driving force, resulting from hormonal and linguistic processes of self-communication, modulated by external controlling factors. Self-motivation produces information – electronic information nowadays – which can be detected and analyzed by intelligent agents processing information and knowledge. Reciprocally, the information which is captured can be produced, which is an approach of generation and therefore potential creation of consciousness.

Bibliography

[ADA 06] ADDA-DECKER M., "De la reconnaissance automatique de la parole à l'analyse linguistique de corpus oraux", *26ᵉ Journées d'étude sur la Parole*, JEP 2006, p. 877-888, Dinard, France, 12-16 June 2006.

[AFA 12] AFANTENOS S., ASHER N., BENAMARA F., BRAS M., FABRE C., HO-DAC L.M., LE DRAOULEC A., MULLER P., PÉRY-WOODLEY M.P., PRÉVOT L., REBEYROLLE J., TANGUY L., VERGEZ-COURET M. and VIEU L., "An empirical resource for discovering cognitive principles of discourse organization: the ANNODIS corpus", *8th International Conference on Language Resources and Evaluation – LREC*, Istanbul, Turkey, May 2012.

[AGR 94] AGRAWAL R., SRIKANT R., "Fast algorithms for mining association rules", *Proc. of the 20th VLDB Conference*, p. 487-499, Santiago, Chile, 1994.

[AHM 03] AHMAD K., ROGERS M., "System Quirk", www.mcs.surrey.ac.uk/SystemQ/, 2003.

[ALB 99] ALBERT R., JEONG H., BARABÁSI A.L., "The Diameter of the WWW", *Nature*, 401(6749), p. 130-131, 1999.

[ALE 63] ALEKSEEV P.M, KALININA E.A, CHERNYADEVA E.A., *O statiticheskikh zakonomernostyakh v sovremenikh russkikh i angliskikh tekstakh po elektronike*, VR series 8, 3, S.97-112, 1963.

[ALS 10] ALSUMAIT, L., PU W., DOMENICONI C., BARBARA D., "Embedding Semantics in LDA Topic Models", BERRY M., KOGAN J. (eds), *Text Mining: Application and Theory*, p. 183-204, Wiley, Chichester, 2010.

[ALT 08] ALTMAN R.B., BERGMAN C.M., BLAKE J., BLASCHKE C., COHEN A., GANNON F., VALENCIA A., "Text mining for biology – the way forward: opinions from leading scientists", *Genome Biology*, 9, Suppl 2(S7), 2008.

[ALT 80] ALTMANN G., "Prolegomena to Menzerath's law", *Glottometrika*, 2, p. 1-10, 1980.

[ALT 90] ALTSCHUL S.F., GISH W., MILLER W., MYERS E.W., LIPMAN D.J., "Basic local alignment search tool", *J. Mol. Biol.*, 215, p. 403-410, 1990.

[AMA 06] AMAN E.E., DEMENKOV P.S., PINTUS S.S., NEMIATOV A.I., APASIEVA N.V., KOROTKOV R.O., IGNATIEVA E.V., PODKOLODNY N.L., IVANISENKO V.A., "Development of a computer system for the automated reconstruction of molecular genetic interaction networks", *Fifth International Conference on Bioinformatics of Genome Regulation and Structure (BGRS)*, vol. 3, p. 15-18, Novossibirsk, Russia, 2006.

[AMI 04] AMIN A., COHENDET P., *Architecture of Knowledge*, Oxford University Press, 2004.

[AN 08] AN J.J.*et al.*, *Mol. Cells*, 2008.

[ANA 06] ANANIADOU S., MCNAUGHT J. (eds), *Text Mining for Biology and Biomedicine*, Artech House Books, London, 2006.

[ANA 09] ANANIADOU S., WEISSENBACHER D., REA B., PIERI E., LIN Y., VIS F., PROCTER R., HALFPENNY P., "Supporting Frame Analysis using Text Mining", *5th International Conference on e-Social Science*, Cologne, Germany, 2009.

[ANA 10] ANANIADOU S., PYYSALO S., TSUJII J., KELL D.B., "Event extraction for systems biology by text mining the literature", *Trends Biotechnol.*, 28(7), p. 381-90, July 2010.

[AND 78] ANDERSEN F.I., FORBES A.D., "Jeremiah: A Linguistic Concordance: I Grammatical Vocabulary and Proper Nouns", *The Computer Bible*, 14, Biblical Research Associates, Wooster, OH, 1978.

[AND 94] ANDREWS R., GEVA S., "Rule extraction from a constrained error backpropagation MLP", *Australian Conference on Neural Networks*, p. 9-12, Brisbane, Queensland, 1994.

[ANG 10] ANGROSH M.A., "Modelling argumentation structures in scientific discourse through context identification: towards intelligent information retrieval systems", *Bulletin of IEEE Technical Committee on Digital Libraries*, vol. 6, Issue 2, Fall 2010

[ANT 07] ANTHONY L., "AntConc3", www.antlab.sci.waseda.ac.jp/software.html, 2007.

[APP 88] APPELT D., KONOLIGE K., "A practical nonmonotonic theory for reasoning about speech acts", *Proceedings of ACL-88*, 1988.

[ARE 65] ARENS H., *Verborgene Ordnung*, Pädagogischer Verlag Schwann, Düsseldorf, 1965.

[ARM 03] ARMINGTON T.C., *Best Practices in Developmental Mathematics*, NADE Mathematics Special Professional Interest Network, 2003.

[ARO 07] AROLES S., *L'Enigme des enfants-loups*, Publibook, Paris, 2007.

[ASH 47] ASHBY W.R., "Principles of the self-organizing dynamic system", *Journal of General Psychology*, vol. 37, p. 125-128, 1947.

[ASS 97] ASSADI H., "Knowledge acquisition from texts: using an automatic clustering method based on noun-modifier relationship", *Proceedings of the 35th Annual Meeting of the Association for Computational Linguistics*, Madrid, Spain, 1997.

[ATW 07] ATWELL E., ARSHAD J., LAI C., NIM L., REZAPOUR ASHREGI N., WANG J., WASHTELL J., "Which English dominates the World Wide Web, British or American?", *Proceedings of Corpus Linguistics*, 2007.

[AUG 70] AUGUSTSON J.G., MINKER J., "Deriving term relations for a corpus by graph theoretical clusters", *Journal of the American Society for Information Science*, vol. 21, n 2, 1970.

[AUS 95] AUSSENAC-GILLES N., BOURIGAULT D., CONDAMINES A., "How can knowledge acquisition benefit from terminology?", *Proc. of 9th KAW*, Banff, Canada, 1995.

[AXE 60] AXELROD J., WEISSBACH H., "Enzymatic O-methylation of N-acetylserotonin to melatonin", *Science*, 131, 1312, 29 April 1960.

[AXE 84] AXELROD R., *The Evolution of Cooperation*, Basic Books, New York, 1984.

[AXE 97] AXELROD R., "The dissemination of culture: A model with local convergence and global polarization", *The Journal of Conflict Resolution*, 41, p. 203-226, 1997.

[BAA 03] BAADER F., CALVANESE D., MCGUINESS D.L., NARDI D., PATEL-SCHNEIDER P.F., *The Description Logic Handbook: Theory, Implementation, Applications*, Cambridge University Press, Cambridge, 2003.

[BAA 08] BAAYEN R.H., *Analyzing Linguistic Data: A Practical Introduction to Statistics Using R.*, Cambridge University Press, Cambridge, 2008.

[BAC 38] BACHELARD G., *La formation de l'esprit scientifique,* 1938.

[BAC 00] BACHELIER L., "Théorie de la spéculation", *Annales scientifiques de l'Ecole Normale Supérieure*, troisième série 17, p. 12-88, 1900.

[BAE 99] BAEZA-YATES R., RIBEIRO-NETO B., *Modern Information Retrieval*, Addison-Wesley, Boston, 1999.

[BAK 98] BAKER L., MCCALLUM A., "Distributional clustering of words for text classification", *Special Interest Group on Information Retrieval Conference (ACM-SIGIR)*, 1998.

[BAN 86] BANDURA A., *Social Foundations of Thought and Action: A Social Cognitive Theory*, Prentice Hall, Englewood Cliffs, 1986.

[BAN 89a] BANDURA A., Wood R., "Effect of perceived controllability and performance standards on self-regulation of complex decision-making", *Journal of Personality and Social Psychology*, vol. 56, n 5, 805-814, 1989.

[BAN 89b] BANDURA A., "Human agency in social cognitive theory", *The American Psychologist*, vol. 44, n° 9, 1175-1184, 1989.

[BAN 89c] BANDURA A., "Social cognitive theory", VASTA R. (ed.), *Annals of Child Development, Six Theories of Child Development*, vol. 6, p. 1-60, JAI Press, Greenwich, CT, 1989.

[BAN 05] BANDURA A., "Adolescent development from an agentic perspective", PAJARES F., URDAN T. (eds), *Self-efficacy Beliefs of Adolescents*, Ben Kirshner, University of Colorado School of Education, 2005.

[BAR 99] BARABÁSI A.L., ALBERT R., "Emergence of scaling in random networks", *Science*, 286, 509-512, 1999.

[BAR 03] BARABÁSI A.L., *Linked: How Everything is Connected to Everything Else and What it Means for Business, Science, and Everyday Life*, Plume, New York, 2003.

[BAR 11] BARIRANI A., BEAUDRY C., AGARD B., "Segmentation sociale d'inventeurs : le cas de l'industrie de la nanotechnologie au Canada", *9ème Congrès International de Génie Industriel – GI 2011*, Saint Sauveur, Canada, 12-14 October 2011.

[BAR 54] BARNES J., "Class and committees in a Norwegian island parish", *Human Relations*, (7), p. 39-58, 1954.

[BAR 25] BARTLETT F.C., "Feeling, imaging, and thinking", *British Journal of Psychology*, 16, p. 16-28, 1925.

[BAS 96] BASILI R., PAZIENZA M.T., VELARDI P., "A context driven conceptual clustering method for verb classification in corpus", BOGURAEV B., PUSTEJOVSKY J. (eds), *Processing for Lexical Acquisition*, MIT 1996.

[BAT 02] BATES M.J., "The cascade of interactions in the digital library interface", *Information Processing & Management*, 38 (3), p. 381-400, 2002.

[BAY 87] BAYER A.E., "The Biglan model and the smart messenger – a case study of eponym diffusion", *Research in Higher Education*, 26 (2), p. 212-223, 1987.

[BEC 06] BECKER C., LESSMANN N., WACHSMUTH I., "Connecting feelings and thoughts – modeling the interaction of emotion and cognition in embodied agents", *Proceedings of the Seventh International Conference on Cognitive Modeling* (ICCM-06), 2006.

[BÉD 91] BEDECARRAX C., HUOT C., "Analyse relationnelle : des outils pour la documentation automatique", *La veille technologique : l'information scientifique, technique et industrielle*, Dunod, Paris, 1991.

[BEH 32] BEHAGHEL O., *Deutsche Syntax. Eine geschichtliche Darstellung: Wortstellung, Periodenbau*, Universitätsverlag Winter, Heidelberg, 1932.

[BEN 73] BENZECRI J.P., *La taxinomie* (tome 1), *L'analyse des correspondances* (tome 2), Dunod, Paris, 1973.

[BEÖ 84] BEÖTHY E., ALTMANN G., "The diversification of meaning of Hungarian verbal prefixes. II. ki-", *Finnisch-Ungarische Mitteilungen*, 8, 29-37, 1984.

[BER 89] BERGSON H., *Essai sur les données immédiates de la conscience*, 1889.

[BER 67] BERTIN J., BARBUT M., *Sémiologie Graphique. Les diagrammes, les réseaux, les cartes*, Gauthier-Villars, Paris, 1967.

[BHA 79] BHASKAR R.A., *The Possibility of Naturalism*, Routledge, London, 1979.

[BIL 08] BILISOLY R., *Practical Text Mining with Perl*, Wiley, New York, 2008.

[BIS 67] BISHOP E., *Foundation of Constructive Analysis*, McGraw Hill, New York, 1967.

[BLA 04] BLANCHARD E., FRASSON C., "An autonomy-oriented system design for enhancement of learner's motivation – in eLearning", *International Conference on Intelligent Tutoring Systems*, Maceió, Brazil, 2004.

[BLA 87] BLANCHE-BENVENISTE C., JEANJEAN C., *Le français parlé : transcription et édition*, Publication du Trésor de la langue française, INALF, Didier Erudition, Paris, 1987.

[BLA 55] BLAU P., *The Dynamics of Bureaucracy*, University of Chicago Press, Chicago, 1955.

[BLA 56] BLAU P., *Bureaucracy in Modern Society*, Random House, New York, 1956.

[BLA 60] BLAU P., "A theory of social integration", *The American Journal of Sociology*, (65)6, p. 545-556, May 1960.

[BLA 64] BLAU P., *Exchange and Power in Social Life*, Wiley, New York, 1964.

[BLE 09] BLEI D., LAFFERTY J., "Text mining: theory and applications, topic models", SRIVASTAVA A., SAHAMI M. (eds.), *Text Mining: Theory and Applications*, chap. 1, p. 1-24, Taylor and Francis, London, 2009.

[BLO 04] BLONDEL V.D., GAJARDO A., HEYMANS M., SENELLART P., VAN DOOREN P., "A measure of similarity between graph vertices. With applications to synonym extraction and web searching", *SIAM Review*, 46:4, p. 647-666, 2004.

[BLO 35] BLOOMFIELD L., *Language*, Henderson and Spalding, London, 1935.

[BOO 75] BOORMAN S.A., "A combinatorial optimization model for transmission of job information through contact networks", *Bell Journal of Economics*, 6, 216-249, 1975.

[BOR 97] BORG I., GROENEN P., "Modern multidimensional scaling: theory and applications", *Springer Series in Statistics*, 1997.

[BOR 09] BORGATTI S.P., MEHRA A., BRASS D.J., LABIANCA G., "Network analysis in the social sciences", *Science*, 323 (5916), p. 892-895, 2009.

[BÖR 03] BÖRNER K., CHEN C., BOYACK K., "Visualizing knowledge domains", *Annual Review of Information Science and Technology*, 37, p. 179-255, 2003.

[BOS 01] BOSSON J.K., SWANN W.B., "The paradox of the sincere chameleon: strategic self-verification in close relationships", HARVEY J., WENZEL A. (eds), *Close Romantic Relationships: Maintenance and Enhancement*, Erlbaum, Mahwah, NJ, p. 67-86, 2001.

[BOT 57] BOTT E., *Family and Social Network. Roles Norms and External Relationships in Ordinary Urban Families*, Tavistock, London, 1957.

[BOU 12] BOULLIER D., LOHARD A., *Opinion mining et sentiment analysis*, Open Press, Marseille, 2012.

[BOU 94] BOURIGAULT D., LEXTER un extracteur terminologique, doctoral thesis, University Paris 8, 1994.

[BOW 00] BOWKER G.C., STAR S.L., *Sorting Things Out: Classification and Its Consequences Inside Technology*, MIT Press, Cambridge, 2000.

[BRA 91] BRAAM R.R., MOED H.F., VAN RAAN A.F.J., "Mapping of Science by combined co-citation and word analysis", *Journal of the American Society for Information Science (JASIS)*, 42, p. 252-266, 1991.

[BRA 34] BRADFORD S.C., "Sources of information on specific subjects", *Engineering: An Illustrated Weekly Journal*, 137, p. 85-86, 26 January 1934.

[BRI 93] BRILL E., A corpus-based approach to language learning, PhD Thesis, University of Pennsylvania, 1993.

[BRI 98] BRIN S., PAGE L., "The anatomy of a large-scale hypertextual web search engine", *Proceedings of the Seventh International Conference on World Wide Web*, p. 107-117, 1998.

[BRO 96] BROCK W.A., LeBARON B.D., "A dynamic structural model for stock return volatility and trading volume", *The Review of Economics and Statistics*, MIT Press, vol. 78(1), p. 94-110, February 1996.

[BRO 97] BRODER A., GLASSMAN S., MANASSE M., ZWEIG G., Syntactic Clustering of the Web, SRC Technical Note #1997-015, 1997.

[BRO 89] BROWN J.S., COLLINS A., DUGUID S., "Situated cognition and the culture of learning", *Educational Researcher*, 18 (1), p. 32-42, 1989.

[BRO 92] BROWN P., PIETRA V.J.D., DESOUZA P.V., LAI J.C., MERCER R.L., "Class-based N-gram models for natural language", *Computational Linguistics*, vol.18, n° 4, 1992.

[BRU 06] BRUECKNER J.K., "Friendship networks", *Journal of Regional Science*, Wiley Blackwell, vol. 46(5), p. 847-865, 2006.

[BRU 56] BRUNER J.S., GOODNOW J.J. and AUSTIN G.A., *A Study of Thinking*, New York, Wiley, 1956.

[BUS 45] BUSH V., "As we may think", *Athlantic Monthly*, 176, p. 101-216, July 1945.

[CAL 83] CALLON M., COURTIAL J.P., TURNER W.A., BAUIN S., "From translations to problematic networks: an introduction to co-word analysis", *Social Science Information*, 22, p. 191-235, 1983.

[CAL 93a] CALLON M., "The use of patent titles for identifying the topics of invention and forecasting trends", *Scientometrics*, (26) 2, 1993.

[CAL 93b] CALLON M., COURTIAL J.P., PENAN H., *La scientométrie*, Presses Universitaires de France, Collection "Que Sais-Je ?", Paris, 1993.

[CAM 01] CAMAZINE S., DENEUBOURG J.L., FRANKS N.R., SNEYD J., THERAULAZ G., BONABEAU E., *Self-Organization in Biological Systems*, Princeton University Press, Princeton, 2001.

[CAM 05] CAMILLO F., TOSI M., TRALDI T., "Semiometric approach, qualitative research and text mining techniques for modelling the material culture of happiness", *Knowledge Mining*, p. 230 255, Springer, Heidelberg, 2005.

[CAR 04] CARAYOL N., MATT M., "Does research organization influence academic production? Laboratory level evidence from a large European university", *Research Policy*, vol. 33, Issue 8, p. 1081-1102, October 2004.

[CAR 97] CARPENTER G.A., "Distributed learning, recognition, and prediction by ART and ARTMAP neural networks", *Neural Networks*, vol. 10, n° 8, p. 1473-1494, 1997.

[CAR 96] CARPINETO C., ROMANO G., "A lattice conceptual clustering system and its application to browsing retrieval", *Machine Learning*, vol. 24, 95, 1996.

[CAY 79] CAYLEY A., "On the colourings of maps", *Proc. Royal Geographical Society*, 1, 259-261, 1879.

[CAY 57] CAYLEY A., "On the theory of the analytical forms called trees", *Phil. Mag.*, p. 172-176, 1857.

[CHA 94] CHALUPSKY H., SHAPIRO S.C., "SL: a subjective, intensional logic of belief", *Proceedings of the Sixteenth Annual Conference of the Cognitive Science Society*, Hillsdale, NJ, United States, 1994.

[CHA 02] CHANG J., SCHUTZE H., ALTMAN R., "Creating an online dictionary of abbreviations from medline", *Journal of the American medical information association*, 9:612-620, 2002.

[CHA 93] CHARNIAK E., *Statistical Language Learning*, MIT Press, Cambridge, 1993.

[CHE 98] CHEN H., HOUSTON A.L., SEWEL R.R., SCHATZ B.R., "Internet browsing and searching: user evaluations of category map and concept space techniques", *Journal of the American Society for Information Science*, 49(7), p. 582-603, 1998.

[CHE 02] CHEN H.H., "Multilingual summarization and question answering. Workshop on Multilingual Summarization and Question Answering", *COLING'02*, Taipei, Taiwan, 2002.

[CHE 08] CHEN B.T., BOWERS M.S., MARTIN M., HOPF F.W., GUILLORY A.M., CARELLI R.M., CHOU J.K., BONCI A., "Cocaine but not natural reward self-administration nor passive cocaine infusion produces persistent LTP in the VTA", *Neuron*, 31, 59(2), p. 288-97, July 2008.

[CHI 93] CHITASHVILI R.J., BAAYEN R.H., "Word frequency distributions", ALTMANN G., HREBICEK L. (eds), *Quantitative Text Analysis*, p. 54-135, WVT, Trier, 1993.

[CHO 65] CHOMSKY N., *Aspects of the Theory of Syntax*, MIT Press, Cambridge, 1965.

[CHU 95] CHURCH K., GALE W., "Poisson mixtures", *Natural Language Engineering*, vol. 1(2), 1995.

[CHU 86] CHURCHLAND P., *Neurophilosophy: Toward a Unified Science of the Mind-Brain*, MIT Press, Cambridge, 1986.

[CIA 93] CIALDINI R.B., *Influence: Science and Practice*, Harper Collins, New York, 1993.

[CIC 11] CICCARESE P., OCANA M., GARCIA CASTRO L.J., DAS S., CLARK T., "An open annotation ontology for science on web 3.0", *Journal of Biomedical Semantics*, 2 (Suppl 2), S4, 2011.

[COH 95] COHEN W., Learning rules that classify email, Technical Report ATT, 1995.

[COL 90] COLEMAN J.S., *Foundations of Social Theory*, The Belknap Press of Harvard University Press, Cambridge, London, 1990.

[COM 30] COMTE A., *Cours de philosophie positive*, 1830.

[CON 91] CONNELL J.P., WELLBORN J.G., "Competence, autonomy and relatedness: a motivational analysis of self-system processes", GUNNAR R., SROUFE L.A. (eds), *Minnesota Symposia on Child Psychology*, 23. p. 43-77, Erlbaum. Hillsdale, NJ, 1991.

[CON 06] CONWAY J., KOCHEN S., "The free will theorem", *Foundations of Physics*, 36, 1441-1473, 2006.

[COO 02] COOLEY C.H., *Human Nature and the Social Order*, Scribner, New York, 1902.

[COR 93] CORNO L., "The best-laid plans: modern conceptions of volition and educational research", *Educational Researcher*, 22, p. 14-22, 1993.

[COR 01] CORNUEJOLS A., MICLET L., "Aprentissage artificiel", *Concepts et algorithmes*, 2001.

[COU 90] COURTIAL J.P., MICHELET B., "A Mathematical-Model of Development in a Research Field", *Scientometrics*, 19 (1-2), 127-141, July 1990.

[COV 89] COVEY S., *The Seven Habits of Highly Effective People*, Running Press, Philadelphia, 1989.

[CRA 72] CRANE D., *Invisible Colleges: Diffusion of Knowledge in Scientific Communities*, University of Chicago Press, Chicago, 1972.

[CRA 11] CRANMER SKYLER J., DESMARAIS B.A., "Inferential network analysis with exponential random graph models", *Political Analysis*, 19(1), p. 66-86, 2011.

[CRO 10] CRONA B., HUBACEK K. (eds), "Special Issue: Social network analysis in natural resource governance", *Ecology and Society*, 48, 2010.

[CZI 75] CZIKSZENTMIHALYI M., *Beyond Boredom and Anxiety*, Jossey-Bassn, San Francisco, 1975.

[DAM 94] DAMASIO A., *Descartes' Error*, Putnam, New York, 1994.

[DAW 76] DAWKINS R., *The Selfish Gene*, New York, Oxford University Press, 1976.

[DEE 90] DEERWESTER S., DUMAIS S.T., LANDAUER T.K., FURNAS G.W., HARSHMAN R.A., "Indexing by latent semantic analysis", *Journal of the American Society of Information Science*, 41 (6), 391-407, 1990.

[DEL 04] DELFS, R., DOMS, A., KOZLENKOV, A., SCHROEDER, M., "GoPubMed: Ontology-based literature search applied to Gene Ontology and PubMed.", *German Conference on Bioinformatics*, pp. 1–9 (2004)

[DEL 95] DEL SOLDATO T., DU BOULAY B., "Formalisation and implementation of motivational tactics in tutoring systems", *Journal of Artificial Intelligence in Education*, 6, p. 337-378, 1995.

[DEM 67] DEMPSTER A., "Upper and Lower probabilities by multiple valued mappings", *Annals of Mathematical Statistics*, 38, 325-339, 1967.

[DEM 77] DEMPSTER A.P., LAIRD N.M., RUBIN D.B., "Maximum likelihood from incomplete data via the EM algorithm", *Journal of the Royal Statistical Society*, B, 39, 1-38, 1977.

[DEP 99] DEPUE R.A., COLLINS P.F., "Neurobiology of the structure of personality: dopamine, facilitation of incentive motivation, and extraversion", *Behavioral and Brain Sciences*, 22, 491–517, 1999.

[DER 06] DERRYBERRY D., TUCKER D., "Motivation, Self-regulation and Self-organization", CICCHETTI D., COHEN D. (eds), *Developmental Psychopathology*, vol. 2, Developmental neuroscience, p. 502-533, Wiley, Hoboken, 2006.

[DES 37] DESCARTES R., *Discours de la Méthode*, 1637.

[DES 73] DESCARTES R., *Œuvres philosophiques*, textes établis, présentés et annotés par Ferdinand Alquié, 3 volumes (I: 1618-1637, II: 1638-1642, III: 1643-1650), Classiques Garnier, 1963-1973.

[DES 03] DESCLÈS J.P., "Une classification aspectuelle des schémes sémantico-cognitifs", *Studia Kognitywne*, 5, SOW, Warsaw, Poland, 53-70, 2003.

[DES 78] DE SOLA POOL I., KOCHEN M., "Contacts and Influence", *Social Networks*, 1, 5-51, 1978.

[DEV 02] DE VICENTE A., PAIN H., "Informing the detection of the students' motivational state: an empirical study", CERRI S.A., GOUARDERES G., PARAGUACU F. (eds), *Proceedings of the Sixth International Conference on Intelligent Tutoring Systems*, vol. 2363 of Lecture Notes in Computer Science, p. 933-943, Springer, Berlin, Heidelberg, 2002.

[DHI 03] DHILLON I.S., MALLELA S., MODHA D.S., "Information-theoretic co-clustering", *Proceedings of the Ninth ACM SIGKDD International Conference on Knowledge Discovery and Data Mining (KDD)*, p. 89-98, August 2003.

[DID 84] DIDEROT D., *Jacques le fataliste*, 1784.

[DIE 03] DIEDERICH J., KINDERMANN J., LEOPOLD E., PAAß G., "Authorship attribution with support vector machines", *Applied Intelligence*, 19 (1-2), 109-123, 2003.

[DIN 03] DINGLI A., CIRAVEGNA F., GUTHRIE D., WILKS Y., "Mining web sites using adaptive information extraction", *Proceedings of the 10th Conference of the EACL*, Budapest, Hungary, 2003.

[DIT 81] DITTENBERGER W., *Sprachliche Kriterien fur die Chronologie der Platonischen Dialogue*, Hermès, p.321-345, 1881.

[DON 99] DONATH J., KARAHALIOS K., VIEGAS F., "Visualizing conversation", *Proceedings of 32th Hawaii International Conference on System Sciences (HICSS-32)*, Hawaii, 5-8 January 1999.

[DUB 01] DUBOIS M., *La nouvelle sociologie des sciences*, Paris, PUF, 2001.

[DUM 98] DUMAIS S., PLATT J., HECKERMAN D., SAHAMI M., "Inductive learning algorithms and representations for text categorization", *Proceedings of the 7th International Conference on Information and Knowledge Management*, ACM, p. 148-155, 1998.

[DUR 93] DURKHEIM E., *De la division du travail social: étude sur l'organisation des sociétés supérieures*, F. Alcan, Paris, 1893.

[DUR 01] DURKHEIM E., The *Elementary Forms* of *Religious Life*, Oxford University Press, Oxford, 1912, 2001.

[EAS 10] EASLEY D., KLEINBERG J., "Overview", *Networks, Crowds, and Markets: Reasoning about a Highly Connected World*, p. 1-20, Cambridge University Press, Cambridge, 2010.

[ECC 98] ECCLES J.S., WIGFIELD A., SCHIEFELE U., "Motivation to succeed", EISENBERG N. (ed.), *Handbook of Child Psychology, 3. Social, Emotional, and Personality Development*, 5th edition, p. 1017-1095, Wiley, New York, 1998.

[ECC 02] ECCLES J.S., WIGFIELD A., *Development of Achievement Motivation*, Academic Press, San Diego, 2002.

[EDE 87] EDELMAN G., *Neural Darwinism. Selection Neural Groups Theory*, Wiley, New York, 1987.

[EDE 92] EDELMAN G., *Bright Air, Brilliant Fire: On the Matter of the Mind*, Basic Books, New York, 1992.

[EDM 97] EDMONDS P., "Choosing the word most typical in context using a lexical co-occurrence network", *Proc. 35th annual meeting ACL*, Madrid, Spain, 1997.

[EGR 98] EGRET D., MOTHE J., DKAKI T., DOUSSET B., "Information mining in Astronomical Literature with Tétralogie", *Seventh Annual Conference on Astronomical Data Analysis Software and Systems, ADASS 98*, Astronomical Society of the Pacific Conference, Urbana-Champaign, United States, January 1998.

[EHR 78] EHRLICH S., BRAMAUD DU BOUCHERON G., FLORIN A., *Le développement des connaissances lexicales à l'école primaire*, Presses Universitaires de France, Paris, 1978.

[ELK 06] ELKAN C., "Clustering documents with an exponential-family approximation of the Dirichlet compound multinomial distribution", *Proceedings of the 23rd International Conference Machine Learning (ICML)*, Pittsburgh, United States, 2006.

[ENG 92] ENGUEHARD C., Apprentissage naturel automatique d'un réseau sémantique, doctoral thesis, University of Compiègne, 1992.

[ERA 45] ERASMUS D., *On Free Will*, [De libero arbitrio], 1524.

[ERD 59] ERDŐS P., RÉNYI A., "On random graphs. I", *Publicationes Mathematicae*, 6, p. 290-297, 1959.

[ERM 59] ERMOLAYEV V., JENTZSCH E., KARSAEV O., KEBERLE N., MATZKE W.E., AMOILOV V., *Modeling Dynamic Engineering Design Processes in PSI. ER*, Workshops, 119-130, 2005.

[ERN 10] ERNSTSON H., "Reading list: Using social network analysis (SNA) in social-ecological studies", *Resilience Science*, 2010.

[EUL 36] EULER L., "Solutio problematis ad geometriam situs pertinentis", *Comment. Academiae Sci. I. Petropolitanae*, 8, 128-140, 1736.

[FAY 96] FAYYAD U., PIATETSKY-SHAPIRO G., SMYTH P., "From Data Mining to Knowledge Discovery in Databases", *AI Magazine*, 17(3), 37-54, Fall 1996.

[FES 57] FESTINGER L., *A Theory of Cognitive Dissonance*, Stanford University Press, Stanford, 1957.

[FIR 68] FIRTH J.R., "A Synopsis of linguistic theory 1930-1955", *Studies in Linguistic-Analysis*, p. 1-32, Oxford Philological Society, Reprinted in PALMER F.R. (*ed.*), *Selected Papers of J.R Firth, 1952-1959*, 1968.

[FOD 75] FODOR J., *The Language of Thought*, Harvard University Press, Cambridge, 1975.

[FON 87] FONSEGRIVE G.L., Essai sur le libre-arbitre ; sa théorie et son histoire, Félix Alcan, Paris, 1887.

[FOR 07] FOROOTAN FARIDEH M.A., Thesis, Research and Science Center, Islamic Azad University, Tehran, 2007.

[FOR 11] FOROSTYAK S. *et al., Cytotherapy*, 2011.

[FOW 94] FOWLES D.C., "A motivational theory of psychopathology", SPAULDING W.G. (ed.), *Nebraska Symposium on Motivation: Integrative Views of Motivation, Cognition and Emotion*, vol. 41, p. 185-238, University of Nebraska press, Lincoln, 1994.

[FRA 02] FRALEY C., RAFTERY A.E., "Model-based clustering, discriminant analysis, and density estimation", *Journal of the American Statistical Association*, 97, 458, June 2002.

[FRA 10] FRANZOSI R., *Quantitative Narrative Analysis (Quantitative Applications in the Social Sciences)*, Sage, Beverly Hills, 2010.

[FRE 01] FREDRICKSON B.L., "The role of positive emotions in positive psychology", *American Psychologist*, 56 (3), p. 218-226, 2001.

[FRE 77] FREEMAN L.C., "A set of measures of centrality based on betweenness", *Sociometry*, 40, 35-41, 1977.

[FRE 95] FREEMAN L.C., WELLMAN B., "A note on the ancestoral Toronto home of social network analysis", *Connections*, 18(2), p. 15-19, 1995.

[FRE 98] FREEMAN C.L., WEBSTER C.M., KIRKE D.M., "Exploring social structure using dynamic three-dimensional color images", *Social Networks*, 20, Part 2, 109-18, 1998.

[FRE 04] FREEMAN L., *The Development of Social Network Analysis: A Study in the Sociology of Science*, Empirical Press, Vancouver, 2004.

[FRE 92] FREGE F., "Über Sinn und Bedeutung", *Zeitschrift für Philosophie und philosophische Kritik*, 100, p. 22-50, 1892.

[FRE 23] FREUD S., *The Ego and the ID*, Norton, New York, 1923.

[FRE 96] FREUND Y., SCHAPIRE R.E., "Experiments with a new boosting algorithm", *Machine Learning: Proceedings of the Thirteenth International Conference*, p. 148-156, 1996.

[FRE 97] FREY B., *Not Just for The Money. An Economic Theory of Personal Motivation*, Edward Elgar, Cheltenham-Brookfield, 1997.

[FRI 07] FRIENDLY M., "A brief history of data visualization", CHEN C., HÄRDLE W., UNWIN A. (eds), *Handbook of Computational Statistics: Data Visualization*, vol. III, chap. 1, p. 1-34, Springer-Verlag, Heidelberg, 2007.

[FRU 62] FRUMKINA R.M., "O zakonach raspredelenija slov i klassov slov", MOLOŠNAJA T.N. (ed.), *Strukturno-tipologičeskie issledovanija*, 124-133, ANSSSR, Moscow, 1962.

[FUK 98] FUKUDA K., TAMURA A., TSUNODA T., TAKAGI T., "Toward information extraction: identifying protein names from biological papers", *Pac. Symp. Biocomput.*, 707-18, 1998.

[GAL 92] GALE W.A., CHURCH K.W., YAROWSKY D., "A method for disambiguating word senses in a large corpus", *Computers and the Humanities*, vol. 26, n° 5-6, 1992.

[GAO 07] GAO Q., *et al.*, *Comp. Biochem. Physiol. B Biochem. Mol. Biol.*, 2007

[GAO 08] GAO Q., *et al.*, *Fish Shellfish Immunol.*, 2008

[GAR 82] GARDNER H., *Art, Mind and Brain: A Cognitive Approach to Creativity*, Basic Books, New York, 1982.

[GAR 70] GARFIELD E., "Citation indexing for studying science", *Nature*, 227, p. 669-671, 1970.

[GAZ 92] GAZZANIGA M.S., *Nature's Mind: The Biological Roots of Thinking, Emotions, Sexuality, Language and Intelligence*, BasicBooks, New York, 1992.

[GIB 94] GIBBONS M., LOGES C., NOWOTNY H., SCHWATRZMAN S., SCOTT P., TROW M., *The New Production of Knowledge. The Dynamics of Science and Research in Contemporary Societies,* Sage, London, 1994.

[GIB 79] GIBSON J.J., *The Ecological Approach to Visual Perception*, Houghton Mifflin, Boston, 1979.

[GID 84] GIDDENS A., *The Constitution of Society. Outline of the Theory of Structuration*, Polity Press, Cambridge, 1984.

[GIE 83] GIERYN T., "Boundary-work and the demarcation of science from non-science: strains and interests in professional ideologies of scientists", *American Sociological Review*, vol. 48, n° 6, 781-795, 1983.

[GIO 04] GIOVANNI PEZZULO G., CALVI G., "A pandemonium can have goals", *Proceedings of International Conference on Cognitive Modeling ICCM*, Pittsburgh, United States, 2004.

[GÖD 31] GÖDEL K., "Über formal unentscheidbare Sätze der Principia Mathematica und verwandter Systeme, I. (On formally undecidable propositions of the Principia Mathematica and of apparent systems)", *Monatshefte für Mathematik und Physik*, 38, p. 173-198, 1931.

[GOE 84] GOEBL H., *Dialektometrische Studien anhand italoromanischer, rätoromanischer und galloromanischer Sprachmaterialien aus AIS und ALF*, Bd.1 (Bd.2 und 3 enthalten Karten und Tabellen), Max Niemeyer, Tübingen, 1984.

[GOF 59] GOFFMAN E., *The Presentation of Self in Everyday Life*, Doubleday Anchor, New York, 1959.

[GOF 81] GOFFMAN, E., *Forms of Talk*, University of Pennsylvania Press, Philadelphia, 1981.

[GOL 85] GOLDBERG G., "Supplementary motor area structure and function: Review and hypotheses", *Behavioral and Brain Science*, 8, 567-616, 1985.

[GOL 39] GOLDSTEIN K., *The Organism*, American Book Company, New York, 1939.

[GON 11] GONÇALVES B., PERRA N., VESPIGNANI A., "Modeling users' activity on Twitter networks: validation of Dunbar's number", *Plos One*, 6(8), e22656, 2011.

[GOV 03] GOVAERT G., NADIF M., "Clustering with block mixture models", *Pattern Recognition*, 36(2), p. 463-473 2003.

[GOV 09] GOVAERT G., *Data Analysis*, ISTE Ltd, London, and John Wiley and Sons, New York, 2009.

[GÖV 99] GÖVERT B., LALMAS M., FUHR N., "A probabilistic description–oriented approach for categorising Web documents", *Proceedings of CIKM-99, 8th ACM International Conference on Information and Knowledge Management*, p. 475-482, ACM, Kansas City, Missouri, 1999.

[GRA 96] GRAHAM S., WEINER B., "Theories and principles of motivation", BERLINER D.C., CALFEE R.C. (eds.), *Handbook of Educational Psychology*, 63-84, Macmillan, New York, 1996.

[GRA 85] GRANOVETTER M., "Economic action and social structure – The problem of embeddedness", *Amer. J. Sociology*, 91, 481-510, 1985.

[GRA 73] GRANOVETTER M.S., "The strength of weak ties", *American Journal of Sociology*, 78:1360, 1973.

[GRA 05] GRANOVETTER M., "The impact of social structure on economic outcomes", *The Journal of Economic Perspectives*, 19(1), p. 33-50, 2005.

[GRA 07] GRANOVETTER M., "Introduction for the French Reader", *Sociologica*, 2, p. 1-8, 2007.

[GRE 98] GREENO J.G., "The situativity of knowing, learning, and research", *American Psychologist*, 53(1), p. 5-26. 1998.

[GRE 85] GREENWALD A.G., BRECKLER S.J., "To whom is the self presented?", SCHLENKER B.R. (ed.), *The Self and Social Life*, p. 126-145, McGraw-Hill, New York, 1985.

[GRE 94] GREFENSTETTE G., "SEXTANT: extracting semantics from raw text: implementation details, heuristics", *Integrated Computer-Aided Engineering*, vol. 1, n 6, p. 527-536, 1994.

[GRE 96] GREFENSTETTE G., "Evaluation techniques for automatic semantic extraction: comparing syntactic and window based approaches", BOGURAEV B., PUSTEJOVSKY J. (eds.), *Corpus Essing for Lexical Acquisition*, MIT Press, Cambridge, 1996.

[GRO 94] GROSS G., "Classes d'objets et description des verbes", *Language*, vol. 115, 1994.

[GRU 93] GRUBER T.R., "A translation approach to portable ontology specifications", *Knowledge Acquisition*, 5, p. 199-220, 1993.

[GUI 74] GUITER H., "Les rélations fréquence – longueur – sens des mots (langues romanes et anglais)", *14ᵉ congresso internazionale di linguistica e filologia romanza*, p. 373-381, Naples, Italy, 1974.

[GUO 12] GUO Y., CHEN X., LU H., PORTER A., "Empirically informing a technology delivery system model for an emerging technology: illustrated for dye-sensitized solar cells", *R&D Management*, vol. 42, Issue 2, p. 133-149, March 2012.

[GUT 04] GUT U., BAYERL P.S., "Measuring the reliability of manual annotations of speech corpora", *Proceedings of Speech Prosody*, p. 565-568, Nara, Japan, 2004.

[HAB 96] HABERT B., NAULLEAU E., NAZARENKO A., "Symbolic word classification for medium-size corpora", *Computational Linguistics Conference (COLING)*, Copenhagen, Denmark, 1996.

[HAH 99] HAHN U., REIMER U., "Knowledge-based text summarization", MANI I., MAYBURY M.T. (eds), *Advances in Automated Text Summarization*, p. 215-232, MIT Press, Cambridge, London, 1999.

[HAH 97] HAHN U., SCHNATTINGER K., "Knowledge Mining from Textual Sources", *Proceedings of the International Conference on Information and Knowledge Management (CIKM)*, 1997.

[HAH 07] HAHN U., WERMTER J., BLASCZYK R., HORN P., "Text mining: powering the database revolution", *Nature*, 12, 448(7150), 130, July 2007.

[HAL 10] HALL J.H., STANTON S.J., SCHULTHEISS O.C., "Biopsychological and neural processes of implicit motivation", SCHULTHEISS O., BRUNSTEIN J. (eds), *Implicit Motives*, Oxford Scholarship, Oxford, May 2010.

[HAL 85] HALLIDAY M.A.K., *Introduction to Functional Grammar*, Edward Arnold, London, 1985.

[HAN 06] HAN J.W., KAMBER M., *Data Mining: Concepts and Techniques*, 2nd edition, Morgan Kauffman, San Francisco, 2006.

[HAN 01] HAND D., MANNILA H., SMYTH P., *Principles of Data Mining*, MIT Press, Cambridge, 2001.

[HAR 69] HARARY F., *Graph Theory*, Addison-Wesley, Reading, 1969.

[HAR 65] HARARY F., NORMAN R.Z., CARTWRIGHT D., *Structural Models: An Introduction to the Theory of Directed Graphs*, Wiley, New York, 1965.

[HAR 54] HARRIS Z., "Distributional structure", *Word*, 10(23), p. 146-162, 1954.

[HAR 68] HARRIS Z., *Mathematical Structure of Language*, Wiley, New York, 1968.

[HAR 80] HART B., RISLEY T.R., "*In vivo* language intervention: Unanticipated general effects", *Journal of Applied Behavior Analysis*, 13, p. 407-432, 1980.

[HAR 72] HARTIGAN J.. "Direct clustering of a data matrix", *JASA*, 67(337), p. 123-129, 1972.

[HAR 75] HARTIGAN J.A., *Clustering Algorithms*, Wiley, New York, 1975.

[HAR 04] HARTMANN J., SPYNS P., MAYNARD D., CUEL R., CARMEN SUAREZ DE FIGUEROA M., SURE Y., "Methods for ontology evaluation", *Knowledge Web Deliverable*, D1.2.3, Karlsruhe, 2004.

[HAS 01] HASTIE T., TIBSHIRANI R., FRIEDMAN J., *The Elements of Statistical Learning*, Springer, New York, 2001.

[HAT 97] HATZIVASSILOGLOU V., MCKEOWN K., "Predicting the semantic orientation of adjectives", *Proceedings of the 8th Conference on European Chapter of the Association for Computational Linguistics*, Stroudsburg, United States, p. 174-181, 1997.

[HEA 94] HEARST M., Contextualizing Retrieval of Full-Length Documents, Report No. UCB/CSD 94/789, University of California, 1994.

[HEA 98] HEARST M.A., "Automated discovery of WordNet relations", FELLBAUM C. (ed.), *Wordnet: An Electronic Lexical Database*, MIT Press, Cambridge, 1998.

[HEA 99] HEARST M.A., "Untangling text mining", *Proceedings of the Annual Meeting of the Association for Computational Linguistics*, University of Maryland, Baltimore, United States, June 1999.

[HED 00] HEDSTRÖM P., SANDELL R., STERN C., "Mesolevel networks and the diffusion of social movements: the case of the Swedish Social Democratic party", *American Journal of Sociology*, 106(1), p. 145-72, 2000.

[HEG 16] HEGEL G.W.F., *Wissenschaft der Logik*, 1816.

[HEI 27] HEIDEGGER M., *Sein und Zeit*, 1927.

[HEI 10] HEIDEN S., "The TXM platform: building open-source textual analysis software compatible with the TEI encoding scheme", *24th Pacific Asia Conference on Language, Information and Computation*, Sendai, Japan, 2010.

[HEI 58] HEIDER F., *The Psychology of Interpersonal Relations*, Wiley, New York, 1958.

[HEI 06] HEINE S.J., PROULX T., VOHS K.D., "The meaning maintenance model: on the coherence of social motivations", *Personality and Social Psychology Review*, vol. 10, n 2, p. 88-110, 2006.

[HEL 11] HELBING D., YU W.J., RAUHUT H., "Self-organization and emergence in social systems: modeling the coevolution of social environments and cooperative behavior", *The Journal of Mathematical Sociology*, vol. 35, n° 1-3, 2011.

[HEN 99] HENDERSON R., ROBERTSON M., "Who wants to be an entrepreneur? Young adult attitudes to entrepreneurship as a career", *Education & Training*, 41(4/5), p. 236-245, 1999.

[HEN 04] HENRICH J., BOYD R., BOWLES S., CAMERER C., FEHR E., GINTIS H. (eds), *Foundations of Human Sociality: Economic Experiments and Ethnographic Evidence from Fifteen Small-Scale Societies*, Oxford University Press, Oxford, 2004.

[HER 64] HERDAN G., *Quantitative Linguistics*, Butterworth, Washington, 1964.

[HEW 73] HEWITT C., BISHOP P., STEIGER R., "A universal modular actor formalism for artificial intelligence", *Third International Joint Conference on Artificial Intelligence IJCAI'73*, Stanford, United States, 1973.

[HIG 88] HIGGINS D.G., SHARP P.M., "CLUSTAL: a package for performing multiple sequence alignment on a microcomputer", *Gene*, 73, p. 237-244, 1988.

[HIL 49] HILGARD E.R., "Human motives and the concept of the self", *American Psychologist*, 4, p. 135-142, 1949.

[HIN 90] HINDLE D., "Noun classification from predicate argument structures", *Association for Computational Linguistics (ACL)*, 1990.

[HIR 05] HIRSCHMAN L., YEH A., BLASCHKE C., VALENCIA A., "Overview of BioCreAtIvE: critical assessment of information extraction for biology", *BMC Bioinformatics*, 6, Suppl 1:S1, 24 May 2005.

[HJE 37] HJELMSLEV L., *Catégorie des cas* (2 volumes), Acta Jutlandica VII, IX, 1935, 1937.

[HOB 51] HOBBES T., *Leviathan*, Suhrkamp, Neuwied, Berlin, [1651] 1984.

[HOF 01] HOFMAN T., "Unsupervised learning by probabilistic latent semantic analysis", *Machine Learning*, 42, p. 177-196, 2001.

[HOL 10] HOLLEY R., "Crowdsourcing: how and why should libraries do it?", *D-Lib Magazine*, vol. 6, n° 3/4, March/April 2010.

[HOL 95] HOLMES D.I., FORSYTH R.S., "The Federalist revisited: New directions in authorship attribution", *Literary and Linguistic Computing*, 10 (2), 111-127, 1995.

[HOL 98] HOLMES D.I., "The evolution of stylometry in Humanities Scholarship", *Literary and Linguistic Computing*, 13 (3), 111-117, 1998.

[HUE 12] HUE I., DEGRELLE S.A., TURENNE N., "Conceptus elongation in cattle: Genes, models and questions", *Anim. Reprod. Sci.*, http://dx.doi.org/10.1016/j.anireprosci.2012.08.007, 2012.

[HUL 98] HULL D., "The TREC-7 Filtering Track: Description and Analysis", *Text Retrieval Conference (TREC)*, University of Maryland, 1998.

[HUM 48] HUME D., *Enquête sur l'entendement humain*, 1748.

[IND 10] INDURKHYA N., DAMERAU F., *Handbook Of Natural Language Processing*, 2ndedition, CRC Press, Boca Raton, 2010.

[IVA 07] IVANISENKO V.A., DEMENKOV P.S., AMAN E.E., PINTUS S.S., KOLCHANOV N.A., "Associative network and protein structure discovery: a software complex for facilitating search of targets for drugs, drug design, and evaluation of molecular toxicity", *3rd International Conference "Basic Science for Medicine"*, Novossibirsk, Russia, p. 92, 2007.

[JAC 01] JACCARD P., "Etude comparative de la distribution florale dans une portion des Alpes et des Jura", *Bulletin de la Société Vaudoise des Sciences Naturelles*, 37, p. 241-272, 1901.

[JAI 88] JAIN A.K., DUBES R.C., *Algorithms for Clustering Data*, Prentice Hall, New Jersey, 1988.

[JAK 56] JAKOBSON R., "Two aspects of language and two types of aphasic disturbances", JAKOBSON R., HALLEM. (eds), *Fundamentals of Language*, 4thedition, Mouton, The Hague, 1956.

[JAM 90] JAMES W., *ThePrinciples of Psychology*, vol. 1, Macmillan, London, 1890.

[JAS 85] JASANOFF S., GERALD E., MARKLE J., PETERSEN C., PINCH T. (eds), *Handbook of Science and Technology Studies*, Sage, London-New Delhi, 1985.

[JEO 09] JEOFFRION C., "Santé et représentations sociales: une étude "multi-objets" auprès de Professionnels de Santé et Non-Professionnels de Santé / Christine Jeoffrion", *Les cahiers internationaux de psychologie sociale*, 2009/2, no. 82, April-May-June 2009.

[JOA 98a] JOACHIMS T., Making large-scale SVM learning practical, Technical report University of Dortmund, 1998.

[JOA 98b] JOACHIMS T., "Text categorization with Support Vector Machines: learning with many relevant features", *Proceedings of the 10th European Conference on Machine Learning*, Lecture Notes in Computer Science,Springer, vol. 1398, p. 137-142, 1998.

[JON 10] JONNALAGADDA S.R., TOPHAM P., "NEMO: Extraction and normalization of organization names from PubMed affiliations", *Journal of Biomedical Discovery and Collaboration*, vol. 5, 2010.

[JOR 70] JORDAN C., *Traité des substitutions et des équations algébriques*, Gauthier-Villars, Paris, 1870.

[JUA 99] JUARRERO A., *Dynamics in Action*, MIT Press, Cambridge, 1999.

[JUN 53] JUNG C.G., *Collected Works*, Routledge and Kegan Paul, London, 1953.

[KAB 55] KABASHIMA T., "Ruibetsu sita hinshi no hiritsu ni mirareru kisokusei", *Kokugo Kokubun*, 24:6, p. 385-387, 1955.

[KAK 04] KAKABADSE N.K., KUZMIN A., CHATHAM R., "IS/IT professionals' personality difference: A case of selection or predisposition?", *Australasian Journal of Business and Social Inquiry*, 2(1), 1-16, 2004.

[KAL 05] KALAMPALIKIS N., MOSCOVICI S., "Une approche pragmatique de l'analyse Alceste", *Les Cahiers Internationaux de Psychologie Sociale*, 66, p. 15-24, 2005.

[KAL 08] KALMAR B., *J. Neurochem.*, 2008.

[KAN 07] KANDYLAS V., PHINEAS UPHAM S., UNGAR L.H., "Finding cohesive clusters for analyzing knowledge communities", *Seventh IEEE International Conference on Data Mining*, p. 203-212, Pisa, Italy, 2007.

[KAN 81] KANT E., *Kritik der reinen Vernunft*, 1781.

[KAN 95] KANTER I., KESSLER I., "Markov processes: linguistics and Zipf's law", *Physical Review Letters*, 1995.

[KAR 97] KARTTUNEN L., CHANOD J.P., GREFENSTETTE G., SCHILLER A., "Regular expressions for language engineering", *Natural Language Engineering*, 1-24, 1997.

[KAT 94] Katz J.S., "Geographical proximity and scientific collaboration", *Scientometrics*, vol. 31, n° 1, p. 31-34, 1994.

[KAU 97] KAUTZ H., SELMAN B., SHAH M., "The hidden Web", *AI Magazine*, 18(2), p. 27-36, 1997.

[KEL 87] KELLER J.M., "Development and use of the ARCS model of instructional design", *Journal of Instructional Development*, 10(3), p. 2-10, 1987.

[KEL 94A] KELLER, J.M., "Trends and tactics for employee motivation", *HR Horizons*, 115 (Winter 94), 5-10, 1994.

[KEL 94b] KELLER R., *On Language Change: The Invisible Hand in Language*, Routledge, New York, 1994.

[KEL 58] KELMAN H.C., "Compliance, identification, and internalization: three processes of attitude change?", *Journal of Conflict Resolution*, 2, 51-60, 1958.

[KIM 09] KIM M. *et al.*, *Cell Stress Chaperones*, 2009

[KIR 45] KIRCHHOFF G.R., "Ueber den Durchgang eines elektrischen Stromes durch eine Ebene, insbesondere durch eine kreisförmige", *Annalen der Physik und Chemie*, Band LXIV, p. 497-514, 1845.

[KIR 99] KIRMAN A., "Quelques réflexions à propos du point de vue des économistes sur le rôle de la structure organisationnelle dans l'économie", *Revue d'économie industrielle*, n° 88, 1999.

[KIR 98] KIRSHNER D., WHITSON J.A., "Obstacles to understanding cognition as situated", *Educational Researcher*, 27(8), 22-28, 1998.

[KIR 97] KIRSHNER D., WHITSON J.A., *Situated Cognition: Social, Semiotic, and Psychological Perspectives*, Erlbaum, Mahwah, 1997.

[KLE 90] KLEIBER G., *La sémantique du prototype*, Paris, PUF, 1990.

[KLE 99] KLEINBERG J.M., "Authoritative sources in a hyperlinked environment", *Journal of the ACM*, vol. 46/5, p. 604-632, 1999.

[KOD 99] KODRATOFF Y., "Knowledge discovery in texts: a definition, and applications", *Proc. ISMIS'99*, Warsaw, June 1999.

[KÖH 86] KÖHLER R., *Zur linguistischen Synergetik. Struktur und Dynamik der Lexik*, Brockmeyer, Bochum, 1986.

[KÖH 05] KÖHLER R., "Synergetic linguistics", KÖHLER R., ALTMANN G., PIOTROWSKI R.G. (eds.), *Quantitative Linguistik. Ein internationals Handbuch*, 760-775, Walter de Gruyter, Berlin, New York, 2005.

[KOH 80] KOHONEN T., *Content-adressable Memories*, Springer, New York, 1980.

[KOH 89] KOHONEN T., *Self-Organization and Associative Memory*, Springer-Verlag, Berlin, 1989.

[KOJ 99] KOJIMA M., HOSODA H., DATE Y., NAKAZATO M., MATSUO H., KANGAWA K., "Ghrelin is a growth-hormone-releasing acylated peptide from stomach", *Nature*, vol. 402, n° 6762, p. 656-60, 1999.

[KÖN 36] KÖNIG D., *Theorie der endlichen und unendlichen Graphen*, Akademische Verlagsgesellschaft, Leipzig, 1936.

[KON 89] KONOLIGE K., MYERS K., "Representing defaults with epistemic concepts", *Computational Intelligence*, 5, p. 32-44, 1989.

[KOS 00] KOSALA R., BLOCKEEL H., "Web mining research: a survey", BRADLEY P.S., SARAWAGI S., FAYYAD U.M. (eds), *SIGKDD Explorations: Newsletter of the Special Interest Group (SIG) on Knowledge Discovery & Data Mining*, ACM, 2, p. 1-15, ACM Press, New York, 2000.

[KOT 10] KOTEYKO N., "Mining the Internet for linguistic and social data: An analysis of "carbon compounds" in web feeds", *Discourse & Society*, 21(6), p. 655-674, 2010.

[KRA 02] KRAAIJ W., SPITTERS M., HULTH A., "Headline extraction based on a combination of uni- and multi-document summarization techniques", *Proceedings of the ACL Workshop on Automatic Summarization/Document Understanding Conference DUC 2002*, Philadelphia, United States, June 2002.

[KRA 08] KRALLINGER M., MORGAN A., SMITH L., LEITNER F., TANABE L., WILBUR J., HIRSCHMAN L., VALENCIA A., "Evaluation of text-mining systems for biology: overview of the Second BioCreative community challenge", *Genome Biol.*, 9, Suppl 2, S1, 2008.

[KRY 82] KRYLOV J.K., "Eine Untersuchung statistischer Gesetzmäßigkeiten auf der paradigmatischen. Ebene der Lexik natürlicher Sprachen", GUITER H., ARAPOV M.V. (eds), *Studies on Zipf's Law*, p. 234-262, 1982.

[KUC 67] KUCERA H., FRANCIS W.N., *Computational Analysis of Present-Day American English*, Brown University Press, Providence, 1967.

[KUH 87] KUHL J., "Action control: The maintenance of Motivational states", HALISCH F., KUHL J. (eds), *Motivation, Intention and Volition*, p. 279-307, Springer-Verlag, Berlin, 1987.

[KUH 96] KUHN T., *The Structure of Scientific Revolutions*, 3rd edition, University of Chicago Press, Chicago, [1962], 1996.

[KUR 30] KURATOWSKI G.K., "Sur le problème des courbes gauches en topologie", *Fund. Math*, 15, p. 271-283, 1930.

[LAB 68] LABOV W., WEINREICH U ., HERZOG M., "Empirical foundations for a theory of language change", LEHMANN W., MALKIEL Y., *Direction for Historical Linguistics*, University of Texas Press, Austin, 1968.

[LAB 68] LABOV W., "The social motivation of a sound change", *Word*, 19: 279-309, 1968.

[LAF 01] LAFFERTY J., MCCALLUM A., PEREIRA F., "Conditional random fields: Probabilistic models for segmenting and labeling sequence data", *Proc. 18th International Conf. on Machine Learning (ICML)*, p. 282-289, Morgan Kaufmann, San Francisco, 2001.

[LAH 96] LAHLOU L., "A method to extract social representations from linguistic corpora", *Japanese Journal of Experimental Social Psychology*, 36, p. 278-291, 1996.

[LAI 08] LAIRD F.M. *et al.*, *J. Neurosci.*, 2008

[LAL 07] LALLMAHAMOOD M., "An examination of individual's perceived security and privacy of the Internet in Malaysia and the influence of this on their intention to use E-commerce: using an extension of the technology acceptance model", *Journal of Internet Banking and Commerce*, vol. 12, n° 3, December 2007.

[LAN 97] LANDAUER T.K., DUMAIS S.T., "A solution to Plato's problem: The latent semantic analysis theory of acquisition, induction, and representation of knowledge", *Psychological Review*, 104 (2), p. 211-240, 1997.

[LAN 95] LANG K., "Newsweeder: Learning to filter netnews", PRIEDITIS A., RUSSELL S. (eds.), *Proceedings of the 12th International Conference on Machine Learning*, p. 331-339, Morgan Kaufmann, San Francisco, 1995.

[LAN 06] LANG P.J., DAVIS M., "Emotion, Motivation, and the brain: reflex foundations in animal and human research", *Prog. Brain Res.*, 156, p. 3-29, 2006.

[LAN 10] LANG P.J., BRADLEY M., "Emotion and the motivational brain", *Biological Psychology*, vol. 84, Issue 3, p. 437-450, July 2010.

[LAT 92] LATOUR B., MAUGUIN P., TEIL G., "A note on socio-technical graphs", *Social Studies of Science*, 22, (1), p. 33-59 and p. 91-94, 1992.

[LAT 86] LATOUR B., WOOLGAR S., *Laboratory Life: the Construction of Scientific Facts*, 2nd edition, Princeton University Press, Princeton, 1986.

[LAT 79] LATOUR B., WOOLGAR S., *Laboratory Life: The Social Construction of Scientific Facts*, Sage, Beverly Hills, 1979.

[LAV 88] LAVE J., *Cognition in Practice: Mind, Mathematics, and Culture in Everyday Life*, Cambridge University Press, Cambridge, 1988.

[LAV 91] LAVE J., WENGER E., *Situated Learning: Legitimate Peripheral Participation*, Cambridge University Press, Cambridge, 1991.

[LEB 03] LEBART L., PIRON M., STEINER J.F., *La Sémiométrie*, Dunod, Paris, 2003.

[LEB 98] LEBART L., SALEM A., BERRY L., *Exploring Textual Data*, Kluwer Academic Publishers, Boston, 1998.

[LED 96] LE DOUX J., *The Emotional Brain*, Simon and Schuster, New York, 1996.

[LEE 02] LEE K.W. *et al., Int. J. Dev. Neurosci.*, 2002

[LEE 97] LEECH G., "Introduction corpus annotation", GARSIDE R., LEECH G., MCENERY A. (eds), *Corpus Annotation: Linguistic Information from Computer Text Corpora*, 1:18, Longman, London, 1997.

[LEI 05] LEIBNIZ G.W., *Nouveaux essais sur l'entendement humain*, 1705.

[LEI 89] LEIGH STAR S., GRIESEMER J.R., "Institutional ecology, "translations" and boundary objects: amateurs and professionals in Berkeley's Museum of Vertebrate Zoology", 1907-39, *Social Studies of Science*, 19, 387, 1989.

[LEI 10] LEITZELMAN M., "La veille 2.0, Outiller les interactions sociales au sein du processus de veille", *Les Cahiers du numérique*, 2010/1, vol. 6, p. 119-133, 2010.

[LEN 97] LENT B., AGRAWAL R., SRIKANT R., "Discovering Trends in Text Databases", *Knowledge Discovery and Data Mining (KDD-97)*, KDD, Newport Beach, United States, 1997.

[LEO 12] LEONELLI S., "When humans are the exception: cross-species databases at the interface of biological and clinical research", *Social Studies of Science*, 23, February 2012.

[LEO 02] LEOPOLD E., KINDERMANN J., "Text categorization with support vector machines. How to represent texts in input space?", *Machine Learning*, 46, 423-444, 2002.

[LES 09] LESKOVEC J., BACKSTROM L., KLEINBERG J., "Meme-tracking and the dynamics of news cycle", *KDD '09 Proceedings of the 15th ACM SIGKDD International Conference on Knowledge Discovery and Data Mining*, Paris, 2009.

[LÉV 67] LÉVI-STRAUSS C., *Les structures élémentaires de la parenté*, Mouton, Paris, La Haye, [1947], 1967.

[LEV 02] LEVY J., PESCOSOLIDO B., *Social Networks and Health*, JAI Press, Boston, MA, 2002.

[LEW 35] LEWIN K., *A Dynamic Theory of Personality*, McGraw Hill, New York, 1935.

[LEY 97] LEYDESDORFF L., "Why words and co-words cannot map the development of the sciences", *Journal of the American Society for Information Science*, 48 (5), p. 418-427, 1997.

[LEY 98] LEYDESDORFF L., "Theories of citation?", *Scientometrics*, 43(1), p. 5-25, 1998.

[LIC 68] LICHTENBERG G.C., *Schriften und Briefe*, Promies, Hanser, Munich, 1968 [Sudelbuch A. Erstes bis fünftes Heft (1765-1770)].

[LIC 92] LICHTENBERG J., LACHMANN F., FOSSHAGE J., *Self and Motivational Systems: Toward a Theory of Psychoanalytic Technique*, The Analytic Press, Hillsdale, 1992.

[LIN 12] LIN Y., "Transdisciplinarity and digital humanities: lessons learned from developing text-mining tools for textual analysis", BERRY D. (ed.), *Understanding Digital Humanities*, Palgrave, Basingstoke, 2012.

[LIS 08] LISSONI F., MONTOBBIO F., Guest authorship or ghost inventors? Inventorship attribution in academic patents, Working Paper, CESPRI, University Bocconi, 2008.

[LIX 09] LIXIA Y., EVANS J.A., RZHETSKY A., "Benchmarking ontologies: Bigger or better?", *Trends Biotechnol*, 27(9), p. 531-540, September 2009.

[LOC 90] LOCKE J., An Essay Concerning Human Understanding, 1690.

[LOR 70] LORENZ K., *Essais sur le comportement animal et humain: Les leçons de l'évolution de la théorie du comportement*, Le Seuil, Paris, [Über tierisches und menschliches Verhalten. Aus dem Werdegang der Verhaltenslehre, 1965], 1970.

[LOR 71] LORRAIN F., WHITE H.C., "Structural equivalence of individuals in social networks", *Journal of Mathematical Sociology*, 1, p. 49-80, 1971.

[LOT 26] LOTKA A.J., "The frequency distribution of scientific productivity", *Journal of the Washington Academy of Sciences*, 16(12), p. 317-324, 1926.

[LOW 95] LOWE D., MATTHEWS R., "Shakespeare vs. Fletcher: A stylometric analysis by radial basis functions", *Computers and the Humanities*, 29, 449-461, 1995.

[LUC 09] LUCIO-ARIAS D., LEYDESDORFF L., "An indicator of research front activity: Measuring intellectual organization as uncertainty reduction in document sets", *Journal of the American Society for Information Science and Technology*, vol. 60, Issue 12, p. 2488-2498, December 2009.

[LUH 88] LUHMANN N., "The Autopoiesis of Social Systems", GEYER F., VAN DER ZOUWEN J. (ed.), *Sociocybernetic Paradoxes Observation, Control and Evolution of Self-steering Systems*, Sage, London, p. 172-192, 1988.

[LUR 80] LURIA A.R., *Higher Cortical Functions in Man*, 2nd edition, Basic Books, New York: 1980.

[LUS 09] LUSHER D., ACKLAND R., "A relational hyperlink analysis of an online social movement: Asylum seeker advocacy groups in Australia", *Journal of Social Structure*, 2009.

[LUT 25] LUTHER M., *De servo arbitrio* (Du serf arbitre), 1525.

[LUT 98] LUTOSLAWSKI W., LEROUX E., *Principes de stylométrie appliqués à la chronologie des œuvres de Platon*, Ernest Leroux, Paris, 1898.

[LYN 85] LYNCH M., "Art and artifact in laboratory science: a study of shop work and shop talk in a research laboratory", *Coll. Studies in Ethnomethodology*, Routledge & Kegan Paul, Boston, 1985.

[MAC 08] MACMULLEN W.J., "Searching for uses and users in gene ontology research", *ASIS&T 2008 Annual Meeting (AM08)*, Columbus, Ohio, 24-29 October 2008.

[MAK 07] MAKRI S., BLANDFORD A., GOW J., RIMMER J., WARWICK C., BUCHANAN E., "A library or just another information resource? A case study of users' mental models of traditional and digital libraries", *JASIST*, 58 (3), p. 433-445, 2007.

[MAL 13] MALINOWSKI B., *The Family Among the Australian Aborigines: A Sociological Study*, University of London Press, London, 1913.

[MAL 29] MALINOWSKI B., *The Sexual Life of Savages in North-Western Melaneisa; An Ethnographic Account of Courtship, Marriage and Family Life Among the Natives of Trobriand Islands*, British New Guinea, Halcyon House, New York, 1929.

[MAL 01] MALMIVUORI M.L., The dynamics of affect, cognition, and social environment in the regulation of personal learning processes: the case of mathematics, Doctoral dissertation, University of Helsinki, 2001.

[MAN 94] MANBER U., "Finding Similar Files in a Large File System", *Proceedings WTEC'94 Proceedings of the USENIX Winter 1994 Technical Conference on USENIX Winter 1994 Technical Conference*, San Francisco, United States, 1994.

[MAN 99] MANNING C.D., SCHÜTZE H., *Foundations of Statistical Natural Language Processing*, MIT Press, Cambridge, London, 1999.

[MAR 91] MARCOTORCHINO F., La classification automatique aujourd'hui, Technical Report IBM, 1991.

[MAR 16] MARKOV A.A., "Ob odnom primenenii statistitcheskogo metoda (une application de méthode statistique)", *Izvestia Imperialisticheskoï Akademii Naouk*, 6(4), p. 239-42, 1916.

[MAR 04] MARSHALL J., BLANK D., MEEDEN L., "An emergent framework for self-motivation in developmental robotics", *Proceedings of the Third International Conference on Development and Learning (ICDL)*, p. 104-111, 2004.

[MAR 92] MARTIN J.R., *English text. System and Structure*, Benjamins, Amsterdam, 1992.

[MAS 43] MASLOW A.H., "A dynamic theory of human motivation", *Psychological Review*, 50, 370-96, 1943.

[MAS 87] MASLOW A.H., *Motivation and Personality*, 3rd edition, Harper and Row, New York, 1987.

[MAT 88] MATSUMOTO D., SANDERS M., "Emotional experiences during engagement in intrinsically and extrinsically motivated tasks", *Motivation and Emotion*, 12, p. 353-369, 1988.

[MAT 06] MATSUO Y., HAMASAKI M., TAKEDA H., MORI J., BOLLEGARA D., NAKAMURA Y., NISHIMURA T., HASIDA K., ISHIZUKA M., "Spinning multiple social networks for semantic web", *Proceedings of the Twenty-First National Conference on Artificial Intelligence (AAAI2006)*, 2006.

[MAU 08] MAUREL S., CURTONI P., DINI L., "L'analyse des sentiments dans les forums", *Atelier Fouille des Données d'Opinions (FODOP 08)*, 2008.

[MAW 96] MAWAL-DEWAN M. *et al.*, *J. Neuropathol. Exp. Neurol.*, 1996.

[MCC 08] McCARTY W., "Knowing true things by what their mockeries be: Modelling in the humanities", SIEMENS R.G., SCHREIBMAN S. (eds), *A Companion to Digital Literary Studies*, p. 391-401, 2008.

[MCC 43] McCULLOCH W., PITTS W., "A logical calculus of ideas immanent in nervous activity", *Bulletin of Mathematical Biophysics*, 5, p. 115-133, 1943.

[MCF 03] McFARLAND K., KALIVAS P.W., "Motivational systems", in GALLAGHER M., NELSON R.J., (eds), *Handbook of Psychology*, vol. 3, p. 379-404, John Wiley & Sons, Hoboken, NJ, 2003.

[MEA 34] MEAD G.H., *Mind, Self and Society*, University of Chicago Press, Chicago, 1934.

[MEI 05] MEI Q., ZHAI C., "Discovering evolutionary theme patterns from text – an exploration of temporal text mining", *Proceedings of the 2005 ACM SIGKDD International Conference on Knowledge Discovery and Data Mining, (KDD'05)*, Chicago, Illinois, 198-207, 2005.

[MEL 84] MEL'ČUK I.A., ZOLKOVSKIJ A.K., APRESIAN Y.D., *Tolkovo-kombinatornyj slovar' sovremennogo russkogo jazyka: Opyty semantiko-sintaksičeskogo opisanija russkoj leksiki*, Wiener Slavistischer Almanach, Vienna, 1984.

[MEN 98] MENDEL G., *L'acte est une aventure. Du sujet métaphysique au sujet de l'acte pouvoir*, La Découverte, Paris, 1998.

[MEN 11] MENEZES DE OLIVEIRA E PAIVA V.L., "Identity, motivation, and autonomy from the perspective of complex dynamical systems", MURRAY G., GAO X. , LAMB T. (eds), *Identity, Motivation and Autonomy in Language Learning*, Multilingual Matters, Bristol, Buffalo, Toronto, 2011.

[MER 94] MERKL D., TJOA A.M., "The representation of semantic similarity between documents by using maps: Application of an artificial neural network to organize software libraries", *Proc. FID'94, General Assembly Conf. and Congress of the Int. Federation for Information and Documentation*, Tokyo, Japan, 1994.

[MER 73] MERTON R.K., "The normative structure of science", STORER N.W. (ed.), *The Sociology of Science*, p. 267-278, University of Chicago Press, Chicago, 1973.

[MER 79] MERTON R.K., *The Sociology of Science: Theoretical and Empirical Investigations*, New Edition, University of Chicago Press, Chicago, 1979.

[MIC 88] MICHELET B., L'analyse des associations, doctoral thesis Paris 7, 1988.

[MID 05] MIDDLETON S.C., MARSH H.W., MARTIN A.J., RICHARDS G., PERRY C., "Discovering mental toughness: a qualitative study of mental toughness in elite athletes", *Psychology Today*, 22, 60-72, 2005.

[MIK 07] MIKA P., "Ontologies are us: A unified model of social networks and semantics", *Journal Web Semantics: Science, Services and Agents on the World Wide Web archive*, vol. 5, Issue 1, p. 5-15, March 2007.

[MIK 95] MIKHEEV A., FINCH S., "Towards a workbench for acquisition of domain knowledge", *Proceedings of EACL '95 Proceedings of the Seventh Conference on European Chapter of the Association for Computational Linguistics*, p. 194-201, Dublin, Ireland, 1995.

[MIL 82] MILARDO R.M., "Friendship networks in developing relationships, converging and diverging social environments", *Social Psychology Quarterly*, 45, p. 162-172, 1982.

[MIL 67] MILGRAM S., "The small world problem", *Psychology Today*, 1(1). p. 60-67, May 1967.

[MIL 56] MILLER G.A., "The magical number seven, plus or minus two: Some limits on our capacity for processing information", *Psychological Review*, 63 (2), p. 81-97, 1956.

[MIL 10] MILLSON S.H. *et al., Biochem. Pharmacol.*, 2010.

[MIM 01] MIMA H., ANANIADOU S., NENADIC G., "The ATRACT workbench: automatic term recognition and clustering for terms", *Proceedings of the 4th International Conference of Text, Speech and Dialogue*, vol. 2166, p. 126-133, Zelezná Ruda, Czech Republic, 2001.

[MIN 12] MINER G., ELDER J., FAST A., HILL T., NISBET R., ELDER D., DELEN G., *Practical Text Mining and Statistical Analysis for Non-structured Text Data Applications*, Academic Press, Waltham, 2012.

[MIN 72] MINKER J., WILSON G., ZIMMERMAN B., "An evaluation of query expansion by addition of clustered terms for a document retrieval system", *Information, Storage and Retrieval*, vol. 8, 1972.

[MIN 75] MINSKY M., "A framework for representing Knowledge", WINSTON P.H. (ed.), *The Psychology of Computer Vision*, McGraw-Hill, New York, 1975.

[MIT 85] MITCHELL J.C., "Configurational similarity in three class contexts in British society", *Sociology*, vol. 19, 1985.

[MIT 97] MITCHELL T., *Machine Learning*, McGraw-Hill, Boston, 1997.

[MIZ 82] MIZUTANI S., *Mathematical Linguistics (Lectures on modern mathematics D-3)*, Baifukan, Tokyo, 1982.

[MLA 99] MLADENIC D., GROBELNIK M., "Feature selection for unbalanced class distribution and naive Bayes", BRATKO I., DZEROSKI S. (ed.), *Proceedings of the Sixteenth International Conference on Machine Learning (ICML 1999)*, p. 258-267, Morgan Kaufmann, San Francisco, 1999.

[MOE 04] MOED H.F., GLÄNZEL W., SCHMOCH U., *Handbook of Quantitative Science and Technology Research. The Use of Publication and Patent Statistics in Studies of S&T Systems*, Kluwer Academic Publishers, Dordrecht, London, 2004.

[MON 70] MONTAGUE R., "Universal grammar", *Theoria*, 36, p. 373-98, 1970.

[MOO 04] MOORMAN C., DIEHL K., BRINBERG D., BLAIR KIDWELL B., "Subjective Knowledge, Search Locations, and Consumer Choice", Journal of *Consumer Research, vol. 31, December 2004.*

[MOR 06] MOREIRA A.A., DEMÉTRIUS R.P., RAIMUNDO N., COSTA F., ANDRADE JR. J.S., "Competitive cluster growth in complex networks", *Physical Review*, E 73(6), 2006.

[MOR 34] MORENO J.L., *Who Shall Survive?*, Nervous & Mental Disease Publishing Co, Washington, 1934.

[MOT 07] MOTHE J., HERNANDEZ N., "Mining a thesaurus and texts to build and update a domain ontology. Data mining with ontologies: implementations, findings, and frameworks", NIGRO H.O., CÍSARO S.G., XODO D. (eds.), *Information Science Reference*, VII, p. 123-144, October 2007.

[MUH 04] MUHM M., "Abolito il libero arbitrio - Colloquio con Wolf Singer", *L'Espresso*, 19 August 2004.

[MUR 91] MURAY P., *L'Empire du Bien*, Les Belles Lettres, Paris, 1991.

[MUR 87] MURTAGH F., *Mutivariate Data Analysis*, Kluwer Academic Publishers, Dordrecht, 1987.

[MUS 92] MUSEN M.A., "Dimensions of knowledge sharing and reuse", *Computers and Biomedical Research*, 25, p. 435-467, 1992.

[MYE 80] MYERS I.B., *Introduction to type*, Consulting Psychological Press, Palo Alto, 1980.

[NAG 11] NAGLER J., LEVINA A., TIMME M., "Impact of single links in competitive percolation", *Nature Physics*, 7, p. 265-270, 2011.

[NAT 06] NATARAJAN J., BERRAR D., DUBITZKY W., HACK C., ZHANG Y.H., DESESA C., VAN BROCKLYN J.R., BREMER E.G., "Text mining of full-text journal articles combined with gene expression analysis reveals a relationship between sphingosine-1-phosphate and invasiveness of a glioblastoma cell line", *BMC Bioinformatics*, 2006.

[NEE 61] NEEDHAM R.M., Research on Information Retrieval, Classificaton and Grouping, PhD CLRU Cambridge University, 1961.

[NEU 02a] NEUMANN G., PISKORSKI J., "A shallow text processing core engine", Computational Intelligence, 18(3), p. 451-476, 2002.

[NEU 02b] NEUMANN G., SCHMEIER S., "Shallow natural language technology and text mining", Künstliche Intelligenz, 2002(2), p. 23-26, 2002.

[NEW 01] NEW B., PALLIER C., FERRAND L., MATOS R., "Une base de données lexicales du français contemporain sur Internet: lexique", L'Année Psychologique, 101, 447-462, 2001.

[NEW 94] NEWMAN R.S., "Adaptive help-seeking: a strategy of self-regulated learning", SCHUNK D.H., ZIMMERMAN B.J. (ed.), Self-Regulation of Learning and Performance: Issues and Educational Applications, p. 283-301, Erlbaum, Hillsdale, 1994.

[NEW 01] NEWMAN M.E.J., "The structure of scientific collaboration networks", Proceedings of the National Academy of Sciences, 98 (2), p. 404-409, 2001.

[NEW 04] NEWMAN M.E.J., "Coauthorship networks and patterns of scientific collaboration", PNAS, vol. 101, 6 April 2004.

[NEW 06] NEWMAN M., BARABÁSI A.L., WATTS D.J., The Structure and Dynamics of Networks, Princeton Studies in Complexity, Princeton University Press, Oxford, 2006.

[NG 06] NG S.K., "Integrating text mining with data mining", Chapter 10, p. 247-266, STAPLEY B., ANANIADOU S. (eds.), Text Mining for Biology and Biomedicine, Artech House Books, London, January 2006.

[NIC 93] NICHOLS D.M., Intelligent Student Systems: an Application of Viewpoints to Intelligent Learning Environments, PhD thesis, Lancaster University, 1993.

[NIE 10] NIE L., "Individual motivation and meaning construction of collective action in self-organization", Lanzhou Academic Journal, July 2010.

[NIE 82] NIETZSCHE F., Die fröhliche Wissenschaft, 1882.

[NIG 99a] NIGAM K., LAFFERTY J., MCCALLUM A., "Using maximum entropy for text classification", IJCAI-99 Workshop on Machine Learning for Information Filtering, p. 61-67, 1999.

[NIG 99b] NIGAM K., MCCALLUM A.K., THRUN S., MITCHEL T., "Text classification from labeled and unlabeled documents using EM", Machine Learning, 39 (1/2), p. 103-134, 1999.

[NIW 94] NIWA Y., NITTA Y., "Co-occurrence vectors from corpora vs. distance vectors from dictionaries", Computational Linguistics Conference (COLING), 1994.

[NOR 04] NORMAN D.A., Emotional Design: Why We Love (or Hate) Everyday things, Basic Books, New York, 2004.

[NOY 99] NOYONS E.C.M., MOED H.F., VAN RAAN A.F.J., "Integrating research performance analysis and science mapping", Scientometrics, (46)3, 1999.

[OHA 98] O'HARA K., SMITH F., NEWMAN W., SELLEN A., "Student readers' use of library documents: Implications for library technologies", *Proceedings of the SIGCHI Conference on Human Factors in Computing Systems*, ACM Press/Addison-Wesley, Los Angeles/New York, 1998.

[OAK 98] OAKES M., "Statistics for corpus linguistics", *Edinburgh Textbooks in Empirical Linguistics*, 1998.

[OAR 98] OARD D.W., KIM J., "Implicit feedback for recommender systems", *AAAI Workshop on Recommender Systems*, Madison, United States, available at www.glue.umd.edu/, 1998.

[OON 56] OONO S., "Kihon-goi ni kansuru ni-san no kenkyuu", *Kokugogaku*, 24, 34-46, 1956.

[ORE 03] O'REGAN K., "Emotion and e-Learning", *Journal of Asynchronous Learning Network*, 7(3), p. 78-92, 2003.

[ORE 05] O'REILLY T., "What Is Web 2.0. Design Patterns and Business users as co-developers", available at http://oreilly.com/pub/a/web2/archive/what-is-web-20.html?page=1, 30 September 2005.

[PAA 02] PAAß G., LEOPOLD E., LARSON M., KINDERMANN J., EICKELER S., "SVM Classification using sequences of phonemes and syllables", ELOMAA T., MANNILA H., TOIVONEN H. (*eds.*), *Proceedings of the 6th European Conference on Principles of Data Mining and Knowledge Discovery (PKDD 2002)*, Helsinki, Finland, 19-23 August 2002, Lecture Notes in Artificial Intelligence, 2431, p. 373-384, Springer, Berlin, Heidelberg, 2002.

[PAI 08] PAIJMANS J.J., WUBBEN S., "Preparing archeological reports for intelligent retrieval", POSLUSCHNY A., LAMBERS K., HERZOG I. (eds.), *Layers of Perception, Proceedings of the 35th International Conference on Computer Applications and Quantitative Methods in Archaology*, Bonn, Germany, 2008.

[PAJ 00a] PAJARES F., BRITNER S.L., VALIANTE G., "Relation between achievement goals and self-beliefs of middle school students in writing and science", *Contemporary Educational Psychology*, 25, p. 406-422, 2000.

[PAJ 00b] PAJARES F., LAPIN ZELDIN A., "Against the odds: self-efficacy beliefs of women in mathematical scientific and technological careers", *American Educational Research Journal*, 2000.

[PAN 98] PANKSEPP J., *Affective Neuroscience*, Oxford University Press, New York, 1998.

[PAP 77] PAPOUSEK H., PAPOUSEK M., "Mothering and cognitive head start: Psychobiological considerations", in SCHAFFER H.R. (ed.), *Studies in Mother-Infant Interaction: The Loch Lomond Symposium*, p. 63-85, Academic Press, London, 1977.

[PAR 25] PARK R.E., "The city", PARK R., BURGESS R. (eds), *Community Organization and Juvenile Delinquency*, University of Chicago Press, 1925.

[PAR 51] PARSONS T., *The Social System*, The Free Press, New York, 1951.

[PAR 49] PARSONS T., *The Structure of Social Action: A Study in Social Theory with Special Reference to a Group of European Writers*, The Free Press, New York, [1937], 1949.

[PAT 64] PATTERSON C.H., "A unitary theory of motivation and its counseling implications", *Journal of individual psychology*, 10, p. 17-31, 1964.

[PAW 97] PAWLOWSKI A., "Time-serics analysis in linguistics. Application of the ARIMA method to some cases of spoken Polish", *Journal of Quantitative Linguistics*, 4 (1-3), 203-221, 1997.

[PAZ 07] PAZZANI M.J. *et al.*, "Content-based recommendation systems", *The Adaptive Web*, p. 327-328, Springer, 2007.

[PEA 88] PEARL J., *Probabilistic Reasoning in Intelligent Systems: Networks Of Plausible Inference*, Morgan Kaufmann, San Francisco, 1988.

[PĚC 02] PĚCHOUČEK M., MAˇRÍK V., JAROSLAV B.J., "A knowledge-based approach to coalition formation", *IEEE Intelligent Systems*, 2002.

[PER 93] PEREIRA F., TISHBY N., LEE L., "Distributional clustering of English words", *30th Conference of the Association for Computational Linguistics (ACL)*, Jerusalem, Israel, 1993.

[PET 96] PETRI H.L., *Motivation: Theory, Research and Applications*, 4th edition, Brooks/Cole, Pacific Grove, 1996.

[PHI 89] PHILLIPS M., "Lexical structure of text discourse analysis", *Monograph*, 12, English Language Research, University of Birmingham, 1989.

[PIA 75] PIAGET J., *L'équilibration des structures cognitives: problème central du développement*, PUF, Paris, 1975.

[PIA 23] PIAGET J., *Le Langage et la pensée chez l'enfant*, Delachaux et Niestlé, Paris, 1923.

[PIA 52] PIAGET J., *The Origins of Intelligence in Children*, International Universities Press, New York, 1952.

[PIA 10] PIANINI D., VIRRUSO S., MENEZES R., OMICINI A., VIROLI M., "Self organization in coordination systems using a wordnet-based ontology", *SASO'2010*, p. 114-123, 2010.

[PIC 02] PICARD D., *Cell. Mol. Life Sci.*, 2002.

[PIC 01] PICKERING A.D., GRAY J.A., "Dopamine, appetitive reinforcement, and the neuropsychology of human learning: An individual differences approach", ELIASZ A. and ANGLEITER A. (eds.), *Advances Research on Temperament*, p. 113-146, PABST Science, Lengerich, 2001.

[PIN 90] PINTRICH P.R., DE GROOT E.V., "Motivational and self-regulated learning components of classroom academic performance", *Journal of Educational Psychology*, vol. 82, n°1, p. 33-40, 1990.

[PIO 68] PIOTROWSKIY R.G., *Informatsionye izmerenija yazika*, Naouka, Leningrad, 1968.

[PIS 05] Pisetta V., Hacid H., Zighed D., "Automatic Juridical Texts Classification and Relevance Feedback", *First IEEE International Workshop on Mining Complex Data (IEE MCD05)*, Texas, United States, 2005.

[PIU 07] Piu M., Bove R., *Annotation des disfluences dans les corpus oraux*, Récital, Toulouse, 2007.

[PLA 09] Plantevit M., Charnois T., Kléma J., Rigotti C., Crémilleux B., "Combining sequence and itemset mining to discover named entities in biomedical texts: a new type of pattern", *Int. J. of Data Mining, Modelling and Management*, 1(2), p. 119-148, 2009.

[PLO 98] Ploux S., Victorri B., "Construction d'espaces sémantiques à l'aide de dictionnaires de synonymes", *Traitement Automatique de la Langue (TAL)*, 1998.

[POI 03] Poibeau T., *Extraction automatique d'information. Du texte brut au web sémantique*, Hermès, Paris, 2003.

[POI 90] Poincaré H., "Sur le problème des trois corps et les équations de la Dynamique (Mémoire couronné du Prix de S. M. le roi Oscar II de Suède)", *Acta Math.*, t. 13, p. 1-270, 1890.

[POP 34] Popper K., *The Logic of Scientific Discovery*, 1934.

[POR 80] Porter M.F., "An algorithm for suffix stripping", *Program (Automated Library and Information Systems)*, 14 (3), p. 130-137, 1980.

[POR 07] Portera-Cailliau C. *et al.*, *J. Neuropathol. Exp. Neurol.*, 2007

[POS 92] Posner M.I., Rothbart M.K., "Attentional mechanisms and conscious experience", Milner A.D., Rugg M.D. (eds), *The Neuropsychology of Consciousness*, Academic Press, London, 1992.

[POT 04] Pothier P., Pothier B., Echelle d'Acquisition en Orthographe Lexicale EOLE. Pour l'école élémentaire du CP au C.M.2., Retz, Paris, 2004.

[PRA 08] Prassinos C. *et al.*, *Plant Mol. Biol.*, 2008

[PRI 76] Pribram K.H., Morton G.M., *Freud's "Project" Re-Assessed: Preface to Contemporary Cognitive Theory and Neuropsychology*, Basic Books, New York, 1976.

[PRI 65] Price D., "Networks of scientific papers", *Science*, 149, p. 510-515, 1965.

[PRI 66] Price D., Beaver D., "Collaboration in an invisible college", *American Psychology*, vol. 21, p. 1011-1018, 1966.

[PRI 84] Prigogine I., Stengers I., *Order out of chaos*, Bantam Books, New York, 1984.

[PRO 98] Proux D., Rechenmann F., Julliard L., Pillet V., Jacq B., "Detecting gene symbols and names in biological texts: a first step toward pertinent information extraction", *Proceedings of the Paper Presentation at the Ninth Workshop on Genome Informatics*, 1998.

[PUS 91] Pustejovsky J., "The generative lexicon", *Computational Linguistics*, 17, 4, 1991.

[QUI 86] Quinlan J.R., "Induction of decision trees", *Machine Learning*, p. 81-106, 1986.

[RAD 30] RADCLIFFE-BROWN A.R., "The social organization of Australian tribes", *University of Sydney Oceania Monographs*, n° 1, Sydney, 1930.

[RAD 33] RADCLIFFE-BROWN A.R., *The Andamen Islanders*, Cambridge University Press, Cambridge, 1933.

[RAF 10] RAFOLS I., MEYER M., "Diversity and network coherence as indicators of interdisciplinarity: Case studies in bionanoscience", *Scientometrics*, 2010.

[RAJ 97] RAJMAN M., BESANÇON R., "Text mining: natural language techniques and text mining applications", *Proc. of the 7th IFIP 2.6 Working Conference on Database Semantics (DS-7)*, Chapman and Hall, 1997.

[RAN 03] RANK O., *Psychology and the Soul*, Johns Hopkins University Press, Philadelphia, 2003.

[RAS 87] RASTIER F., *Sémantique interprétative*, Paris, 1987.

[RAS 95] RASTIER F., "Le terme: entre ontologie et linguistique", *La Banque des Mots*, vol. 7, 1995.

[RAS 01] RASTIER F., *Arts et sciences du texte*, PUF, Paris, 2001.

[RAU 09] RAUHUT H., WINTER F., "A sociological perspective on measuring social norms by means of strategy method experiments", *Jena Economic Research Papers*, 54, p. 1-27, 2009.

[RED 11] REDDY P.S. *et al.*, *Gene.*, 2011

[REI 03] REINBERGER M.L., SPYNS P., DAELEMANS W., MEERSMAN R., "Mining for lexons: Applying unsupervised learning methods to create ontology bases", MEERSMAN R., TARI Z., SCHMIDT D. *et al.* (*ed.*), *On the Move to Meaningful Internet Systems 2003: CoopIS, DOA and ODBASE*, LNCS 2888, p. 803-819, Springer, 2003.

[REI 86] REINERT M., "Un logiciel d'analyse lexicale (Alceste)", *Les Cahiers de l'Analyse des Données*, vol. 4, p. 471- 484, 1986.

[REN 03] REN L.M., "Scientific development and the regime innovation of science community", *Journal of Beijing University of Technology*, Social Sciences Edition, Issue 2, p. 61-64, 2003.

[REN 91] RENOUF A., SINCLAIR J., "Collocational frameworks in English", *English Corpus Linguistics*, AIJMER K., ALTENBERG B., (eds), 128-143, Longman, New York, 1991.

[RES 92] RESNIK P., "Wordnet and distributional analysis. A class-based approach to lexical discovery", *Workshop Notes, Statistically-Based NLP Techniques*, p. 54-64, AAAI, 1992.

[RIL 98] RILOFF E., SCHMELZENBACH M., "An empirical approach to conceptual case frame acquisition", *Proceedings of the Sixth Workshop on Very Large Corpora*, Montreal, Canada, August 1998.

[RIL 97] RILOFF E., SHEPHERD J., "A corpus-based approach for building semantic lexicons", *Proceedings of the Second Conference on Empirical Methods in Natural Language Processing (EMNLP-2)*, 1997.

[ROG 61] ROGERS C.R., *On Becoming a Person*, Houghton Mifflin, Boston, 1961.

[ROG 62] ROGET P.M., *The Original Roget's Thesaurus of English Words and Phrases* (Americanized ed.), Dell, New York, 1962.

[ROS 58] ROSENBLATT F., "The perceptron: a probabilistic model for information storage and organization in the brain", *Psychological Review*, vol. 65, n 6, November 1958.

[ROU 09] ROUVIÈRE J.M., *Adam ou l'innocence en personne*, L'Harmattan, Paris, 2009.

[ROW 07] ROWE J.P., MCQUIGGAN S.W., MOTT B.W., LESTER J.C., "Motivation in narrative-centered learning environments", Proceedings of the AIED'07, 2007.

[RUD 98] RUDMAN J., "The state of authorship attribution studies: some problems and solutions", *Computers and the Humanities*, 31, p. 351-365, 1998.

[RUS 03] RUSSELL B., *The Principles of Mathematics*, vol. 1, Cambridge University Press, Cambridge, 1903.

[RYA 00] RYAN R.M., DECI E.L., "Self-determination theory and the facilitation of intrinsic motivation, social development, and well-being", *American Psychologist*, 55, p. 68-78, 2000.

[SAA 12] SAAD MISSEN M.M., BOUGHANEM M., CABANAC G., "Opinion mining: reviewed from word to document level", *Social Network Analysis and Mining*, Springer-Verlag, Vienna, Austria, 2012.

[SAC 00] SACK W., "Conversation map: a content-based usenet newsgroup browser", LIEBERMAN H. (ed.), *International Conference on Intelligent User Interfaces 2000*, p. 233-240, New Orleans, United States, 9-12 January 2000.

[SAC 04] SACK W., DÉTIENNE F., DUCHENEAUT N., BURKHARDT J.M., MAHENDRAN D., BARCELLINI F., "A methodological framework for socio-cognitive analyses of collaborative design of open source software", *Workshop "Distributed Collective Practices" CSCW'04*, Chicago, United States, 5-10 November 2004.

[SAG 75] SAGER N., Computerized discovery of semantic word classes in scientific fields, Directions in Artificial Intelligence: Natural Language Processing, Courant Computer Science Report, n°7, 27-48, Courant Institute of Mathematical Sciences, New York University, 1975.

[SAG 11] SAGLIMBENI F., PARISI D., "Input from the external environment and input from within the body", KAMPIS G., KARSAI I., SZATHMÁRY E. (ed.), *Advances in Artificial Life. Darwin Meets Von Neumann,* Lecture Notes in Computer Science, vol. 5777, p. 213-221, Springer Verlag, Berlin, 2011.

[SAH 12] SAHADEVAN S., HOFMANN-APITIUS M., SCHELLANDER K., TESFAYE D., FLUCK J., FRIEDRICH C.M., "Introducing the potential of text mining to animal sciences", *J. Anim. Sci.*, 4 June 2012.

[SAI 98] SAINT AUGUSTIN, "Les confessions", *Œuvres*, tome 1, n 448, La Pléiade, Paris, 1998.

[SAL 83] SALTON G., MCGILL M.J., *Introduction to Modern Information Retrieval*, McGraw-Hill, New York, 1983.

[SAN 08] SANSORES C., PAVÓN J., "A motivation-based self-organization approach", *International Symposium on Distributed Computing and Artificial Intelligence (DCAI)*, University of Salamanca, Spain, p. 259-268, 2008.

[SAP 21] SAPIR E., *Language: An Introduction to the Study of Speech*, Harcourt, Brace, New York, 1921.

[SAP 88] SAPORTA G., *Probabilités, analyse de données et statistique*, Technip, Paris, 1988.

[SAR 07] SARMIENTO T., HARTE V., PICKFORD R., WILLOUGHBY L., "Enterprise skills for undergrads – never too early to start?", *Italics*, 6(2), p. 10-21, 2007.

[SAR 01] SARWAR B.M., KARYPIS G., KONSTAN J., RIEDL J., "Item-based collaborative filtering recommendation algorithms", *Proceedings of the 10th International World Wide Web Conference (WWW10)*, 285-295, Hong Kong, May 2001.

[SAU 77] SAUSSURE DE F., *Cours de linguistique générale*, compiled by BALLY C. and SECHEHAYE A. (eds.), with the collaboration of RIEDLINGER A., Payot Lausanne, Paris, 1916; [translated by BASKIN W., *Course in General Linguistics*, Fontana, Collins, Glasgow, 1977].

[SAV 08] SAVAGE M., "Elizabeth Bott and the formation of modern British sociology", *The Sociological Review*, 56(4), p. 579-605, 2008.

[SCH 00] SCHAPIRE R., SINGER Y., "BoosTexter: A boosting-based system for text categorization", *Machine Learning*, 39(2/3), p. 135-168, 2000.

[SCH 71] SCHELLING T.C., "Dynamic models of segregation", *Journal of Mathematical Sociology*, 1, p. 143-186, 1971.

[SCH 78] SCHELLING T.C., *Micromotives and Macrobehavior*, Norton, New York, 1978.

[SCH 19] SCHOPENHAUER A., *Die Welt als Wille und Vorstellung*, 1819.

[SCH 38] SCHOPENHAUER A., *Über die Freiheit des Willens*, 1838.

[SCH 03] SCHUNK D.H., "Self-efficacy for reading and writing: Influence of modeling, goal setting, and self-evaluation", *Reading and Writing Quarterly*, 19, 159-172, 2003.

[SCH 97] SCHÜTZE H., SILVERSTEIN C., "A comparison of projections for efficient document clustering", *Proceedings of ACM SIGIR*, p. 74-81, Philadelphia, United States, 1997.

[SCH 92] SCHWARZ G., TRUSZCZYFISKI M., "Modal logic S4F and the minimal knowledge paradigm", *Proceedings of the Third Conference on Theoretical Aspects of Reasoning about Knowledge (TARK-92)*, Monterey, United States, 1992.

[SCH 02] SCHWEITZER F., "Brownian agent models for swarm and chemotactic inter-action", in POLANI D., KIM J., MARTINETZ T. (eds.), *Proceedings of the Fifth German Workshop on Artificial Life. Abstracting and Synthesizing the Principles of Living Systems*, Akademische Verlagsgesellschaft Aka, Berlin, p. 181-190, 2002.

[SCO 00] SCOTT J.P., *Social Network Analysis: A Handbook*, 2nd edition, Sage Publications, Thousand Oaks, 2000.

[SCO 03] SCOTT W.R., DAVIS G.F., "Networks in and around organizations", *Organizations and Organizing*, Prentice Hall, Pearson, 2003.

[SEK 98] SEKIMIZU T., PARK H.S., TSUJII J., "Identifying the interaction between genes and gene products based on frequently seen verbs in Medline abstracts", *Genome Inform. Ser. Workshop Genome Inform.*, 9, p. 62-71, 1998.

[SHA 76] SHAFER G., *A Mathematical Theory of Evidence*, Princeton University Press, Princeton, 1976.

[SHA 11] SHAH C., FILE C., "InfoExtractor – a tool for social media data mining", *JITP 2011: The Future of Computational Social Science*, Seattle, United States, 2011.

[SHA 03] SHAMSFARD M., BARFOROUSH A., "The state of the art in ontology learning: a framework for comparison", *Knowledge Engineering Review*, 18(4), p. 293-316, 2003.

[SHA 77] SHANK R., ABELSON R., *Scripts, Plans, Goals and Understanding*, Lawrence Erlbaum and associates, Hillsdale, 1977.

[SHI 00] SHIBATA N. *et al.*, *Amyotroph. Lateral. Scler. Other Motor. Neuron. Disord.*, 2000

[SHI 79] SHIBUYA M., "Generalized hypergeometric, digamma and trigamma distributions", *Annals of the Institute for Statistical Mathematics*, 31, p. 373-390, 1979.

[SID 08] SIDERA K. *et al.*, *Cell Cycle*, 2008

[SIL 92] SILLINCE J.A.A., "Argumentation-based indexing for information retrieval from learned articles", *Journal of Documentation*, vol. 48, p. 387-405, 1992.

[SIM 08] SIMMEL G., *Soziologie*, Duncker & Humblot, Leipzig, 1908.

[SIM 12] SIMPSON M.S., DEMNER-FUSHMAN D., "Biomedical text mining: a survey of recent progress", AGGARWAL C.C., ZHAI C.X. (eds.), *Mining Text Data*, p. 465-517, Springer, 2012.

[SIN 07] SINCLAIR S., ROCKWELL G., "Reading tools, or text analysis tools as objects of interpretation", *Digital Humanities Conferences*, University of Illinois, Urbana-Champaign, United States, 2-8 June 2007.

[SKI 57] SKINNER B.F., *Verbal Behavior*, Prentice Hall, Englewood Cliffs, 1957.

[SKI 95] SKINNER E.A., *Perceived Control, Motivation, and Coping*, Sage, Thousand Oaks, 1995.

[SKU 91] SKUCE D., MEYER I., "Terminology and knowledge acquisition: exploring a symbiotic relationship", *Proceedings of 6th Knowledge Acquisition Workshop (KAW)*, Banff, Canada, 1991.

[SMA 90] SMADJA F., MCKEOWN K., "Automatically extracting and representing collocations for language generation", *Association for Computational Linguistics Conference (ACL)*, Pittsburgh, United States, 1990.

[SMA 74] SMALL H., GRIFFITH B.C., "The structure of scientific literatures, I. identifying and graphing specialties", *Science Studies*, 4, p. 17-40, 1974.

[SMA 75] SMALL H.G., "Citation model for scientific specialities", *Proceedings of the American Society for Information Science*, 12, p. 34-35, 1975.

[SOK 63] SOKAL R.R., SNEATH P.H.A., *Principles of Numerical Taxonomy*, W.H. Freeman, San Francisco, 1963.

[SOL 12] SOLDATOS T.G., O'DONOGHUE S.I., SATAGOPAM V.P., BARBOSA-SILVA A., PAVLOPOULOS G.A., WANDERLEY-NOGUEIRA A.C., SOARES-CAVALCANTI N.M., SCHNEIDER R., "Caipirini: using gene sets to rank literature", *BioData Mining*, 5:1, 2012.

[SOM 10] SOMMER B., TIYS E.S., KORMEIER B., HIPPE K., JANOWSKI S.J., IVANISENKO T.V., BRAGIN A.O., ARRIGO P., DEMENKOV P.S., KOCHETOV A.V., IVANISENKO V.A., KOLCHANOV N.A., HOFESTÄDT R., "Visualization and analysis of a cardio vascular disease- and MUPP1-related biological network combining text mining and data warehouse approaches", *Journal of Integrative Bioinformatics*, 7(1), p. 148, 11 November 2010.

[SOW 84] SOWA J.F., *Conceptual Structures: Information Processing in Mind and Machine*, Addison-Wesley Longman, Boston, 1984.

[SPA 99] SPARCK-JONES K., "Automatic summarizing: factors and directions", MANI I., MAYBURY M.T. (eds.), *Advances in Automated Text Summarization*, MIT Press, Cambridge, 1999.

[SPA 87] SPARCK-JONES K., Synonymy and Semantic Classification, PhD thesis (1964), Edinburgh University Press, 1987.

[SPY 05] SPYNS P., "Adapting the object role modelling method for ontology modelling", HACID M.S., RAS Z., TSUMOTO S. (eds), *Proceedings of the 15th International Symposium on Methodologies for Intelligent Systems (ISMIS 2005)*, LNAI 3488, p. 276-284, Springer, 2005.

[SRI 09] SRIVASTAVA A., SAHAMI M., *Text Mining: Classification, Clustering, and Applications*, Chapman and Hall/CRC Press, Boca Raton, 2009.

[SRI 00] SRIVASTAVA J., COOLEY R., DESHPANDE M., TAN P.N., "Web usage mining: discovery and applications of usage patterns from Web data", *Proceedings of the ACM Conference on Knowledge Discovery and Data Mining*, 1(2), p. 12-23, 2000.

[STA 11] STACEY J., "Text mining Wikipedia for misspelled words", http://jonsview.com/text-mining-wikipedia-for-misspelled-words, 2011.

[STA 07] STAVRIANOU A., ANDRITSOS P., NICOLOYANNIS N., "Overview and semantic issues of text mining", *SIGMOD Record*, vol. 36, n 3, p. 23-34, September 2007.

[STA 08] STAVRIANOU A., BAHRI E., NICOLOYANNIS N., "Text mining issues and noise handling in health care systems", *9th International Conference on System Science in Health Care*, Lyon, France, September 2008.

[STE 06] Steel P., König C.J., *Integrating Theories of Motivation*, vol. 31, Issue 4, p. 889-913, Academy of Management, 2006.

[STÖ 00] Stöber K., Wagner P., Helbit J., Köster S., Stall D., Thomae M., Blauert J., Hess W., Hoffmann R., Mangold H., "Speech synthesis by multilevel selection and concatenation of units from large speech corpora", Wahlster W. (ed.), *Verb-mobil*, Springer, 2000.

[STO 05] Stoilova L., Holloway T., Markines B., Maguitman A.G., Menczer F., "GiveALink: mining a semantic network of bookmarks for web search and recommendation", *LinkKDD '05: Proceedings of the 3rd International Workshop on Link Discovery*, p. 66-73, 2005.

[STR 96] Strassman R.J., "Human psychopharmacology of N,N-dimethyltryptamine", Behav. Brain Res., 73(1-2), p. 121-124, 1996.

[STR 00] Stricker M., Vichot F., Dreyfus G., Wolinski F., "Vers la conception de filtres d'informations efficaces", *Reconnaissance des Formes et Intelligence Artificielle (RFIA'2000)*, p. 129-137, Paris, 2000.

[STR 01] Strogatz S.H., "Exploring complex networks", *Nature*, 410, p. 268-276, 2001.

[SUS 95] Sussna M., Information Retrieval using Semantic Distance in Wordnet, Technical Report, University of California, San Diego, 1995.

[SWA 02] Swann W.B., Pelham B., "Who wants out when the going gets good? Psychological investment and preference for self-verifying college roommates", *Journal of Self and Identity*, p. 219-233, 1 July 2002.

[SWA 86] Swanson D.R., "Fish oil, Raynaud's syndrome, and undiscovered, public knowledge", *Perspectives in Biology and Medicine*, 30, p. 7-18, 1986.

[SYL 78] Sylvester J.J., "Chemistry and algebra", *Nature*, n 17, p. 284, 7 February 1878.

[TAI 10] Taipale M. et al., *Nat. Rev. Mol. Cell. Biol.*, 2010.

[TAN 96] Tanguy L., Thlivitis T., "PASTEL: un protocole informatisé d'aide à l'interprétation des textes", *Conférence terminologie et intelligence artificielle TIA'96*, Paris, 1996.

[TEN 97] Tennant M., *Psychology and Adult Learning*, 2nd edition, Routledge, 1997.

[TES 34] Tesnière L., "Comment construire une syntaxe", *Bulletin de la Faculté des Lettres de Strasbourg, 7*, 12th year, 219-229, 1934.

[TEZ 05] Tezuka T., Tanaka K., "Landmark extraction: A Web mining approach. Spatial information theory", *Lecture Notes in Computer Science*, vol. 3693/2005, p. 379-396, 2005.

[THE 01] Thelwall M., "A Web crawler design for data mining", *Journal of Information Science*, vol. 27, n 5, p. 319-325, 2001.

[THI 87] Thisted R., Efron B., "Did Shakespeare write a newly discovered poem?", *Biometrika*, 74(3), p. 445-55, 1987.

[THI 88] THISTED R., *Elements of statistical computing*, Chapman & Hall, London, 1988.

[TIN 12] TING I.H., TZUNG-PEI HONG T.P., WANG L.S.L., "Social network mining, analysis and research trends: techniques and applications", *IGI Global*, p. 1-501, 6 July 2012.

[TIS 99] TISHBY N., PEREIRA F., BIALEK W., "The information bottleneck method", *37th Annual Allerton Conference on Communication Control and Computing*, Monticello, United States, p. 368-377, 1999.

[TÖN 87] TÖNNIES F., *Gemeinschaft und Gesellschaft*, Fues's Verlag, Leipzig, 1887.

[TOW 98] TOWSEY M., DIEDERICH J., SCHELLHAMMER I., CHALUP S., BRUGMAN C., "Natural language learning by recurrent neural networks: A comparison with probabilistic approaches", *Computational Natural Language Learning Conference, Australian Natural Language Processing Fortnight*, Macquarie University, Sydney, Australia, 15-17 January 1998.

[TRA 69] TRAVERS J., MILGRAM S., "An experimental study of the small world problem", *Sociometry*, vol. 32, n 4, (1), p. 425-443, 1969.

[TRI 31] TRIER J., *Der Deutsche Wortschatz im Sinnbezirke des Verstandes*, Die Geschichte eines Sprachlichen Feldes, Heidelberg, 1931.

[TUF 01] TUFTE E., *The Visual Display of Quantitative Information*, 2nd edition, Graphics Press, Cheshire, 2001.

[TUK 77] TUKEY J., WILDER J., *Exploratory Data Analysis*, Addison-Wesley, Reading, 1977.

[TUR 98a] TURENNE N., ROUSSELOT F., "Evaluation of 4 Clustering Methods used in Text-Mining", *Actes du colloque TextMining, 10th European Conference on Machine Learning (ECML)*, Chemnitz, Germany, 1998.

[TUR 98b] TURENNE N., ROUSSELOT F., "A new Reformulation System: the SAROS Tool", *11th Knowledge Acquisition Workshop (KAW)*, Banff, Canada, 1998.

[TUR 98c] TURENNE N., *Dictionnaire des sciences et de l'informatique*, CD-ROM LexPRo 3.0, La Maison du Dictionnaire, Paris, 1998.

[TUR 99] TURENNE N., "Apprentissage d'un ensemble pré-structuré de concepts d'un domaine: l'outil GALEX", *Mathématiques, Informatique et Sciences Humaines*, vol. 148, p. 41-71, 1999.

[TUR 00] TURENNE N., "Term clusters evaluation by MonteCarlo sampling", *5e Congrès Journées Internationales d'Analyse Statistique des Données Textuelles (JADT)*, Lausanne, Switzerland, 2000.

[TUR 02a] TURENNE N., "Bayesian discriminant analysis for lexical semantic tagging", *16th European Meeting on Cybernetics and Systems Research (EMCSR)*, Vienna, Austria, 2002.

[TUR 02b] TURENNE N., "Nommage de classes de termes par consensus", *6e congrès Journées Internationales d'Analyse Statistique des Données Textuelles (JADT)*, Saint-Malo, France, 2002.

[TUR 03] TURENNE N., "Learning semantic classes for improving mail classification", *IJCAI Workshop Text Mining and Link Analysis*, Acapulco, Mexico, 2003.

[TUR 04] TURENNE N., BARBIER M., "BELUGA : un outil pour l'analyse dynamique des connaissances de la littérature scientifique d'un domaine. Première application au cas des maladies à prions", HEBRAIL G., LEBARTL. (eds), *Proceedings of Extraction et Gestion de Connaissances*, Clermont-Ferrand, France, 2004.

[TUR 06] TURENNE N., MESZAROS B., "KASKAD: a plat-form to extract temporal and interaction relations for genes in texts", *Proceedings of International Workshop on NanoBioTechnology (NanoBio'06)*, St Petersburg, Russia, 2006.

[TUR 08] TURENNE N., SCHWER S.R., "Temporal representation of gene interaction networks from text databases - drosophila melanogaster and bacillus subtilis cases", *International Journal of Data Mining and Bioinformatics (IJDMB)*, 2(1), p. 36-53, 2008.

[TUR 09a] TURENNE N., HUE I., "A combinatorics-based data-mining approach to time-series microarray alignment", *Informacionnyj Vestnik VOGiS (The Herald of Vavilov Society for Geneticists and Breeding Scientists)*, 13(1), March 2009.

[TUR 09b] TURENNE N., "Data mining, a tool for systems biology or a systems biology tool", *Journal of Computer Science & Systems Biology (JCSB)*, vol. 2, 4, p. 216-218, July-August 2009.

[TUR 10] TURENNE N., "Modeling noun-phrases dynamics in specialized text collections", *Journal of Quantitative Linguistics*, vol. 17, Issue 3, p. 212-228, 2010.

[TUR 11a] TURENNE N., Apprentissage statistique et extraction de concepts à partir de corpus, doctoral thesis, University of Strasbourg, 2011.

[TUR 11b] TURENNE N., "Role of a Web-based software platform for systems biology", *Journal of Computer Science & Systems Biology (JCSB)*, 4, p. 035-041, 2011.

[TUR 12] TURENNE N., TIYS E., IVANISENKO V., YUDIN N., IGNATIEVA E., VALOUR D., DEGRELLE S.A., HUE I.,"Finding biomarkers in non-model species: literature mining of transcription factors involved in bovine embryo development", *Journal of Bio Data Mining*, 2012.

[TUR 03] TURNEY P., LITTMAN M., "Measuring praise and criticism: inference of semantic orientation from association", *ACM TOIS*, 21(4), p. 315-346, 2003.

[TWE 96] TWEEDIE F.J., SINGH S., HOLMES D.I., "Neural network applications in stylometry: the federalist paper", *Computers and the Humanities*, 30, 1-10, 1996.

[UVN 03] UVNÄS-MOBERG K., *The Oxytocin Factor. Tapping the Hormone of Calm, Love, and Healing*, Da Capo Press, Cambridge, 2003.

[VAL 09] VALENZUELA S., PARK N., KEE K.F., "Is there social capital in a social network site? Facebook use and college students' life satisfaction, trust, and participation", *Journal of Computer-Mediated Communication*, 14(4), p. 875-901, 2009.

[VAN 10] VAN LOOY B. *et al.*, Exploring the feasibility and accuracy of Latent Semantic Analysis based text mining techniques to detect similarity between patent documents and scientific publications, UCL Louvain, Faculty of Business and Economics, 2010.

[VAN 79] VAN RIJSBERGEN C.J., *Information Retrieval*, Butterworths, London, Boston, 1979.

[VAP 98] VAPNIK V.N., *Statistical Learning Theory*, Wiley, New York, 1998.

[VAS 07] VASILEIOS K., UPHAM S.P., UNGAR L.H., "Finding cohesive clusters for analyzing knowledge communities", *Seventh IEEE International Conference on Data Mining*, p. 203-212, 2007.

[VEL 11] VELLINGIRI J., PANDIAN S.C., "A survey on web usage mining", Journal of Computer Science and Technology, vol. 11 (4), 67-72, 2011.

[VIN 07] VINCK D., *Sciences et société. Sociologie du travail scientifique*, Armand Colin, Paris, 2007.

[VOH 07] VOHS K.D., BAUMEISTER R.F., "Can satisfaction reinforce wanting? A new theory about long-term changes in strength of motivation", SHAH J., GARDNER W. (eds), *Handbook of Motivational Science*, Guilford, New York, 2007.

[VON 79] VON CRANACH M., FOPPA K., LEPENIES W., PLOOG D. (eds), *Human Ethology: Claims and Limits of a New Discipline*, Cambridge University Press, Cambridge, 1979.

[VYG 78] VYGOTSKY L.S., *Mind in Society: The Development of Higher Psychological Processes*, Harvard University Press, Cambridge, 1978.

[WAG 09] WAGNER G., DIACONESCU M., "AOR-Simulation.org – cognitive agent simulation", *AAMAS 2009 8th International Conference on Autonomous Agents and Multiagent Systems*, Budapest, Hungary, 10-15 May 2009.

[WAN 99] WANG K., LIU H., "Discovering structural association of semi structured data", *IEEE Transactions on Knowledge and Data Engineering*, 1999.

[WAS 94] WASSERMAN S., FAUST K., "Social network analysis in the social and behavioral sciences", *Social Network Analysis: Methods and Applications*, p. 1-27, Cambridge University Press, Cambridge, 1994.

[WAT 96] WATERMAN S., "Distinguished usage", BOGURAEV B., PUSTEJOVSKY J. (eds), *Corpus Processing for Lexical Acquisition*, MIT Press, Cambridge, 1996.

[WAT 98] WATTS D.J., STROGATZ S.H., "Collective dynamics of 'small-world' networks", *Nature*, 393, 440-442, 1998.

[WEI 85] WEINER B., "An attributional theory of achievement motivation and emotion", *Psychological Review*, 92. p. 548-573, 1985.

[WEI 90] WEISBUCH G., *Complex Systems Dynamics*, Addison Wesley, Redwood City, 1990.

[WEI 99] WEISS S.M., APT C., DAMERAU F., JOHNSON D.E., OLES F.J., GOETZ T., HAMPP T., "Maximizing textmining performance", *IEEE Intelligent Systems*, 14(4), p. 63-69, 1999.

[WEI 05] WEISS S.M., INDURKHYA N., ZHANG T., DAMEREAU F.J., *Text Mining. Predictive Methods for Analyzing Unstructured Information*, Springer-Verlag, New York, 2005.

[WEL 83] WELLMAN B., "Network analysis: some basic principles", *Sociological Theory*, 1, p. 155-99, 1983.

[WEL 88] WELLMAN B., "Structural analysis: From method and metaphor to theory and substance", WELLMAN B., BERKOWITZ S.D. (eds), *Social Structures: A Network Approach*, p. 19-61, Cambridge University Press, Cambridge, 1988.

[WEL 08] WELLMAN B., "Review: The development of social network analysis: A study in the sociology of science", *Contemporary Sociology*, 37, p. 221-222, 2008.

[WEN 12] WENNER MOYER M., "TOC: le cerveau déréglé", *Cerveau et Psycho*, n° 50, March-April 2012.

[WHI 59] WHITE R.W., "Motivation reconsidered: the concept of competence", *Psychological Review*, 66, p. 297-333, 1959.

[WHI 73] WHITE H.C., "Everyday life in stochastic networks", *Sociological Inquiry*, 43, p. 43-49, 1973.

[WHI 76] WHITE H.C., BOORMAN S.A., BREIGER R.L., "Social structure from multiple networks I", *American Journal of Sociology*, 81, p. 730-780, 1976.

[WHI 81] WHITE H.D., GRIFFITH B.C., "Author co-citation: a literature measure of intellectual structure", *Journal of the American Society for Information Science*, 32, p. 163-171, 1981.

[WHI 32] WHITNEY H., "Congruent graphs and the connectivity of graphs", *Am. J. Math.*, 54, p. 150-168, 1932.

[WIE 72] WIERZBICKA A., *Semantic Primitives*, Athenäum, Frankfurt, 1972.

[WIE 02] WIESENFELD-HALLIN Z., XU X.J., HOKFELT T., "The role of spinal cholecystokinin in chronic pain states", *Pharmacol. Toxicol.*, 91(6), p. 398-403, 2002.

[WIN 08] WINNENBURG R., WACHTER T., PLAKE C., DOMS A., SCHROEDER M., "Facts from text: can text mining help to scale-up high-quality manual curation of gene products with ontologies?", *Brief Bioinform*, 9(6), p. 466-478, 2008.

[WIN 09] WINTER F., HEIKO R., HELBING D.. "How norms can generate conflict", *American Journal of Sociology*, 2009.

[WIT 05] WITTEN I., FRANK E., *Data Mining: Practical Machine Learning Tools and Techniques*, 2nd edition, Morgan Kaufmann, San Francisco, 2005.

[WIT 01] WITTGENSTEIN L., *Philosophical Investigations*, Blackwell, London, 2001.

[WOO 97] WOOD W., CHRISTENSEN P.N., HEBL M.R., ROTHGERBER H., "Conformity to sex-typed norms, affect, and the self-concept", *Journal of Personality & Social Psychology*, 1997.

[WOO 90] WOOLGAR S., LYNCH M. (eds.), *Representation in Scientific Practice*, Routledge, New York, 1990.

[YAN 99] YANG Y., "An evaluation of statistical aproaches to text categorization", *Information Retrieval*, 1 (1/2), p. 60-69, 1999.

[YAO 09] YAO L.X., EVANS J.A., RZHETSKY A., "Novel opportunities for computational biology and sociology in drug discovery", *Trends Biotechnol*, 27(9), p. 531-540, September 2009.

[YAR 92] YAROWSKY D., "Word-sense disambiguation using statistical models of Roget's categories trained on large corpora", *Computational Linguistics Conference (COLING)*, Nantes, France, 1992.

[YOU 95] YOUNG M., MCNEESE M., "A situated cognition approach to problem solving", FLACH J., HANCOCK P., CAID J., VICENTE K. (eds), *The Ecology of Human-Machine Systems*, Chapter 12, Erlbaum, Hillsdale, 1995.

[YOU 07] YOUNG H.P., Self-knowledge and self-deception, Technical Report, Johns Hopkins University, 2007.

[YUL 44] YULE G.U., *The Statistical Study of Literacy Vocabulary*, Cambridge University Press, 1944.

[YUS 12] YUSUF D. *et al.*, "The transcription factor encyclopedia", *Genome Biology*, 13:R24, 2012.

[ZER 91] ZERNIK U., "Train 1 vs train 2: tagging word sense in a corpus", ZERNIK U. (ed.), *Lexical Acquisition: Exploiting on-Line Resources to Build a Lexicon*, Lawrence Erlbaum Associates, Hillsdale, 1991.

[ZHA 94] ZHANG Y., PROENCA R., MAFFEI M., BARONE M., LEOPOLD L., FRIEDMAN J.M., "Positional cloning of the mouse obese gene and its human homologue", *Nature*, 372, 425-432, 1994.

[ZIM 89] ZIMMERMAN B.J., "A social cognitive view of self regulated learning", *Journal of Educational Psychology*, 81, p. 329-339, 1989.

[ZIP 35] ZIPF G.K., *The Psychology of Language, an Introduction to Dynamic Philology*, Houghton-Mifflin, Boston 1935.

[ZWE 07] ZWEIGENBAUM P., DEMNER-FUSHMAN D., YU H., COHEN K.B., "Frontiers of biomedical text mining: current progress", *Brief Bioinform*, 8(5), p. 358-375, September 2007.

Index